THE NEW CAMBRIDGE SHAKESPEARE

GENERAL EDITOR: Brian Gibbons, *University of Münster*
ASSOCIATE GENERAL EDITOR: A. R. Braunmuller, *University of California, Los Angeles*

From the publication of the first volumes in 1984 the General Editor of the New Cambridge Shakespeare was Philip Brockbank and the Associate General Editors were Brian Gibbons and Robin Hood. From 1990 to 1994 the General Editor was Brian Gibbons and the Associate General Editors were A. R. Braunmuller and Robin Hood.

THE MERRY WIVES OF WINDSOR

This new edition of Shakespeare's citizen comedy focuses at every point on a theatrical understanding. While emphasising the liveliness of the play in stage terms, David Crane also claims that it needs to be taken much more seriously than in the past, as an expression of Shakespeare's fundamental understanding of human life, conveyed centrally in the character of Falstaff. In the process he also examines Shakespeare's free and vigorous use of different linguistic worlds within the play.

Together with a freshly edited text, a new account of the play's textual history is provided. Crane concludes that at the time of its earliest performances Shakespeare's text was in the process of adaptation to specific theatrical needs, and as much in the possession of its players as of its author.

THE NEW CAMBRIDGE SHAKESPEARE

All's Well That Ends Well, edited by Russell Fraser
Antony and Cleopatra, edited by David Bevington
The Comedy of Errors, edited by T. S. Dorsch
Hamlet, edited by Philip Edwards
Julius Caesar, edited by Marvin Spevack
The First Part of King Henry IV, edited by Herbert Weil and Judith Weil
The Second Part of King Henry IV, edited by Giorgio Melchiori
King Henry V, edited by Andrew Gurr
The First Part of King Henry VI, edited by Michael Hattaway
The Second Part of King Henry VI, edited by Michael Hattaway
The Third Part of King Henry VI, edited by Michael Hattaway
King Henry VIII, edited by John Margeson
King John, edited by L. A. Beaurline
King Lear, edited by Jay L. Halio
King Richard II, edited by Andrew Gurr
Measure for Measure, edited by Brian Gibbons
The Merchant of Venice, edited by M. M. Mahood
The Merry Wives of Windsor, edited by David Crane
A Midsummer Night's Dream, edited by R. A. Foakes
Much Ado About Nothing, edited by F. H. Mares
Othello, edited by Norman Sanders
The Poems, edited by John Roe
Romeo and Juliet, edited by G. Blakemore Evans
The Sonnets, edited by G. Blakemore Evans
The Taming of the Shrew, edited by Ann Thompson
Titus Andronicus, edited by Alan Hughes
Twelfth Night, edited by Elizabeth Story Donno
The Two Gentlemen of Verona, edited by Kurt Schlueter

THE EARLY QUARTOS
The First Quarto of King Lear, edited by Jay L. Halio
The First Quarto of King Richard III, edited by Peter Davison

THE MERRY WIVES OF WINDSOR

Edited by
DAVID CRANE

Research Fellow in the University of Wales at Lampeter

CAMBRIDGE
UNIVERSITY PRESS

Published by the Press Syndicate of the University of Cambridge
The Pitt Building, Trumpington Street, Cambridge CB2 IRP
40 West 20th Street, New York, NY 10011–4211, USA
10 Stamford Road, Oakleigh, Melbourne 3166, Australia

First published 1997

Printed in the United Kingdom at the University Press, Cambridge

A catalogue record for this book is available from the British Library

Library of Congress cataloguing in publication data

Shakespeare, William, 1564–1616.
The Merry Wives of Windsor/edited by David Crane.
  p.   cm. – (The new Cambridge Shakespeare)
Includes bibliographical references (p.   ).
ISBN 0 521 22155 2. – ISBN 0 521 29370 7 (pbk.)
1. Falstaff, John, Sir (Fictitious character) – Drama.   2. Married women – England – Windsor –
Drama.   I. Crane, David Lisle.   II. Title.   III. Series: Shakespeare, William, 1564–1616.   Works.
1984. Cambridge University Press.
PR2826.A2C74   1997
822.2'3 – dc20   96–12545 CIP

ISBN 0 521 22155 2 hardback
ISBN 0 521 29370 7 paperback

BT

CONTENTS

List of illustrations   *page* vi

Preface   vii

List of abbreviations and conventions   viii

Introduction   1

    The date and first occasion of the play   1

    The world of the play   6

    Some moments in the play   13

    The play on the stage   16

Note on the text   28

List of characters   30

THE PLAY   33

Textual analysis   151

Reading list   163

ILLUSTRATIONS

1   Queen Elizabeth viewing a performance of *The Merry Wives of Windsor*. Painted by David Scott, 1840, reproduced by permission of the Trustees of the Victoria and Albert Museum.   *page* 2

2   Brewster Mason as Falstaff in Terry Hands' 1968 production by the Royal Shakespeare Company, reproduced by permission of the Shakespeare Centre Library: the Tom Holte Theatre Photographic Collection.   12

3   Brenda Bruce and Barbara Leigh-Hunt as Mistress Page and Mistress Ford in Terry Hands' 1975 Royal Shakespeare Company production. Photo: Nobby Clark.   14

4   Title page of Q1.   18

5   Act 3, Scene 3. Painted by the Revd W. Peters, 1789.   21

6   Act 5, Scene 5. Painted by Robert Smirke, 1789.   23

7   Beerbohm Tree as Falstaff, Ellen Terry as Mistress Page, and Madge Kendall as Mistress Ford in Beerbohm Tree's 1902 production. Portrait by J. Collier, 1904, reproduced by permission of the Garrick Club (ET Archive).   25

8   From a page of the 1623 Folio showing 'massed entry' stage directions.   27

PREFACE

The Merry Wives of Windsor has at most times been a popular play on the stage, but it has not been one by which Shakespeare is chiefly known and thought about. Even the presence of Falstaff has often merely invited somewhat slighting comparison with the two great histories, *The First Part* and *The Second Part of King Henry IV*, in which he also appears. I hope this edition will emphasise the degree to which *The Merry Wives of Windsor* is alive in stage terms, but that it will also bring to the reader's attention how great a linguistic triumph the play is and how profound an understanding it conveys of what it means to be alive and not dead.

My old friend, Tom Craik, published his edition of *The Merry Wives of Windsor* for the Oxford Shakespeare in 1990, and I have profited immensely from it, as well as owing a great deal in the preparation of my own edition to frequent discussion with him. Inevitably, and happily, the play seems somewhat different focused through his understanding of it and through mine, but I think neither of us would say we had no need of the other understanding.

My indebtedness is so great, in the pages that follow, both to people I know personally and to those known only in print, that the small space of a preface will not record it in detail; but I could not fail here to thank Brian Gibbons, the General Editor of the New Cambridge Shakespeare, for his constant help and encouragement; nor end without my warmest and most affectionate thanks to the staff of Bishop Cosin's Library in Durham, who gave me an academic home and a place to work in when I badly needed it.

D. L. C.

Durham

ABBREVIATIONS AND CONVENTIONS

Shakespeare's plays, when cited in this edition, are abbreviated in a style modified slightly from that used in the *Harvard Concordance to Shakespeare*. Other editions of Shakespeare are abbreviated under the editor's surname (Rowe, Eccles) unless they are the work of more than one editor. In such cases, an abbreviated series title is used (Cam.). When more than one edition by the same editor is cited, later editions are discriminated with a raised figure (Collier[2]). All quotations from Shakespeare, except those from *The Merry Wives of Windsor*, use the text and lineation of *The Riverside Shakespeare*, under the general editorship of G. Blakemore Evans.

1. Shakespeare's plays

Ado	*Much Ado About Nothing*
Ant.	*Antony and Cleopatra*
AWW	*All's Well That Ends Well*
AYLI	*As You Like It*
Cor.	*Coriolanus*
Cym.	*Cymbeline*
Err.	*The Comedy of Errors*
Ham.	*Hamlet*
1H4	*The First Part of King Henry the Fourth*
2H4	*The Second Part of King Henry the Fourth*
H5	*King Henry the Fifth*
1H6	*The First Part of King Henry the Sixth*
2H6	*The Second Part of King Henry the Sixth*
3H6	*The Third Part of King Henry the Sixth*
H8	*King Henry the Eighth*
JC	*Julius Caesar*
John	*King John*
Lear	*King Lear*
LLL	*Love's Labour's Lost*
Mac.	*Macbeth*
MM	*Measure for Measure*
MND	*A Midsummer Night's Dream*
MV	*The Merchant of Venice*
Oth.	*Othello*
Per.	*Pericles*
R2	*King Richard the Second*
R3	*King Richard the Third*
Rom.	*Romeo and Juliet*
Shr.	*The Taming of the Shrew*
STM	*Sir Thomas More*
Temp.	*The Tempest*
TGV	*The Two Gentlemen of Verona*
Tim.	*Timon of Athens*

Tit.	*Titus Andronicus*
TN	*Twelfth Night*
TNK	*The Two Noble Kinsmen*
Tro.	*Troilus and Cressida*
Wiv.	*The Merry Wives of Windsor*
WT	*The Winter's Tale*

2. Other works cited and general references

Abbott	E. A. Abbott, *A Shakespearian Grammar*, 1883 edn (references are to numbered paragraphs)
Alexander	*Works*, ed. Peter Alexander, 1951
Bentley	G. E. Bentley, *The Jacobean and Caroline Stage*, 7 vols., 1941–68
Bevington	*Works*, ed. David Bevington, 1980
Bowers	*The Merry Wives of Windsor*, ed. Fredson Bowers, 1969 (revised Pelican Shakespeare)
Bullough	*Narrative and Dramatic Sources of Shakespeare*, ed. Geoffrey Bullough, 8 vols., 1957–75
Cam.	*Works*, ed. W. G. Clark, J. Glover and W. A. Wright, 1863–6 (Cambridge Shakespeare)
Capell	*Comedies, Histories, and Tragedies*, ed. Edward Capell, [1768]
Cercignani	Fausto Cercignani, *Shakespeare's Works and Elizabethan Pronunciation*, 1989
Chambers	E. K. Chambers, *The Elizabethan Stage*, 4 vols., 1923
Clarke	*Dramatic Works*, ed. Charles and Mary Cowden Clarke, 1864
Collier	*Works*, ed. John Payne Collier, 1842–4
Collier²	*Plays*, ed. John Payne Collier, 1853
Collier³	*Comedies, Histories, Tragedies, and Poems*, ed. John Payne Collier, 1858
Collier⁴	*Plays and Poems*, ed. John Payne Collier, 1875–8
Colman	E. A. M. Colman, *The Dramatic Use of Bawdy in Shakespeare*, 1974
conj.	conjecture
Craig	*Works*, ed. W. J. Craig, 1891 (Oxford Shakespeare)
Craik	*The Merry Wives of Windsor*, ed. T. W. Craik, 1990 (Oxford Shakespeare)
Daly	*Shakespeare's Comedy of The Merry Wives of Windsor*, A facsimile of the First Quarto . . . prepared for use at Daly's Theatre, 1886
Delius	*Werke*, ed. Nicolaus Delius, 1854–60
Dyce	*Works*, ed. Alexander Dyce, 1857
Dyce²	*Works*, ed. Alexander Dyce, 2nd edn, 1864–7
Evans	*The Riverside Shakespeare*, ed. G. Blakemore Evans *et al.*, 1974
F	*Mr. William Shakespeares Comedies, Histories, and Tragedies*, 1623 (First Folio)
F2	*Mr. William Shakespeares Comedies, Histories and Tragedies*, 1632 (Second Folio)
F3	*Mr. William Shakespears Comedies, Histories and Tragedies*, 1663 (Third Folio)
F4	*Mr. William Shakespears Comedies, Histories and Tragedies*, 1685 (Fourth Folio)
Farmer	Richard Farmer, *An Essay on the Learning of Shakespeare*, 1767
Furnivall	*The Merry Wives of Windsor*, ed. F. J. Furnivall, 1908
Geneva	Geneva translation of the Bible (1560)
Globe	*Works*, ed. W. G. Clark and W. A. Wright, 1864

Greg	*The Merry Wives of Windsor, 1602*, ed. W. W. Greg, 1910
Halliwell	*Works*, ed. James O. Halliwell, 1854
Hanmer	*Works*, ed. Thomas Hanmer, 1743–4
Harness	William Harness, *Dramatic Works*, 8 vols., 1825
Hart	*The Merry Wives of Windsor*, ed. H. C. Hart, 1904 (Arden Shakespeare)
Hibbard	*The Merry Wives of Windsor*, ed. G. R. Hibbard, 1973 (New Penguin Shakespeare)
Hotson	Leslie Hotson, *Shakespeare versus Shallow*, 1931
Hudson	*Works*, ed. Henry Hudson, 1851–6
Irving/Marshall	*Works*, ed. Sir Henry Irving and Frank A. Marshall, 2nd edn, 1906
Jackson	Zachariah Jackson, *Shakespeare's Genuis Justified*, 1819
Johnson	*Works*, ed. Samuel Johnson, 1765
Jowett	John Jowett, textual notes on *The Merry Wives of Windsor* in Stanley Wells and Gary Taylor, *William Shakespeare: A Textual Companion*, 1987
Keightley	*Works*, ed. Thomas Keightley, 1864
Kittredge	*Works*, ed. G. L. Kittredge, 1936
Knight	*Works*, ed. Charles Knight, 1840
Knight[2]	*Works*, ed. Charles Knight, 1842
Lambrechts	Guy Lambrechts, 'Proposed new readings in Shakespeare', *Bulletin de la Faculté des Lettres de Strasbourg* 63 (1965), 946–7
Lyly	John Lyly, *Works*, ed. R. W. Bond, 3 vols., 1902
Malone	*Works*, ed. Edmond Malone, 1790
Munro	*Works*, ed. John Munro, 1958 (London Shakespeare)
N&Q	*Notes and Queries*
Nashe	Thomas Nashe, *Works*, ed. R. B. McKerrow, 5 vols., 1904–10, rev. F. P. Wilson, 1958
Neilson	*Works*, ed. W. A. Neilson, 1906
Noble	Richmond Noble, *Shakespeare's Biblical Knowledge and Use of the Book of Common Prayer*, 1935
NS	*The Merry Wives of Windsor*, ed. J. Dover Wilson and A. Quiller-Couch, 1921 (New Shakespeare)
OED	*The Oxford English Dictionary*, ed. James A. H. Murray *et al.*, 12 vols., and supplement, 1933
Oliver	*The Merry Wives of Windsor*, ed. H. J. Oliver, 1971 (Arden Shakespeare)
Onions	C. T. Onions, *A Shakespeare Glossary*, rev. Robert D. Eagleson, 1986
Oxberry	*The Merry Wives of Windsor*, ed. W. Oxberry, 1820 (Oxberry's New English Drama, vol. 8)
Oxford	*Works*, ed. Stanley Wells and Gary Taylor, 1986 (Oxford Shakespeare)
Partridge	Eric Partridge, *Shakespeare's Bawdy*, rev. edn, 1968
Pope	*Works*, ed. Alexander Pope, 1723–5
Pope[2]	*Works*, ed. Alexander Pope, 2nd edn, 1728
Q, Q1	*A Most pleasaunt and excellent conceited Comedie, of Syr Iohn Falstaffe, and the merrie Wiues of Windsor*, 1602
Q2	*A Most Pleasant and Excellent Conceited Comedy, of Sir Iohn Falstaffe, and the Merry Wiues of Windsor*, 1619
Q3	*The Merry Wives of Windsor*, 1630
Rann	*Dramatic Works*, ed. Joseph Rann, 1786–[94]
Reed	*Works*, ed. Isaac Reed, 1785
Rowe	*Works*, ed. Nicholas Rowe, 1709
Rowe[2]	*Works*, ed. Nicholas Rowe, 1709

Rowe³	*Works*, ed. Nicholas Rowe, 1714
RSC	Royal Shakespeare Company
Schmidt	Alexander Schmidt, *Shakespeare-Lexicon*, 1874–5 edn
SD	stage direction
SH	speech heading
Singer	*Works*, ed. S. W. Singer, 1826
Sisson	*Works*, ed. C. J. Sisson, 1954
SQ	*Shakespeare Quarterly*
S.St.	*Shakespeare Studies*
S.Sur.	*Shakespeare Survey*
Staunton	*Works*, ed. Howard Staunton, 1858–60
Steevens	*Works*, ed. Samuel Johnson and George Steevens, 1773
Steevens²	*Works*, ed. Samuel Johnson and George Steevens, 1778
Steevens³	*Works*, ed. George Steevens and Isaac Reed, 1793
Theobald	*Works*, ed. Lewis Theobald, 1733
Theobald²	*Works*, ed. Lewis Theobald, 1740
Thirlby	Styan Thirlby, MS. notes in eighteenth-century editions of Shakespeare, 1723–51
Tieck	*Dramatische Werke*, ed. Ludwig Tieck, 1831
Tilley	M. P. Tilley, *A Dictionary of the Proverbs in England in the Sixteenth and Seventeenth Centuries*, 1950 (references are to numbered proverbs)
Tyrwhitt	Thomas Tyrwhitt, *Observations and Conjectures upon Some Passages of Shakespeare*, 1766
Walker	W. S. Walker, *A Critical Examination of the Text of Shakespeare*, 3 vols., 1860
Warburton	*Works*, ed. William Warburton, 1747
Wheatley	*The Merry Wives of Windsor*, ed. Henry B. Wheatley, 1886
White	*Works*, ed. Richard Grant White, 1857–66

Biblical references are to the Geneva Bible (1560), with modernised spelling.

INTRODUCTION

In the following introduction I have tried at every point to use information about *The Merry Wives of Windsor* as a way of directly confronting the play.

The date and first occasion of the play

I have argued in the Textual Analysis that the F text of *The Merry Wives of Windsor* is very close to Shakespeare's foul papers, the earliest state of the play, and that the play here shows signs of having been completed in haste.[1] The F text also contains matter of an upper-class and educated kind, such as the heraldic discussion with which the play begins, and William Page's Latin lesson at the beginning of Act 4, which suggests that the play was angled towards an audience specifically of this kind, even though the substantial and fundamental conception of the play, as one might expect with Shakespeare, derived not from this sense of the enthusiasms and snobberies of a particular audience but from a much deeper grasp of the forces generally at work among human beings. The targeting of a play substantially written out of other energies towards a specific audience gives these focusing elements of upper-class and educated matter a detachable quality (and they were duly later detached)[2] but they point interestingly to the circumstances within which, even if not out of which, the play arose. A yet more specific pointer and focuser of this kind is found at the end of the play, to ensure no doubt the audience's approbation as they left it. At 5.5.48–65 there is a long speech by the Queen of Fairies about Windsor Castle and the Garter Chapel which in the specificity of its reference is even more easily detachable from its surroundings than the heraldry or the Latin lesson.

As early as 1790 Malone suggested that the first performance of *The Merry Wives of Windsor* was connected with the Order of the Garter. A yearly feast was held for the Garter knights, in the presence of the Queen, and as Leslie Hotson showed in 1931,[3] there is good reason for dating the first performance of this play to St George's Day (23 April) 1597, the day of the feast held at Westminster, in Whitehall Palace, at which it was virtually certain that George Carey (the second Baron Hunsdon, who had just succeeded his father as patron of the Lord Chamberlain's Men, the company to which Shakespeare belonged) was to be one of the newly elected knights. The probability seems great that the play was commissioned by Lord Hunsdon as his contribution to the festivities, perhaps commissioned at rather short notice (after it had become clear that he was to be elected) and was there acted, as the title page of Q puts it 'by the right Honorable my Lord Chamberlaines seruants . . . before her Maiestie'.

[1] See Textual Analysis, pp. 157–9.
[2] See Textual Analysis, p. 154.
[3] *Shakespeare versus Shallow*, pp. 111–22.

1 Queen Elizabeth viewing a performance of *The Merry Wives of Windsor*.

The tradition that *The Merry Wives of Windsor* was written in response to Queen Elizabeth's desire to see a play about Falstaff in love, which first appears in John Dennis' dedication of his adaptation of the play as *The Comical Gallant* in 1702, may derive from these circumstances of its first performance, or from the title page of the quarto, or may have some truth to it. In the same dedication, Dennis says the play had to be finished in fourteen days and at least that part of his testimony seems borne out by the signs of haste in F.

THE GERMAN ELEMENT

The presence of Germans, and a German Duke, in the play also suggests the Garter celebrations of 1597. On this occasion one of the newly elected knights, elected *in absentia* and so not actually present at the feast (he had not even, indeed, been informed of his election), was Frederick, Duke of Württemberg, who had been touting for election (perhaps in a way that made him seem comic) since he had first visited England in 1592 as Count Mömpelgard (see 4.5.61 n.). It seems conceivable that references of this kind in the play, which would allow a certain private merriment about the persistent German with the funny name, might have been introduced quite late on, when the plot was already shaped and established, as the result of a hint from some of those interested in its coming performance at the feast where Frederick would be an absent presence. That a bit of hasty insertion could come to seem to us important in the play because of its haste and incompleteness[1] is evidence of a genius like Shakespeare's which will take the untidy circumstances of life as they occur and give them permanent significance.

THE BROOM/BROOK SUBSTITUTION

One change, however, Shakespeare had to make very late in the day because of the circumstances of the first performance, which an editor can only unmake. There can be no doubt that Shakespeare's intention was that Master Ford should be called Brook when he appeared in disguise to Falstaff. A ford goes across a brook (that is, the words are cognate) and at 2.2.122 Falstaff decisively quibbles with the name of his mysterious benefactor from whom he has had 'a morning's draught of sack': 'Such brooks are welcome to me, that o'erflows such liquor.'

F's substitution of the name Broom for Q's Brook, occurring because F is directly derived from the foul papers which served as the theatrical text for the first perform-ance,[2] seems the result of a sudden difficulty about the name Brook just before the first performance. We can surmise what that difficulty may have been. George Carey, Lord Hunsdon, became Lord Chamberlain six days before the Garter Feast, following the death in March of the previous holder of the office (and his own father's successor), William Brooke, Lord Cobham. There is evidence that the Brooke family had already objected to Oldcastle, Shakespeare's first name for Falstaff in *The First Part of King Henry IV*, since it was the name of a distinguished ancestor of theirs. That in a play

[1] See Introduction, p. 10.
[2] See Textual Analysis, p. 158.

also about Falstaff their own present family name should occur as the alias of a jealous fool may have provoked sudden objection again from the new Lord Cobham, Henry Brooke, or may indeed have been noticed as an embarrassing coincidence by Lord Hunsdon as he looked through Shakespeare's text before the performance. The performance was, after all, to be in the presence of an audience who would all know the Cobham family name, and who were all going to be asked to chuckle at an absent German duke. The possibility that there might be humour as well at the expense of his recently dead predecessor as Lord Chamberlain had to be ruled out, along with the name Brook. On the public stage, of course, so common a name would not have pointed a finger of fun at the Cobham family. It was only the upper-class coterie who formed the audience for the first performance who had to be prevented from picking up an allusion which was not intended.

THE LUCY FAMILY

One other upper-class allusion in *The Merry Wives of Windsor* clearly was intended, and this derives not from the immediate circumstances of its first performance but from the Stratford of Shakespeare's youth. Shallow's 'dozen white luces' at 1.1.12–13 must be a reference to the Lucy family of Charlecote near Stratford who bore in their coat of arms a rather more modest assemblage of three silver luces (see 1.1.13 n. and 15 n.). We need not accept the tradition, dating only from the early eighteenth century, that Shakespeare had had to leave Stratford because of trouble about stealing deer from Sir Thomas Lucy's park (a tradition which may very well derive from this play and Falstaff's deer-stealing), in order to account for a satiric memory keen enough to adorn Shallow with a touch of Lucy. Important men are often the subject of merriment just because of their importance, and we may have here no more than an echo of the fun Shakespeare and his friends had with the idea of the Lucy family when he was young (see 1.1.15 n.).

LINKS WITH THE MATURE HISTORY PLAYS

The play was probably created amid the circumstances of the Garter feast, then, and of Shakespeare's own private memories; but both Shakespeare and the first audience for the play must also have had memories of what he had already written about Falstaff. The first play in which Falstaff appears, *Henry IV Part One*, can be dated to the winter theatre season of 1596/97. *Henry V*, which contains the account of Falstaff's death, can be dated between March and September 1599; and *Henry IV Part Two*, which continues Falstaff's history from *Part One*, clearly was written between these two bracketing plays. Somewhere within this sequence of histories *The Merry Wives of Windsor* was written, either before, during or after the writing of *Henry IV Part Two*.

It is clear that Shakespeare took no pains to make *The Merry Wives of Windsor* accurately part of the sequence of the three histories when writing about characters who appear in both. Falstaff, for instance, is clearly in *The Merry Wives of Windsor* still of the court and not disgraced (since he fears court gossip about his discomfiture at 4.5.75–9, for instance), but equally clearly Prince Hal's mad days are past, and so presumably Henry V is on the throne, since Fenton is said, in the past tense, to have 'kept company with the wild Prince and Poins' (3.2.56 and see 1.1.86n.). Page speaks disapprovingly of Fenton here, and the suggestion is surely not that Fenton has repented of his association with Prince Hal and left his company, but rather that the wild Prince is no longer available as a companion. In terms of the plot of *Henry IV Part Two* that should mean that Falstaff has been banished the court. Similarly the inconsistent life of Mistress Quickly (who in *The Merry Wives of Windsor* does not know Falstaff, but in the histories has known him for nearly thirty years) makes it clear that *The Merry Wives of Windsor* is not an episode in a soap opera begun in *Henry IV Part One* and concluded in *Henry V*. However, some connections there are between the histories and *The Merry Wives of Windsor* (see notes to the List of Characters), and it seems plain that Shakespeare would not have introduced a number of characters in *The Merry Wives of Windsor* whom the audience would certainly already know from *Henry IV Part One* unless with some approximate intent to run this horse again.

At one interesting point the horse changed course in *The Merry Wives of Windsor* in a way that seems to explain an inconsistency in *Henry IV Part Two*. In the earlier part of *Henry IV Part Two* Falstaff, on his way north to Yorkshire to take part in the campaign against the rebels, calls on Shallow, who is shown in 3.2 talking about cattle prices at Stamford Fair. He clearly lives somewhere near Stamford in Lincolnshire and the Great North Road, a long way from Gloucestershire. By the time we reach 4.3, however, Falstaff is asking permission of Prince John to return through Gloucestershire where, as he says to Bardolph, he intends to visit Shallow. Oliver suggests that Shakespeare moved Shallow's home to Gloucestershire in *The Merry Wives of Windsor* because that was nearer to Windsor and then decided to keep him there for the rest of *Henry IV Part Two*.[1] This would seem to place the hasty writing of *The Merry Wives of Windsor* somewhere between the writing of Act 3 and Act 4 of *Henry IV Part Two*, a dating consistent with the evidence about the Garter Feast of 1597 and explaining, perhaps, the occurrence in *The Merry Wives of Windsor* and *Henry IV Part Two* of various words and phrases not found elsewhere in Shakespeare, and the significant percentage of shared vocabulary between the two plays.[2]

SOURCES
Attempts to suggest a specific literary context for *The Merry Wives of Windsor* beyond the obvious one of Shakespeare's own plays have not, on the whole, been fruitful. We may suppose substantially that *The Merry Wives of Windsor* arose from the demand of

[1] Oliver p. lv.
[2] Oliver p. lv; Eliot Slater, 'Word links with *The Merry Wives*', *N&Q* 220 (1975), 169–71. The links between *Wiv.* and *H5* are also clear, as Elizabeth Schafer notes, contesting the 1597 dating, in 'The date of *The Merry Wives of Windsor*', *N&Q* 235 (1990), 57–60; but this might be expected if *H5* was written shortly after *2H4* and *Wiv.* Barbara Freedman also contests the 1597 dating in 'Shakespearean chronology, ideological complicity, and floating texts: something is rotten in Windsor', *SQ* 45 (1994), 190–210, rightly pointing out that all the argument for this date falls short of proof, that there is no evidence of any other play ever being commissioned or performed for a Garter ceremony, and that Francis Meres does not mention this play in his list of plays in *Palladis Tamia: Wit's Treasury* (1598). On the other hand, Barbara Freedman does not directly address the main arguments in favour of the 1597 dating, which still seem to me to stand. Similarly, Giorgio Melchiori in *Shakespeare's Garter Plays: 'Edward III' to 'Merry Wives of Windsor'*, 1994, placing *Wiv.* after *H5*, does not explain why Shakespeare includes in a play written for the public stage specific lines about the Garter ceremonies.

a particular occasion, and from a mind already creatively involved with a certain period of English history that was both in a sense past history and also present late sixteenth-century reality. It has been often rightly said that *The Merry Wives of Windsor* in particular, although in formal terms set in the reign of Henry V, gives a picture of contemporary Elizabethan life. As such, of course, it reflects attitudes, opinions, popular story-telling of the time on the subject of marital infidelity, and it would be surprising if there were not quite frequent resemblances to be found between this play and other contemporary writing in the area of these common motifs. One possible source for an appreciable part of the plot is, however, usually mentioned, a story from a collection called *Il pecorone* (1558) by Ser Giovanni Fiorentino.[1] Even though the story is not known to have been available to Shakespeare in any English translation, another story from the same collection is generally thought to be the source of the main plot of *The Merchant of Venice*, and this one does resemble the plot of *The Merry Wives of Windsor* in some notable ways. A student is taught the art of seduction by a professor, and practises it on the professor's own wife. The professor suspects that it is his own wife the student is seducing and follows him to his own house where the student escapes by being hidden under some washing. On a second occasion, the professor stabs the washing, but the student has escaped by another method and the professor is treated as a lunatic by the wife's brothers whom he has asked to witness his search.

Nothing, of course, can be done with such a piece of information as this about *Il pecorone* except to acknowledge it. Shakespeare, if he knew this story, plainly transmuted it beyond a point where it is any longer useful to think of it. By contrast, the history plays about Henry IV and Henry V, and the likely circumstances in which the play was first commissioned and conceived, still have something to offer to any attempt at understanding what Shakespeare created in *The Merry Wives of Windsor*.

The world of the play

In formal terms, *The Merry Wives of Windsor* is in a class by itself among Shakespeare's plays because it is his only Citizen Comedy. This can be made a more interesting approach to the play than it sounds, for what we appear to find in *The Merry Wives of Windsor* is that the world of the play is itself not significant. A play with lords and ladies in it, or famous figures from history, or a play that extends from riches and power to great poverty, that encompasses extremes, has about it a significance of shape even before anything starts to happen; and much modern criticism of Shakespeare has concentrated upon the way in which that spatial significance of the play draws upon and returns upon the richness of individual character, so that we have an acute sense that what is said or done is weighty, asks to be understood, tends towards a philosophy. The world of *The Merry Wives of Windsor* is densely populated, full of life and action, but is not in this sense significant. Perhaps Shakespeare felt, as Yeats did, that what distinguished middle-class life was its lack of resonance beyond itself. That lack of

[1] An English translation of the story may be found in Bullough II, 19–26.

resonance is indeed the peculiar strength of *The Merry Wives of Windsor*: everything in this play remains itself, whether a laundry basket, a venison pasty or massively, of course, Falstaff, and when passion or rhetoric or the ingenuities of the plot seem to ask for something more, something beyond, it can never be supplied without a comic emptiness, like Pistol's theatrical speech or Ford's pointless jealousy, or a ludicrous lack of real transforming power, like Falstaff into young lover or little boys into frightening fairies. It is precisely this sense of the untransformability of real life that characterises *The Merry Wives of Windsor*.

And whatever may be the truth of the tale that *The Merry Wives of Windsor* is about Falstaff because Queen Elizabeth wanted to see a play about Falstaff in love, one could argue that in *The Merry Wives of Windsor* Shakespeare found exactly the vehicle he wanted for him. In *Henry IV Part One* and *Part Two*, where Falstaff comes to birth and his first kind of life in Shakespeare's imagination, he is the refuser of chivalry, of honour, the refuser of the fictions that decorate and sometimes transform the lives of lords and kings, but himself seems to produce a counter-fiction, a Rabelaisian icon to stand over against the business of kings and noble wars. By contrast, in *The Merry Wives of Windsor*, Falstaff is just massively himself. The enormous power of his language, which is at the centre of the inexhaustible linguistic vitality of *The Merry Wives of Windsor*, the great energy continually at play within it, has no design to make him more than the fat old man he is, but only to establish a sense of the tremendous, usually unseen, energy which underpins the ordinary; and the various humiliating accidents that occur to him fail to make him less than the fat old man he is, and it is fat old Falstaff who survives to the end of the play, the big man himself, indestructible, untransformable, whether by an old woman's gown or a set of antlers. It may very well be that simple survival, if you like, that comically empty survival, represents Shakespeare's fundamental view of Falstaff, and that *The Merry Wives of Windsor* is Shakespeare's attempt (whether or not the play was written because of the Queen's suggestion or in some sense for a particular occasion) to give the most unvarnished meaning to Falstaff's words in *Henry IV Part One*, at 5.3.58–9: 'I like not such grinning honor as Sir Walter hath. Give me life.'

The play begins in the midst of Shallow's ineffectual protestations of gentility and passes rapidly to the ludicrous and hopeless attempt to transform Slender into a courtly lover. The real people remain who they are, behind the sketched-in rhetoric they persuade themselves or are persuaded into. The whole plot of the play as it develops skilfully and a little untidily (nothing comes, for instance, of Shallow's hostility to Falstaff) is fuelled by the insubstantial rhetoric of love and honour. With the single exception of the lovers, Fenton and Anne Page, who come, as it were, from some other comedy of Shakespeare's, where true love is the final subject, all the characters in this play have as their true subject themselves. There is no enchantment of event which reveals them as different or irrevocably makes them so. So the plot, which offers a wholly ineffectual enchantment of event, is a skilful nothing in this play. Falstaff is not in love and never was, except with money and sack. It would indeed be a massive enchantment by the plot (manipulated by Mistress Page and Mistress Ford) which could find in Falstaff and his belly the great seducer, the young lover; but in reality Falstaff does not, except for the most fleeting moments, believe it. What he believes is not that he is lovable, but that some lucky combination of chance and lust is forwarding his schemes for repairing his ruined fortunes. It is not plausible that a lover who thought himself truly beloved would, at his beloved's suggestion, put on antlers and pretend to be a stag; but a trickster in the hope of gulling money out of a foolish woman might do it.

If plot as a transformer of reality is not to be found in this play, if the gestures of the plot leave the characters fundamentally untouched, then what shall we say of the teeming richness of the language? The first thing to remark is that this abundance of language does not offer itself to the plot, does not offer its energies to the plot. The language each character speaks remains his or her own language, his or her own peculiar property; it never aspires to alter perceptions on a grand scale, as for instance John of Gaunt's speech about England at the beginning of Act 2 of *Richard II*. Gaunt speaks like 'a prophet new inspir'd', his words sweep out from him and into the march of history. Falstaff in *The Merry Wives of Windsor*, by contrast, who is every bit as inspired as to his words, uses them to travel nowhere, to become nothing that he was not already before the words began.

Are we to say, then, that the language of *The Merry Wives of Windsor* is as much a nothing as the plot? I think not. And by trying to understand how language which does nothing can nevertheless be matter of great human substance, we may come to grasp as well how plot which goes nowhere significant can also be the very stuff of life. And see as a consequence that what this play is about is human life lived, not lived for a purpose or in pursuit of a great end.

There is no other play of Shakespeare's which gives us so many characters each with his or her own poetry of speech, utterly distinctive and unrepeatable. Each of these linguistic worlds is both in free and vigorous contact with others and also in a way sealed tight within itself, unaffected by whatever language goes on about it. In some cases, as with Mistress Quickly, or Caius or Evans, these little worlds achieve their intensity by falling short of what would be thought acceptably correct English; and it is astonishing how much energy a language can find within itself when it is broken or fragmented or mishandled. It is as though all the power which would normally hold it in place quietly in a conventional shape of sound or syntax is suddenly nakedly displayed. Only when a building begins to collapse does one realise, as girder springs apart from girder, how much unobtrusively concentrated energy kept it in place, and one may paradoxically have more of a sense of *edifice* in a half-collapsed building, as roof beams swing in the air, than in its quietly complete neighbour. So with the Frenchman, the Welshman, and the garrulously approximate Mistress Quickly; one has an intense sense of language being performed, a poetic sense of it. And as with a poem, one has to stand back and be prepared for a meaning which is not the prosaic sum of all the words used, especially when the words as used do not occur in the dictionary or in the sound or order that would normally be expected.

With Pistol the matter is different. He is *conscious* of resorting to poetic speech in his attempt to claim and hold the energy he wants for his life. He is a conscious poet as the other three are not; but in this he also resembles them: there is something ineluctably fragmentary about the way this poetic force is made present in his speech. By some obscure instinct Pistol knows that complete quotation of passages from plays would not serve his purpose. Lines have to be wrenched from their sockets, and only the dismembered remains of a rhetorical body will suit his end. Fizzing with energy they often are, like a live electric cable torn out of the wall, and it is that kind of dangerous and (in conventional terms) useless energy that he lives by, not only in his speech but in his actions. His sword, the point of it ever ready for a random target (as distinct from a usefully employed knife, or indeed a sword in the service of one's king), is the analogy in bodily terms for the randomly seeking rhetorical live wire (as distinct from a usefully constructed sentence). Speech and action are of a piece with Pistol, as indeed they are with Caius, Evans, and Quickly, and his speech establishes him, as much as his action, as a character who rivets attention while onstage, but who can disappear for good at 2.2.110 with no damage to the plot of the play. Pistol is a peculiarly powerful example of the degree to which this play is about life being lived and not life being significant. He is closer to Falstaff in his implicit acceptance of non-significance, than to Evans or Caius, for instance, both of whom would give a significant account of themselves and their actions (even though the audience would not for a moment accept it).

There are many others in the play, of course, who would give a significant account of themselves, who would reckon that their activities made up an interesting and meaningful plot, most notably the Ford and Page couples, the middle-class core of *The Merry Wives of Windsor*. These middle-class families end the play as they began it, however; their values and attitudes remain unchanged, though the business with Anne Page and Fenton, on the one hand, and with Falstaff and the two wives on the other, has clearly demonstrated with how firm a hold they keep a grip on property, whether that be in terms of money or human beings possessed. The little bit of plot concerned with Fenton and Anne Page (which comes as it were from another comedy by Shakespeare, as I have said) does, it is true, make some significant change to the Page family, because here true love prevails over the love of money, and the victory of love is accepted, though only, one is convinced, on this one occasion. But the whole of the Falstaff plot, his wooing of Mistress Ford and Mistress Page, makes for no change at all. Page trusts his wife anyway, so is not concerned for the security of his property; and Ford gives way to a rage of jealousy, producing rhetorical energy fully in the Pistol and Falstaff league, which is only criticised because it is irrelevant to the situation, which warrants no jealousy. The notion that possessions should be jealously guarded is not called into question, only Ford's belief that the burglar alarm is ringing when it is not. By the end of the play, neither Ford nor Page, nor indeed the audience, have been encouraged to think thoughts about property – the plot has initiated nothing substantial in that line – and we the audience perhaps find that we do not share Ford's and Page's sense that what they do, whatever they do, is solid and significant. That is not our sense of their importance; our sense is that they are important because they are alive.

With Mistress Ford and Mistress Page, we have the emphatic sense of what a joyous thing it is just to be alive; they are wives not husbands and so in a certain contemporary social sense can by definition do nothing of significance. Their husbands are the important people. All they have in life is living it. The adjective applied to them in the title of the play is peculiarly appropriate, for 'merry' suggests an attitude of mind not derived from a sense of engaging in and affecting important matters. It makes good sense that the character in *The Merry Wives of Windsor* with whom they are most intimately involved is Falstaff, for he is as they are, merry. He has no power to affect the world and no wish to do so, he wishes only to survive and to enjoy being himself. Mistress Ford and Mistress Page likewise live in a small arena hedged about by their husbands' power to do things, and so in a way even more emphatic than is the case with Ford and Page (who themselves do nothing of much significance in *The Merry Wives of Windsor*) they do nothing. At the same time, of course, they are the master-plotters behind the main plot, the great doers animating an action which, I have argued, does nothing. Even the two women's expressed desire to teach Falstaff a lesson, which in other circumstances might have produced a 'significant' Morality play, is not in any way central to the delighted energy with which they elaborate and forward their scheme.

Indeed, the measure of how signally *The Merry Wives of Windsor* is about nothing significant is to be found in the degree to which it refuses the Morality play tradition which is lying in wait all about it, as it were, to be brought in. Indignant Virtue punishing Vice is the tradition which might have captured this play, but by merriment Shakespeare's comedy escapes, and with a subtlety typical of him suggests the possibility of a world where it is not the struggle between virtue and vice which has the decisive, the architectural, say; but where rather the play of attraction and escape is what underlies the vigour with which human relationships are conducted, whether in love or any other activity of life. The willingness to be seduced, and then to struggle and throw off seduction so as to be oneself the pursuer, is the game of life in this world, and it is to be seen clearly in the relationship between the merry wives and Falstaff. Although their indignation at Falstaff's attempted seduction expresses itself in Morality play language, it is in reality a delighted indignation, which uses the absurdity of the love situation (fat old man, two women past their best) not its immorality to fuel the response, to reverse the chase, so that hunter becomes hunted, indeed becomes the stag shot down by the end of the play – shot down though not dismembered and eaten but instead invited to supper: a merry world.

The most evident and uncomplicated presence of merriment in the play is, of course, the Host; hosts are by definition merry. His speech in a way resembles Pistol's, in that it is intended to convey, but convey abundantly, little more than the attitude with which he speaks, his angle to the world. It is sometimes suggested that the shreds of plot about Germans and horse-stealing which hang about the Host are evidence of haste or incompleteness on Shakespeare's part; but even if they are, it is somehow very appropriate (especially in a play whose plotting is not central) that the Host should be vividly presented in tattered incompleteness of circumstance matching so well the abrupt inconsequentiality and the casually reached for, highly coloured obscurity of his speech, which nevertheless so marvellously and completely conveys the man:

Go, knock and call. He'll speak like an Anthropophaginian unto thee. Knock, I say . . . Bully knight! Bully Sir John! Speak from thy lungs military. Art thou there? It is thine host, thine Ephesian, calls . . . Here's a Bohemian Tartar tarries the coming down of thy fat woman.

(4.5.7–17)

If Bardolph, Pistol and Nim are Falstaff's sidekicks, then the Host is his front-man and Robin the pennant before him. Falstaff is the great vessel in *The Merry Wives of Windsor*, everywhere accompanied by smaller boats, at least in the earlier part of the play, and any appreciation of *The Merry Wives of Windsor* must begin and end with him:

Have I lived to be carried in a basket like a barrow of butcher's offal, and to be thrown in the Thames? Well, if I be served such another trick, I'll have my brains ta'en out and buttered, and give them to a dog for a new year's gift. The rogues slighted me into the river with as little remorse as they would have drowned a blind bitch's puppies, fifteen i'th' litter! And you may know by my size that I have a kind of alacrity in sinking. If the bottom were as deep as hell, I should down. I had been drowned but that the shore was shelvy and shallow – a death that I abhor, for the water swells a man, and what a thing should I have been when I had been swelled! I should have been a mountain of mummy.

(3.5.4–14)

Falstaff is finally unsinkable. It is less the shelvy shore here which saves him from drowning than the great ballooning of his imagination, which makes possible a kind of resurrection from death in the vast mountain of mummy he sees surfacing amid the waters. *The Merry Wives of Windsor* is not a play about Falstaff's discomfiture, much less his conversion; rather it is about his invincibility, beginning with the easy rebuttal of Shallow and Slender and continuing through a series of resurrections, of resurfacings, which set at nought all that standard middle-class morality with its attendant condign punishments, ridicules, and exposures can throw against him. Even in the very midst of his ridiculing, as in 5.5, he is precariously magnificent, trusting to the emptily fabled extremity of love at the beginning of that scene, regions of desire that no one else in this play has any notion of; and the ridicule over, he recovers a sense of himself as genuine Falstaff very rapidly. He is as massively the genuine article at the end of the play, with his comic despair at Evans' English – 'Have I lived to stand at the taunt of one that makes fritters of English?' (5.5.129–30) – as he was at the beginning by comparison with Shallow's much asserted but fragile gentility (see 1.1.1 n.). As Mistress Page, Page, Ford, and Evans combine at 5.5.132–44 to destroy what they fancy are Falstaff's illusions about himself, they succeed chiefly in demonstrating just how far Falstaff is the cause of imaginative energy in his enemies – not only energetic himself but the cause of energy in others. The play is nothing without him: as he ruefully but, surely, triumphantly admits at 5.5.145: 'I am your theme.' No moralist could be satisfied with Falstaff's response to the final attack upon him; even as he sinks he rises:

I am dejected. I am not able to answer the Welsh flannel. Ignorance itself is a plummet o'er me.

(5.5.145–7)

As a Morality play, *The Merry Wives of Windsor* is a failure, even though the plot does not think so; the values of property and morality are in plot terms affirmed, but

2 Brewster Mason as Falstaff in the 1968 Royal Shakespeare Company production.

Falstaff and his like remain apart from this defended territory; the greatness of the play lies in the fact that by the end of it Falstaff is as he was, and the citizenry round him are as they were. The comic world of the play has offered us no lessons of a kind to suggest that its real usefulness is to point a moral, or even on the other hand to call into question that system of morality. The Windsor world is not presented to us for any purpose, but is simply made present in all its variety of energy, with the glorious meaninglessness of life itself. That is the true success of this play; and indeed in the degree to which life itself is affirmed as real without needing to be affirmed as significant, *The Merry Wives of Windsor* may seem to touch lightly upon Lear's final agonised question about Cordelia:

> Why should a dog, a horse, a rat, have life,
> And thou no breath at all?   (5.3.307–8)

What *The Merry Wives of Windsor* suggests is that the great issue is not there but in the common unity of all life against all death:

>   Master Fenton,
> Heaven give you many, many merry days! –
> Good husband, let us every one go home,
> And laugh this sport o'er by a country fire,
> Sir John and all.   (5.5.210–14)

Some moments in the play

I have chosen three passages in *The Merry Wives of Windsor* for detailed consideration in the following pages, as a way of bringing out shapes and energies in the play which might otherwise escape proper comment, even though they are always vividly present in the relationship between an audience and a good production of the play.

2.1.1–81: THE FLOURISHING OF CHARACTER

The Merry Wives of Windsor is full of characters whose energy derives from caricature, employed to give a sense of the range of energetic possibility that may fall within the compass of ordinary 'insignificant' life. We need only remind ourselves of Pistol, Caius, Evans, or Mistress Quickly, or of Ford in his passion of jealousy. But the art of the play does not stop there. In this passage at the beginning of the second act, a situation of caricatural simplicity at an energetic surface level can be seen flourishing covertly into something a little more complex beneath. Mistress Page and Mistress Ford and their relationship with each other are more extensive, more subtle than what is strictly required by the situation of the play here, and the audience may well pick up resonances, here and elsewhere in *The Merry Wives of Windsor*, which further enliven and enhance a play already very active at its dominant and untransformable surface level.

For Mistress Page to have escaped love-letters in the holiday time of her beauty (2.1.1–2) is the ground of her robust response to Falstaff's late-coming letter; but the energy – the almost delighted energy – of her reply (2.1.17–25) can be seen as deriving

3 Brenda Bruce and Barbara Leigh-Hunt as Mistress Page and Mistress Ford in the 1975 production by the Royal Shakespeare Company.

at least in some part from a sexual response, safely tucked away beneath her ample indignation, on the part of a woman who had escaped that kind of courtship in her youth, when it seems she may have been married to her good husband for reasons not to do with romantic love, just as she designs for her own daughter. That in a hidden way she wishes the world were as it comes to be for Anne and Fenton may explain the generosity of her response to the fact of their marriage at the end of the play (5.5.210–11); and although the sexual element in her response to Falstaff's letter is nowhere explicit, the player of this part could approach it with much greater energy and verve with sexual response in mind.

'Did you ever hear the like?' (2.1.54) – Mistress Ford rushes in excitedly to tell her friend that she is grotesquely wooed, knowing nothing of the letter her friend has also had. And surely at the moment when Mistress Page says 'Letter for letter, but that the name of Page and Ford differs' (2.1.55–6), there is sharp, comic disappointment on Mistress Ford's face for a second before she combines in the spirit of revenge with her friend, as though together they are more secure revengers, less securely to be wooed, than apart. Together in the lines that follow (2.1.57–81) they allow themselves to luxuriate a little in the sexuality of the situation. The security of their position, both psychological and social, is that they have *both* been approached and so can league themselves (without jealousy – contrast Caius and Slender) against the seducer – it is of fundamental importance that this play is about the merry wives and not the merry wife – and because of this security (and deceived successfully by Falstaff into thinking it is lust for them and not their money that is the moving force) they can set in hand a plan which is to punish Falstaff and to teach Ford not to be jealous, but also, as bewitchingly, to arouse Ford's jealousy ('O that my husband saw this letter! It would give eternal food to his jealousy' 2.1.80–1). Of course, Falstaff never intended sex, but is himself seduced by the well-deceived women into the role of lover, which culminates at 5.5.1–23. The tangle of characters here, then, is larger than the plot will allow for, and is trying to write a further plot which absolutely cannot be written, in distant imitation of Anne and Fenton, but whose frustrated attempt at coming to something produces strange harmonics on the edge of what actually does happen. We have an example of the way in which, as elsewhere in Shakespeare's plays, but never so importantly as in *The Merry Wives of Windsor*, characters are larger and more complex than the lives they lead.

2.2.225–45: THE INDEPENDENCE OF WORDS

Words are easily released in this play to glory in their independent moment, because the theatrical structure which encourages them does not draw heavily upon them for a sense of its own significance. Pistol's inconsequential rant, for instance, is truly at home in *The Merry Wives of Windsor* because contributing nothing to the intrigue of the play. By contrast, this passion of jealousy from Ford is in plot terms central; but still it achieves a lyrical freedom from its context that reminds one of Marlowe at his most intense.

There is surely a moment's pause at 2.2.224, after Falstaff has left, an unbridgeable moment of silence, before Ford begins at full volume. And the speech, as it proceeds, does so in the way of lyric poetry rather than of prose. One is acutely aware of the independence of each succeeding self-conscious shape: 'My wife hath sent to him, the hour is fixed, the match is made' (2.2.226–7). There is, for sure, a thread of argument, an overall shape, but not one which dominates all the spaces; rather it is one which allows subsidiary shape to assert itself, as in the echoing threefold repetition which succeeds the sentence I have just quoted, after an interval of two sentences, or 'lines' 'My bed shall be abused, my coffers ransacked, my reputation gnawn at' (2.2.228–9). Sometimes these local shapes are so compact that the space echoes like a great chamber all about them: 'but Cuckold! Wittol! – Cuckold?' (2.2.234). And just in the way that the great echo-chamber of the theatre, when empty of all furnishing but that of an undemandingly significant plot, can immensely amplify the succession of characters and moments, as it does in *The Merry Wives of Windsor*, so here, in miniature, the same echo effect is achieved. The reason, surely, why we are so often aware of the prose of this play as, in reality, poetry is that it is not huddled into the practicality of closely succeeding argument but rather has the air at freedom, to be what it will: to be here Ford jealous, or the Jealous Husband, or Jealousy, each expansion an access of energy:

I will prevent this, detect my wife, be revenged on Falstaff, and laugh at Page. I will about it. Better three hours too soon than a minute too late. Fie, fie, fie! Cuckold, cuckold, cuckold!

(2.2.242–5)

5.5.126–54: THE SHAPE OF POETRY

Not only does *The Merry Wives of Windsor* begin and end with a stolen deer (see 5.5.19 n.), but other shapes and patterns accomplish themselves too, all this at a level below the dominant shape of the plot. We have a sense, in noticing these things, of the play as poem as much as a theatrical structure. In plot terms, the situation in this passage may well remind us of the beginning of the play, with Falstaff invited to Page's house, the ever-incompetent lover, Slender, and Evans as judge of the cause against Falstaff and his followers. But at a more detailed level the pattern returns as well. Page invites Falstaff again to his house (5.5.152–3) in terms that remind us of 1.1.155–7, in neither case being the injured party. Rather more precisely, Evans is here with his cheese, as at 1.2.10, and for only the second time in the play, with his 'pribbles and prabbles' (5.5.144; see 1.1.43); and Mistress Quickly's 'posset' (1.4.7–8) reappears (for the only other time in the play) as part of Page's invitation, and indeed her 'latter end of a sea-coal fire' (1.4.8 n.) does duty at the latter end of this play as the no doubt excellent fire that everyone will sit by in the Pages' house (5.5.213). The detail of repetition and echo here and elsewhere in the play does not ask to be thought of as significant; it is not, for instance, like heavily underscored patterns of repeated imagery in other of Shakespeare's plays; but it asks to be noticed and enjoyed for its own sake, with a lack of insistence upon significance which we are perhaps now familiar enough with, as the distinctive voice of this play.

The play on the stage

It is difficult to say anything vivid and illuminating about a production of a play one has not seen, and this is the reason why stage history is so often a catalogue of names and dates interspersed with snippets of reviewers' opinions. I have tried to do things differently here, to speculate broadly, with what evidence is available, on the kind of presence *The Merry Wives of Windsor* might have been on the stage at various times. The speculation is sometimes very tentative, but the sense of what the play could be, could be seen as, derives of course directly from my own experience of reading and directing it.

THE SEVENTEENTH CENTURY

What Shakespeare created was primarily a presence on the stage.[1] More than is the case perhaps with most other of Shakespeare's plays, *The Merry Wives of Windsor* bears down upon one as a stage presence. It is not a play that resolves itself into issues, rather one that encourages response in the midst of the theatrical experience. In our earliest (much garbled) record of what happened to the play on the stage, which dates from five years after its first production (the quarto of 1602), we can see how its presence, rather than any meaning one might coolly wish to carry away from it, was the important thing. At 1.3.15 (see note), for instance, Q's reading 'gongarian' (which I would dearly have liked to accept into my text) gives us in a small and magnificent moment that sense that *The Merry Wives of Windsor* was so securely upon the stage, so utterly and simply explicit in the way it made sense to the audience (and after all they would not have had difficulty with a tale about jealous husbands and adulterous lovers), that a large word which was in itself a sound without dictionary meaning could carry amply the immediate stage sense of the situation, and carry it all the more amply, indeed, because that sound had never been burdened with significance before. Total originality, then, is here made possible because the play is so confidently and immediately present to the audience, its 'themes' so well known, so little needing to be thought about on the way home.

I have commented in the Textual Analysis (see pp. 151–7) on some other ways in which the 1602 quarto gives us evidence of vigorous stage life, but it is worth pausing here as well to look at the title page of Q (reproduced in illustration 4). Besides suggesting that the play was often acted in these first years, both in the presence of the Queen and elsewhere, the title page gives us a clear idea of what it was about *The Merry Wives of Windsor* that pleased, Falstaff first of all and his entanglement with the merry wives (who are, in the title page, not so much the title of the play as what, after Falstaff, it principally offers the audience). After this, 'Syr *Hugh* the Welch Knight, Iustice *Shallow*, and his wise Cousin M. *Slender*' with their 'sundrie variable and pleasing humors' and then the 'swaggering vaine of Auncient *Pistoll*, and Corporal *Nym*'. We can see that what was memorable about the play to the first audiences was the gallery of characters with their fashionably prevailing 'humours' or dominant characteristics. It may even be that it was because the strangely assorted characters were so much

---

[1] Oliver (pp. ix–xiii) and Craik (pp. 25–48) give accounts of the stage history of *Wiv*. Two unpublished dissertations are also of direct interest: George David Glenn, '*The Merry Wives of Windsor* on the nineteenth-century stage' (PhD thesis, University of Illinois, 1969); and Peter Lindsay Evans, 'The stage history of *The Merry Wives of Windsor* 1874–1933' (MPhil thesis, University of London, 1981). For details of more recent twentieth-century productions, various volumes of *Shakespeare Survey* and *Shakespeare Quarterly* may be consulted, as well as J. C. Trewin, *Shakespeare on the English Stage, 1900–1964: A Survey of Productions*, 1964.

A
Moſt pleaſaunt and
excellent conceited Co-
medie, of Syr *Iohn Falſtaffe*, and the
merrie Wiues of *Windſor*.

Entermixed with ſundrie
variable and pleaſing humors, of Syr *Hugh*
the Welch Knight, Iuſtice *Shallow* , and his
wiſe Couſin M. *Slender*.

With the ſwaggering vaine of Auncient
Piſtoll, and Corporall *Nym*.

By *William Shakeſpeare*.

As it hath bene diuers times Acted by the right Honorable
my Lord Chamberlaines feruants. Both before her
Maieſtie, and elſe-where.

LONDON
Printed by T. C. for Arthur Iohnſon, and are to be ſold at
his ſhop in Powles Church-yard, at the ſigne of the
Flower de Leuſe and the Crowne.
1602.

4   Title page of Q1.

emphasised in the production, at the expense of any plot holding them informatively
together, that whoever wrote the copy for this title page could suppose that Sir Hugh
Evans was a knight and not a clergyman, even though the writer was surely a theatre-
goer because he calls Pistol by a title he has, not in *The Merry Wives of Windsor* but in

Henry IV Part Two (though Q1 (1600) of *Henry V* advertises 'Auntient Pistoll' on the
title page, so he may have got it from there).

In the early years of performance of *The Merry Wives of Windsor*, then, we have the
feeling that it might well have been a play much liked by the actors, with a good
collection of memorable parts and plenty of space for a number of players to make a
vivid impression on the audience. Although we can be sure that the play was frequently put on, the first explicit record of a performance occurs in the Revels Accounts
for 1604, when *The Merry Wives of Windsor* was performed on Sunday 4 November in
the Banqueting House at Whitehall.[1] The only other clear record of a performance
before the Restoration is again of a performance at court, on 15 November 1638.[2]

At the Restoration, *The Merry Wives of Windsor* was one of the first plays to be
revived, for Pepys saw a performance at the Vere Street Theatre on 5 December 1660.
He liked Slender and Caius, but not the rest of the production. It is interesting to
speculate that he may have been echoing what had been a common way of talking
about the play (which found an early expression in the 1602 quarto) by referring in a
rather old-fashioned manner to the 'humours of the country gentleman and the
French doctor'. The great vogue for Nim's favourite word was by this time past, but
in 1660 Pepys may have felt as triumphant about the return of the past as eager for a
new world to open with the return of the King. So he went to see *The Merry Wives of
Windsor*, perhaps because it could show him a whole Elizabethan world again, now that
the Commonwealth was past; but he did not in the event much like what he saw, nor
did he like the play on the two other occasions on which he saw it, 25 September 1661
and 15 August 1667. He went to see it, however, on these two further occasions, and
we may think that Pepys' sense of the play was equivocal. Perhaps he liked the idea of
it, of this large, hearty old world, better than the performing. It may even have been
that acting styles in the Restoration were not robust and unself-conscious enough to
sustain the joyously and directly focused energies of the play.

There is some evidence from elsewhere about Restoration attitudes to *The Merry
Wives of Windsor* which may support this view. John Dennis writes in the Epistle
Dedicatory to his revised version of the play, *The Comical Gallant*, in 1702 that in the
Restoration court 'all those men of extraordinary parts, who were the Ornament of that
Court . . . were in Love with the Beauties of this Comedy', but again that when
revived on the stage in Charles II's times 'this Comedy had never . . . had any great
success'. In writing this, of course, Dennis was in the slightly difficult situation of
wishing to recommend highly a play which he had nevertheless found it necessary to
alter substantially to suit the taste of a later age, and of puffing his own alteration; but
what he says does suggest that the reaction to *The Merry Wives of Windsor* was
complex. It may be, as Oliver suggests,[3] that a play about the final triumph of middle-
class virtue (if that is how the play was presented in performance) seemed boringly
old-fashioned and tame to a sophisticated audience, while the attention of others was
held by a play so delighted about transgression of every sort as *The Merry Wives of*

[1] Chambers IV, 171.
[2] Bentley I, 99.
[3] Oliver p. xi.

Windsor. It may even have seemed in tune with the wit of the time because, just as in much Restoration comedy, trangression, and particularly sexual transgression, is presented as a vivid possibility to the imagination, but does not actually occur; so with the possibility of adultery in the body of Shakespeare's play and the possibility of men having sex with boys which energises its end.[1] This last possibility, of course, could not then have had the kind of vividness it would have had on the Elizabethan stage, where boys actually played the parts of girls, and were no doubt as regularly perceived to be in reality boys as to justify Evans' amazement in Q (see 5.5.179 n.) that Slender did not realise he was being offered a boy disguised as a girl; but nevertheless the idea of forbidden sex surely would have amused and attracted 'those men of extraordinary parts' like Buckingham and Rochester who so much set the tone for an aristocratic coterie in Restoration London.

THE EIGHTEENTH AND NINETEENTH CENTURIES

Dennis' version of 1702 regularised the plot of the play and unified what he complained of as the 'three Actions in it that are independent one of another, which divide and distract the minds of an Audience', thus sacrificing Shakespeare's diversity and bustle to a strained artificiality of shape that reminds us of the serious-minded self-conscious theatricality of the eighteenth-century stage at its most artificial and confident. *The Comical Gallant* did not take, however, and instead it was Shakespeare's play which became popular and remained so through the eighteenth and nineteenth centuries. Although it was James Quin as Falstaff from 1720–51 who made the play so very popular in the first half of the eighteenth century,[2] I think we may understand how *The Merry Wives of Windsor* trumped the artificiality of this theatrical period by laughing at itself, delighting in itself, as a contrived theatrical entity, so making itself invulnerable.

At 3.3.98–100, for instance, Mistress Page urges Mistress Ford, with a desperate urgency for the benefit of the hidden Falstaff, to think of some way of getting him out of the house before Ford rushes in: 'Your husband's here at hand! Bethink you of some conveyance. In the house you cannot hide him.' Then, with a sudden inspiration, she points to the great buck-basket which has been massively and ludicrously to hand on the stage for this purpose since the beginning of the scene: 'Look, here is a basket.' There is some difference between the overwhelming convenience of the laundry basket here and, for instance, the useful magic of Prospero in *The Tempest* or the wriggles of plot that expose a solution in other of Shakespeare's comedies. An errant letter suddenly found or the staying of an assassin's hand with a magic spell surprise the audience with a sudden sense of a possibility they had not envisaged, even open up the possibility of a world, a reality, they had not thought of. The theatre here extends the range of what the audience can believe. With the buck-basket we have a solution comfortably within a world the audience already lives in; its usefulness occurs as a sudden possibility to the characters onstage some time after it has been apparent

[1] See Textual Analysis, p. 156.
[2] See Nancy A. Mace, 'Falstaff, Quin and the popularity of *The Merry Wives of Windsor* in the eighteenth century', *Theatre Survey* 31 (1990), 55–66.

5   Act 3, Scene 3. Painted by the Revd W. Peters, 1789.

to the audience, so the theatrical event is no surprise to them. The magician is sawing the lady in half but the audience can see how the box is contrived to make it possible. And the magician indeed intends that this trick should be transparent. Both the subtlety and the splendidly solid crudity of *The Merry Wives of Windsor* are in its willingness to offer its theatricality openly to the audience.

Frequently, in this play, the audience is allowed to arrive before the play does. So at 5.5.184 Ford summons us to amuse ourselves with a joke we are already laughing at, as he comments on the discomfiture of Slender and Caius: 'This is strange.' And he goes on to ask the big question we all already know the answer to: 'Who hath got the right Anne?'

The Herne the Hunter episode is of exactly this open, delighted, undefended theatricality.[1] The Welsh devil and his boy fairies are to appear suddenly and reveal their lighted candles to Falstaff – 'That cannot choose but amaze him' (5.3.15) – Gosh, yes! – This is important work we are upon, with high purpose:

> Against such lewdsters and their lechery,
> Those that betray them do no treachery.   (5.3.19–20)

Let us thrillingly put the great plan into action: 'To the Oak, to the Oak!' (5.3.21), with as elaborate a rhetorical gesture pointing the way as may be. Think of all those eighteenth-century prints of stage scenes with a character in dramatic pose, legs tensely apart, arm and fingers flung out to point beyond the horizon of the stage.

Evans across the stage with his inadequately transformed boys doing their fairy parts (5.4), hardly the fairies of *A Midsummer Night's Dream*, and then enter Falstaff wearing a buck's head. Falstaff is magnificently equal to the absurdity of the occasion, triumphing amid the ruins of theatrical *vraisemblance*:

> Send me a cool rut-time, Jove, or who can blame me to piss my tallow?   (5.5.10–11)

And after all, is not love absurd, is not copulation physically comic? Very well, let copulation thrive:

> Let the sky rain potatoes, let it thunder to the tune of 'Greensleeves', hail kissing-comfits, and snow eryngoes.   (5.5.14–16)

The play breaks through to a point beyond its evident theatrical absurdity, led by the terrified and undaunted Falstaff. The fairies come in with a noise of horns:

---

[1] Some critics have taken the episode in a more solemn way, responding to the folkloric shape of the story in the play but not to its tone. Northrop Frye, for instance, in the *Anatomy of Criticism*, 1957, saw the rejected Falstaff of the end of *2H4* as a kind of ritual scapegoat and the Falstaff of the end of *Wiv.* as the victim of 'an elaborate ritual of the defeat of winter' (p. 183) (though, as Craik notes at p. 47, seasonal indications in the play are not so consistently focused as to suggest great concern on Shakespeare's part with the season of the year). Jeanne Addison Roberts in *Shakespeare's English Comedy: 'The Merry Wives of Windsor' in Context*, 1979, sees in Falstaff's fortunes at the end of the play both the sacrifice of a fertility god and the scapegoat by means of which a sexually threatened social order is reasserted. John M. Steadman suggests, with a more convincing response to the tone of the play, that Falstaff's disguise is a burlesque of the Actaeon myth, in 'Falstaff as Actaeon: a dramatic emblem', *SQ* 14 (1963), 230–44; and Jan Lawson Hinely in 'Comic scapegoats and the Falstaff of *The Merry Wives of Windsor*', *S.St.* 15 (1982), 37–54 takes Falstaff as a scapegoat for the Garter knights.

6 Act 5, Scene 5. Painted by Robert Smirke, 1789.

MISTRESS PAGE Alas, what noise?
MISTRESS FORD Heaven forgive our sins!
FALSTAFF What should this be?
MISTRESS FORD *and* MISTRESS PAGE Away, away!
FALSTAFF I think the devil will not have me damned, lest the oil that's in me should set
hell on fire. He would never else cross me thus.   (5.5.24–9)

For a moment perhaps, as the fairies burn Falstaff, theatrical absurdity is replaced
by nightmare, even though one of the fairies remains indisputably Welsh (5.5.74–5).
Then after the nightmare the morning suddenly comes, we wake a little ashamed of
our sweating terror at nothing, the theatricality of the episode round Falstaff suddenly
disappears. He is discomfited at being found in so outrageously rhetorical a gesture
and pulls off his buck's head. So might a man take off his crown who had really
believed for a while he was king, while the play lasted, though of course Falstaff never
believed he was a stag, a king of the forest. It is absurd, the theatre, and *The Merry
Wives of Windsor* reminds one of this often; but once handsomely admit the absurdity
and the sensible, 'untheatrical', energies that ordinarily fuel everyday life seem not all
there is to the ordinary business of being alive; perhaps we are alive in order to play
also. The comic emptiness of the untransformed (see p. 7) comes to seem like comic
space, spaciousness. Let copulation thrive then; the theatre too. Falstaff survives after
his moment of discomfiture, as large as before (see Textual Analysis, p. 162).

It seems likely that the kind of celebrated theatricality we see in these instances in
The Merry Wives of Windsor is what kept it alive on stage through the eighteenth and
nineteenth centuries, when showmanship was the vital element in the theatre. In the
two hundred years from 1700 to 1900 there were over thirty productions of the play at
major theatres, involving most of the famous actor-managers and companies of the
time, and one can imagine that a rowdy audience that could be brought to its feet by
the transforming showmanship of the end of Sheridan's *The Critic* would have re-
sponded with equally uninhibited delight to fat Falstaff with the horns on his head
danced round by schoolboy fairies.

THE TWENTIETH CENTURY

And when the lecherous fat king finally came to the throne after the death of
Queen Victoria, Beerbohm Tree celebrated the coronation of Edward VII in 1902 with
a revival of *The Merry Wives of Windsor*, playing the main part himself. The two
leading actresses of the day, Ellen Terry and Madge Kendal, played Mistress Page
and Mistress Ford, and 'though Ellen Terry was fifty-five and Madge Kendal
fifty-three, they romped through the comic scenes to the great delight of the
audiences'.[1] Beerbohm Tree had already played what has been called the best Falstaff
of all (but who can tell?) in his 1889 production of the play at the Haymarket, and here
it was again to greet the new age, to be part of the great enthusiasm that swept the
country at the coronation of the new king, after the long reign of the widow of
Windsor:

[1] Alan Hyman, *The Gaiety Years*, 1975. p. 136.

7   Falstaff (Beerbohm Tree), Mistress Page (Ellen Terry), and Mistress Ford (Madge Kendal). Portrait by J. Collier, 1904.

Tree was the finest Falstaff of them all . . . he revelled in the part. He made it fat, he made it 'lard the earth', and with it all he was a gentleman. He might consort with scum, he might drink the night through in low taverns with lower company, but always he was Sir John.[1]

What distinguished Tree's productions of *The Merry Wives of Windsor* seems to have been the understanding that neither Falstaff nor the play as a whole is finally to be taken as farcical, in spite of the abundance of farcical elements, easy to overplay, and which Tree came close at times to overplaying, for instance with the prolonged chasing of the old women of Brentford through the streets of Windsor. Tree recognised, too, that *The Merry Wives of Windsor* is created as importantly amid the topographical circumstances of a real town as the mature histories are amid the historical circumstances of the reigns of three English kings.

In production the play needs the sense that it happens in a real place, and that extraordinary human characters and reactions to events are within the compass of the real, make-believe fairies included. Tree's account of Falstaff, and his care in the 1902 production to present the play in authentic fifteenth-century costumes 'which

---

[1] W. Macqueen Pope, *Haymarket: Theatre of Perfection*, 1947, pp. 330–1.

have been preferred to the customary Elizabethan habits',[1] show a recognition of that vital ballast of the real, even though arguably Tudor costumes would have done as well for a play which was in reality about the Windsor world of Shakespeare's own day.

The Merry Wives of Windsor has been extremely popular on the stage in the twentieth century, though not until recently much attracting the interest of literary critics.[2] From 1902 onwards to the Second World War there were major productions of the play every two or three years, very occasionally (and not very successfully) in modern dress, as with Oscar Ashe's 1929 version at the Haymarket, where the attempt at modernity, to judge from report, made nonsense of the wit, the social comedy, and the balance of social and linguistic forces in the play, delicately and deeply rooted as it is in Shakespeare's understanding of sixteenth-century small-town life. The great productions of this play have always acknowledged how local it is, how rooted in one time and place, and have allowed it to grow in size and consequence from there. Donald Wolfit at the Strand in 1940 and again in 1942, at the Winter Garden in 1946 and at the Bedford, Camden Town, in 1949 developed a way with the character of Falstaff which demonstrated, too, that however Elizabethan the play properly is, it also (like much of Shakespeare) is about the theatre itself, the energies found in the theatre, and that a certain rhetorical larger-than-lifeness is a language common in all ages to players.

Productions of *The Merry Wives of Windsor* in the second half of the twentieth century have followed every few years, with the Royal Shakespeare Company in particular regularly reviving the play. It is a play which often attracts repeated attention from directors and players alike, so for instance we find Terry Hands directing it in 1968 with Brewster Mason as Falstaff, Brenda Bruce as Mistress Page, Elizabeth Spriggs as Mistress Ford, and Ian Richardson as Ford; and again directing in 1975 with the same Falstaff, Mistress Page and Ford, and with Barbara Leigh-Hunt as Mistress Ford. The first of these two productions ended with more destructive savagery against Falstaff than the second, but neither of them underplayed the size and centrality of Falstaff, the way in which he holds the attention and affection of audiences. He cannot be made a metaphor for anything; he and his world signify nothing beyond themselves. The clue perhaps to the enthusiasm of audiences and the lukewarmness of critics is in the play's untransformable rootedness in a certain defined world. A clearly defined world creates a link between stage and audience which allows

---

[1] *Illustrated London News*, 14 June 1902.
[2] More recently, critical interest has focused on *Wiv.* as a Citizen Comedy, though being the best in that kind it is not very characteristic of the run of such plays (Alexander Leggatt, *Citizen Comedy in the Age of Shakespeare*, 1973); the play has also benefited from new attention given to Shakespeare's prose (Brian Vickers, *The Artistry of Shakespeare's Prose*, 1968) and from fresh exploration of the way Shakespeare exploits the traditions of comedy (Bertrand Evans, *Shakespeare's Comedies*, 1960; Leo Salingar, *Shakespeare and the Traditions of Comedy*, 1974). *Wiv.* has also been fruitful ground for the exploration of various ideologies, to do with women, marriage, money, and the social order, in spite of the fact that this is not a play about ideologies (Alice-Lyle Scoufos, *Shakespeare's Typological Satire*, 1979; Jeanne Addison Roberts, *Shakespeare's English Comedy*). For detailed accounts of criticism of the play, see Jeanne Addison Roberts pp. 61–118 and R. S. White, 'Criticism of the comedies up to *The Merchant of Venice*, 1953–82', *S.Sur.* 37 (1984), 1–11. See also p. 22, n. 1 and the Reading List.

Actus Secundus. Scœna Prima.

Enter Miſtris Page,*Miſtris* Ford,*Maſter* Page, *Maſter*
Ford, Piſtoll, Nim, Quickly,Hoſt,Shallow.

Miſt. Page. What, haue ſcap'd Loue-letters in the
holly.day-time of my beauty , and am I now a ſubiect
for them ? let me ſee?

Aske me no reaſon why I loue you,for though Loue vſe Rea-
ſon for his preciſian, hee admits him not for his (ounſailour :
you are not yong, no more am I: goe to then,there's ſimpathie :
you are merry, ſo am I : ha, ha, then there's more ſimpathie :
you loue ſacke, and ſo do I : would you deſire better ſimpathie?
Let it ſuffice thee (Miſtris Page) at the leaſt if the Loue of
Souldier can ſuffice, that I loue thee : I will not ſay pitty mee ,
'tis not a Souldier-like phraſe; but I ſay, loue me :
       By me, thine owne true Knight,by day or night :
       Or any kinde of light, with all his might ,
       For thee to fight.   Iohn Falſtaffe.

8   From a page of the 1623 Folio showing 'massed entry' stage directions (see Textual Analysis,
pp. 157–8).

for the traffic back and forth of all kinds of subtlety, but it will not yield very easily to
the various metamorphoses of interpretation, and so that characteristic busyness of
much twentieth-century criticism has found little to get a grip on in *The Merry Wives*
of Windsor.

You cannot push this play about much, you must take it as it is, and the best
modern productions have really done that. The relative failure of the 1992 RSC
production demonstrated fairly comprehensively what the play demands of a production if it is to succeed. Peter Holland, reviewing this 1992 revival, makes the important
points:

The play, so often a glittering success for the RSC, became an inglorious catastrophe, devoid
of charm or interest . . . The play's language was ignored in favour of ancient pieces of
business . . . No one had the courage to suggest that the play's prose is an extraordinary comic
achievement . . . [Falstaff] became marginal to the play, never its dominant and dominating
character . . . The exactness of the play's interest in a provincial town, something the RSC has
in the past found and recreated, here disappeared.[1]

Shakespeare never wrote prose better than in *The Merry Wives of Windsor*; the play
gives us his finest, most subtle, most extensive account of Falstaff; and it leaves us with
the lasting conviction that in the detailed, confined circumstances of a known world,
of the kind we move in every day, are to be found in all their vigour the energies that
make the earth go round the sun.

[1] Peter Holland, 'Shakespeare performances in England, 1992', *S.Sur.* 46 (1994), 180–1.

NOTE ON THE TEXT

The copy-text for this edition is provided by the more authoritative of two early texts of *The Merry Wives of Windsor*, that found third in the group of four comedies with which the 1623 Folio begins. This text (F), evidently set from a fair copy provided by a professional scribe called Ralph Crane, like the other comedies in this group, was plainly carefully prepared and printed, but in some respects it is notably deficient and has to be supplemented by recourse to the only other text of the play of independent authority, the first quarto of 1602 (Q). Q gives us a much shorter, more abrupt and disorderly version of the play which is, however, in some respects evidently closer to the early theatrical performance and on occasion preserves a plainly genuine reading in the spoken text, which F requires. A fuller account of the relations between F and Q and a discussion in general and in detail of the textual problems of this play will be found in the Textual Analysis (pp. 151–62).

A first glance at the textual Collation at the foot of each page of text, which records all significant departures from F, will make it clear that what is presented to the reader here is, in most respects, the version of the play appearing in the First Folio. The most notable single exception to this is in the provision of stage directions, where F is seriously inadequate. Square brackets in the body of the text indicate more than superficial departures from the Folio stage directions, and where Q stage directions are adapted or incorporated, this is recorded in the Collation.

The Collation omits mention of the regularisation of spelling, punctuation, and speech headings usually found in a modern edition, except where these are of special interest. In cases where the Collation records a departure from F, the Commentary at the foot of each page should be consulted (an asterisk before the lemma alerts the reader to a note relating to a departure from F), since this provides a fine detail of justification for textual decisions which complements the account in the Textual Analysis.

The Merry Wives of Windsor

LIST OF CHARACTERS

Sir John FALSTAFF
ROBIN, *Falstaff's page*
BARDOLPH ⎫
PISTOL   ⎬ *followers of Falstaff*
NIM   ⎭
Master Francis FORD, *a citizen of Windsor*
MISTRESS *Alice* FORD, *his wife*
JOHN   ⎫ *his servants*
ROBERT ⎭
Master George PAGE, *a citizen of Windsor*
MISTRESS *Margaret* PAGE, *his wife*
ANNE *Page, his daughter*
WILLIAM *Page, his son*
Master Robert SHALLOW, *a country justice of the peace*
Master Abraham SLENDER, *his nephew*
Peter SIMPLE, *Slender's servant*
Doctor CAIUS, *a French doctor*
MISTRESS QUICKLY, *his housekeeper*
John RUGBY, *his servant*
Master FENTON, *a young gentleman*
Sir Hugh EVANS, *a Welsh parson*
HOST *of the Garter Inn at Windsor*
Children of Windsor

Notes
No list of characters appears in either F or Q; Rowe was the first to supply one.

SIR JOHN FALSTAFF Appears also in *1* and *2H4*, and his death is recorded in *H5*. Significantly not characterisable in a phrase like the other characters in the play, he stands somewhat apart from their interwoven social networks. The old (2.1.18) fat (1.3.29–30) knight with the great beard (4.2.158) is a class above most others in this middle-class world (4.5.75–9), a foreign body in their midst.

ROBIN Also appears in *2H4*. He is small (3.2.1) and vividly and gaily dressed (3.2.13; 3.3.20).

BARDOLPH Also appears in *1* and *2H4* and *H5*. He is just born to be the tapster he becomes (1.3.14), with his red face (1.1.135) no doubt red from drink.

PISTOL Also appears in *2H4* and *H5*. He is aware of himself as an exciting and dangerous man, the very opposite of Slender (1.3.56–7).

NIM Also appears in *H5*. Of the lowest officer rank in the infantry (2.1.111), he is ready to trust to his sword (2.1.109), and has an insistent, repetitive form of speech (2.1.117).

MASTER FRANCIS FORD A constitutionally jealous man (2.1.81).

MISTRESS ALICE FORD A black-haired woman (5.5.14), no longer young (2.1.91) nor in any sense giddy (3.3.48).

JOHN *and* ROBERT Servants robustly resigned to the foolishness of their betters.

MASTER GEORGE PAGE Not a jealous or anxious man (2.1.83).

MISTRESS MARGARET PAGE Like her friend, Mistress Ford, she is no longer young (2.1.4–5) or giddy, perhaps never was giddy (2.1.1–2).

ANNE PAGE A young girl not yet seventeen years of age (1.1.42), pretty (1.4.117), with brown hair and a clear high voice (1.1.37–8), rather shy (1.4.128–9).

WILLIAM PAGE A shoolboy reluctantly submitting to the idiocies of adults, both the learned and the ignorant (4.1).

MASTER ROBERT SHALLOW Also appears in *2H4*. He is a justice of the peace, a country gentleman from Gloucestershire, entitled to bear arms, and he is anxious that this should all be known as soon as possible (1.1.3–7). Though a great fighter in his youth, as he boasts (2.3.32–8), he is now over eighty years of age (3.1.45).

MASTER ABRAHAM SLENDER Lives at the moment like a poor gentleman born (1.1.219–20) but has expectations after his mother dies (4.4.82); neatly dressed and fussily aware of it (1.1.121; 1.1.135), with a small face and a little yellow beard (1.4.19–20) and a strutting, head-held-high walk (1.4.25). He is not educated enough to know any Latin (1.1.144), unlike William Page, is a fastidious avoider of drunken knaves (1.1.146–7), and an incompetent and reluctant lover (3.4.55–6).

PETER SIMPLE A young man (1.4.31–2) matching in a lower sphere the incompetence of his master.

DOCTOR CAIUS Very French. Easily angered (1.4.4–5); a skilled fencer (2.1.178), as Frenchmen were reputed to be; rich, and with friends at court (4.4.84–5).

MISTRESS QUICKLY Also appears in *1* and *2H4* and *H5*, but is here not the hostess of the Boar's Head Tavern but Caius' maid of all work (1.2.2–4).

JOHN RUGBY An honest, willing, kind fellow (1.4.9), though given to prayer (1.4.11).

MASTER FENTON Comes closest in the play to Falstaff's social status, and is the one successful lover. He is of high birth (3.4.4) but has wasted his fortune with high living (3.2.55–7; 3.4.5–8); but now he is a youth to fall in love with (3.4.13–18), he smells April and May (3.2.52–3).

SIR HUGH EVANS Very Welsh. Stupid but occasionally accurate in the moralising way of a clergyman and schoolmaster (4.1; 5.5.118–19; 5.5.121).

HOST Larger than life, a smaller version of Falstaff, given to a ranting style of speech (2.1.153). Merrily dedicated to drink and money (2.1.153–4).

THE MERRY WIVES OF WINDSOR

1.1 [*Enter* JUSTICE SHALLOW, SLENDER, *and* SIR HUGH EVANS]

SHALLOW Sir Hugh, persuade me not. I will make a Star Chamber
matter of it. If he were twenty Sir John Falstaffs, he shall not abuse
Robert Shallow, Esquire.

SLENDER In the county of Gloucester, Justice of Peace and Coram.

SHALLOW Ay, cousin Slender, and Custalorum.   5

Title] THE Merry Wiues of Windsor. F; A pleasant conceited Comedie, of Syr *Iohn Falstaffe*, and the merry Wiues of
VVindsor. Q1   Act 1, Scene 1   1.1] *Actus primus, Scena prima.* F   0 SD] *Rowe; Enter Iustice* Shallow, Slender, *Sir* Hugh
Euans, *Master* Page, Falstoffe, Bardolph, Nym, Pistoll, Anne Page, *Mistresse* Ford, *Mistresse* Page, Simple. F; *Enter Iustice*
Shallow, *Syr* Hugh, *Maister* Page, *and* Slender. Q   1–2 Sir . . . it] F; NEre talke to me, Ile make a star-chamber matter of
it Q

Act 1, Scene 1

1 Sir Hugh The clergyman is given the title
'Sir', as would normally be done, to indicate that he
has a university degree, but this is without the
higher *rank* a real knight had. On the title page of
Q1, this title is mistaken for the form of address to a
knight, and Sir Hugh is called 'the Welch Knight'.
Perhaps in ordinary usage the title was understood
as belonging really to a knight, so that Shakespeare
intends us to be aware in this first speech that
Sir Hugh's title is a good deal more fragile than
Falstaff's. The speech indeed begins with that fragile aspiration to gentility and ends with Shallow's
similarly fragile though strongly asserted status. See
3 n.

1 Sir . . . will Q1, at the beginning of a scene
much abbreviated from the Folio text, omits 'Sir
Hugh', thereby abandoning what is Shakespeare's
clear rhetorical intention in the playing with
genuine and not so genuine titles, and alters the
following words. Q1's changes clearly happened for
irresistible theatrical reasons: here Shallow is not
particularly addressing Evans but bursts with dramatic anger onto the stage, in a way that would
delight an actor; and all that need be known about
Sir Hugh in the actual circumstances of the stage
is his Welsh speech, not his name. See Textual
Analysis, p. 155.

1–2 Star Chamber matter The King's Council sitting as a court of law met in a room in Westminster Palace with stars painted on the ceiling;
hence the name of the court. Among cases brought

before the Star Chamber were those concerning
riotous assembly, especially where men of title
were involved.

2 abuse wrong, use ill.

3 Esquire A gentleman one degree below a
knight. As Oliver remarks, Shallow could use this
title not necessarily because he was born to it, but by
virtue of being a justice of the peace. This, then,
would be an occupationally acquired title rather like
Sir Hugh's. The clear irony of the speech is that
Falstaff's title and status, so contemptuously set
aside by Shallow, outweighs that of his opponents;
as indeed he outweighs them in other respects.

4 Coram A common corruption for the Latin
quorum, this being the first word of the commission
by which certain justices of the peace of particular
standing were designated.

5 cousin Often loosely used as a term of friendship, but in this case Shallow does indeed seem to
be Slender's uncle. See 3.4.36.

5 Custalorum A corruption of the Latin
phrase *custos rotulorum*, meaning the 'keeper of the
rolls' or the chief justice of the peace of the county.
Slender in the following line, with the corrupt word
'Ratolorum', is plainly referring to the same office,
not realising that Shallow has already mentioned
it. We may readily suppose, because of Slender's
character in the rest of the play, that his Latin
here is laughably ignorant. What is not so clear is
the flavour of Shallow's 'Custalorum'. It may be
a standard contraction, but it is not recorded in
OED.

33

SLENDER Ay, and Ratolorum too; and a gentleman born, Master Parson, who writes himself Armigero in any bill, warrant, quittance, or
obligation – Armigero.

SHALLOW Ay, that I do, and have done any time these three hundred
years.   10

SLENDER All his successors gone before him hath done't, and all his
ancestors that come after him may. They may give the dozen white
luces in their coat.

SHALLOW It is an old coat.

EVANS The dozen white louses do become an old coat well. It agrees   15
well passant. It is a familiar beast to man, and signifies love.

SHALLOW The luce is the fresh fish. The salt fish is an old coat.

---

17 The salt . . . coat] F; the salt fish is an old cod *NS;* The salt fish is not an old coat *Craik*

---

7 **writes himself** signs himself, uses the title.

7 **Armigero** *Armiger* at this time simply de-
signates a gentleman entitled to bear arms.
Steevens³ suggests that Slender had only ever seen
this word in the ablative case, as it would appear in
the standard legal formula of attestation: *jurat coram
me*, Roberto Shallow, *Armigero*. Slender ignorantly
takes the ablative for the nominative, and may also
have confused the preposition in this formula with
the 'Coram' he used at 4. We know from 1.1.144
that Slender has little or no Latin.

7 **quittance** bill of discharge from a debt or obligation.

9–10 Shallow means that his family have been
entitled to bear arms for three hundred years; but
unintentionally, to comic effect, he speaks of himself as having signed himself *armiger* for all that
time. This is deliberately the speech of an old man
(more than eighty years old; see 3.1.45) so flushed
with his own honourable status that he cannot limit
his sense of his own dignity to the span of a single
human life.

11–12 **All . . . him may** Slender ludicrously
transposes 'successors' and 'ancestors'.

12 **give** display.

13 **luces** pike. There seems little doubt that
there is some reference here to the arms of the
Lucy family of Charlecote near Stratford, three
luces haurient argent (three silver pike set perpen-
dicularly; see Introduction, p. 4). The Lucy arms
were old established, but the Shallow arms, although allegedly dating back a similar three hundred years, in fact have a contemporary and rather
overblown feel to them, with their dozen pike. A
tendency towards overcrowded and elaborate
shields reached something of a climax by about the
middle of the sixteenth century, and was followed

by a marked return to simpler designs after 1570
(see W. H. St John Hope, *A Grammar of English
Heraldry*, rev. ed. Anthony R. Wagner, 1953, pp.
72–3). An aristocratic audience at the end of
the century might well think Shallow's twelve fish
vulgar and amusing.

13 **coat** coat of arms.

15 **louses** Craik's suggestion (p. 7) that Shakespeare remembered the luce/louse pun as a joke he
had known from his schooldays is very attractive. It
seems clear, nevertheless, that Evans himself is not
punning, but takes Slender's 'luces' as the kind of
plural formation for 'lice' that would be familiar to
him in his own Welsh dialect of English.

15 **old coat** Evans' use of a heraldic term in his
next sentence must mean that he understands Shallow's heraldic use of the term 'coat'. Evans makes
the witty remark that an old heraldic coat like an old
garment goes appropriately with lice; but the joke is
on him because he has misunderstood pike as lice in
the first place.

16 **passant** Evans' much undermined joke continues: 'passant' is a heraldic term meaning walking,
and he suggests that lice in an old coat of arms
are appropriately shown walking, just as they walk
about in an old garment.

16 **It . . . love** The undermined bout of wit
reaches its goal: lice cling closely to men, are never
separated from them (see Tilley L471); and so the
louse signifies well, in emblematic terms, the in-
separability of love.

17 Shallow says to Evans, 'It is the luce, the
freshwater fish, that I'm talking about, not the
louse.' Then he takes up the structure of Evans'
joke: just as Evans had remarked that lice were very
suitable animals for an old heraldic coat because
they were found in old coats of another sort, so

SLENDER I may quarter, coz.

SHALLOW You may, by marrying.

EVANS It is marring indeed, if he quarter it.   20

SHALLOW Not a whit.

EVANS Yes, py'r Lady. If he has a quarter of your coat, there is but three
skirts for yourself, in my simple conjectures. But that is all one. If
Sir John Falstaff have committed disparagements unto you, I am of
the Church, and will be glad to do my benevolence to make atone-   25
ments and compromises between you.

SHALLOW The Council shall hear it; it is a riot.

EVANS It is not meet the Council hear a riot. There is no fear of Got in
a riot. The Council, look you, shall desire to hear the fear of Got,
and not to hear a riot. Take your visaments in that.   30

SHALLOW Ha! O'my life, if I were young again, the sword should
end it.

EVANS It is petter that friends is the sword, and end it. And there is also
another device in my prain, which peradventure prings goot
discretions with it. There is Anne Page, which is daughter to   35
Master George Page, which is pretty virginity.

22 py'r Lady] *Capell;* per-lady F   36 George] *Theobald; Thomas* F

Shallow muses that the kind of fish that would suit
an old heraldic coat would be not the fresh one (now
in the other sense of 'fresh', meaning recently dead
rather than found in inland waters) but the salted
and preserved one ('salt' in the sense salted, not in
the sense 'found in the sea'). The reading of F will
just about sustain this interpretation without emendation, I think, but I suggest one might emend 'is'
to 'fits' in the second sentence on the grounds that
this carries the meaning of Evans' verb 'become' at
15 more explicitly, and on the grounds that an actor
playing an eighty-year-old man with no teeth (as we
may suppose) would relish not only three f-sh
sounds in the line, but an f-ts sound that could drift
amusingly towards it. The verb 'fits' would be used
rather in the sense in which it occurs at 2.1.131.

18 **quarter** Slender introduces the idea that by
marrying he might alter the Shallow arms in the
usual way by combining the arms of his wife with
his own, each appearing twice in a cross-pattern on
a quartered shield.

20 Evans doggedly pursues his joke about coats
(heraldic) and coats, and so deliberately takes 'quarter' here to mean that a garment is cut into four
pieces, which would indeed mar it. The additional
quibble on marrying and marring was proverbial at
this time ('Marrying is marring' Tilley M701).

21 **Not a whit** Not at all. Shallow makes no

attempt to follow Evans' joke in kind, but contents
himself with denying the non-heraldic, destructive
sense of 'quarter'.

22 ***py'r Lady** Evans' Welsh speech is indicated often but not with absolute regularity by F;
here the 'p' for 'b' is clearly Welsh.

23 **skirts** The long coat would be divided into
four panels below the waist.

23 **conjectures** Part of Evans' Welsh speech is
a frequent use of plural for singular, as here.

23 **But . . . one** So much for that. At last Evans
abandons his joke, long after everyone else, on the
stage and in the audience, has abandoned it.

25–6 **atonements** reconciliation (with Evans'
plural for singular). Appropriately, the parson uses
a word with a distinct theological flavour here.

27 **Council** The King's Council, sitting in the
Star Chamber. See 1–2 n.

28 **hear a riot** Evans takes Shallow to mean
'hear the riot itself'.

30 **Take . . . that** Take advisement about that,
think well about that.

33 **and end it** and so end the matter.

34–5 **prings . . . it** would make very good
sense.

36 ***George** Elsewhere in the play, Page is consistently given the first name George. Shakespeare
probably forgot he had begun by calling him

SLENDER Mistress Anne Page? She has brown hair, and speaks small like a woman.

EVANS It is that fery person for all the 'orld, as just as you will desire. And seven hundred pounds of moneys, and gold, and silver, is her grandsire upon his death's-bed (Got deliver to a joyful resurrections!) give, when she is able to overtake seventeen years old. It were a goot motion if we leave our pribbles and prabbles, and desire a marriage between Master Abraham and Mistress Anne Page.   40

SLENDER Did her grandsire leave her seven hundred pound?   45

EVANS Ay, and her father is make her a petter penny.

SHALLOW I know the young gentlewoman. She has good gifts.

EVANS Seven hundred pounds, and possibilities, is goot gifts.

SHALLOW Well, let us see honest Master Page. Is Falstaff there?

EVANS Shall I tell you a lie? I do despise a liar as I do despise one that is false, or as I despise one that is not true. The knight Sir John is there; and I beseech you be ruled by your well-willers. I will peat the door for Master Page. [*He knocks*] What ho! Got pless your house here!   50

[Enter PAGE*]*

PAGE Who's there?   55

EVANS Here is Got's plessing and your friend, and Justice Shallow, and here young Master Slender, that peradventures shall tell you another tale, if matters grow to your likings.

---

47 SH SHALLOW] *Capell; Slen.* F   53 SD] *Rowe; not in* F   54 SD] *Rowe; not in* F

Thomas, but it is conceivable, as Jowett suggests, that 'Geo.' in Shakespeare's handwriting could have been misread 'Tho.'.

37 small in a high-pitched voice.

39 as just . . . desire as precisely as you could wish it.

43 pribbles and prabbles quarrelling and bickering. The reduplicated phrase, derived from 'brabbles' (= squabbles, quarrels), serves to emphasise the triviality of Shallow's Star Chamber matter.

44 Abraham As we learn at 186, this is Slender's inappropriately grand first name, and there is no doubt that in performance Evans would indicate Slender here.

46 is . . . penny has left her more still.

47 SH *SHALLOW F assigns this speech to Slender, but he has already, at 37–8, said he knows her. It seems characteristic, too, of the young man to recall Anne's hair and voice, and of the old man to recall her gifts. The mistaken speech heading is easily explained as a scribal or compositorial error;

but there seems less justification for suggesting, as some editors have done, that Slender's speech at 45 should also be given to Shallow. A mechanical repetition of the piece of information just provided by Evans would suit Slender's feeble capacities well.

48 possibilities further prospects.

48 goot gifts Here is another quibble of the coat/coat variety from Evans. Shallow has just commented on Anne Page's qualities of character; Evans deliberately takes the phrase 'good gifts' to mean more tangible possessions.

52 well-willers well-wishers. Hart demonstrates that this is a common phrase and not an example of Evans' dialect.

57–8 tell . . . tale have something further to say to you.

58 likings Shakespeare generally prefers the singular form, but here, as Craik notes, the reference may be to the approval of both Slender and Page, so that the plural form may not be an example of Evans' dialect.

PAGE I am glad to see your worships well. I thank you for my venison,
  Master Shallow.   60

SHALLOW Master Page, I am glad to see you. Much good do it your
  good heart! I wished your venison better; it was ill killed. How doth
  good Mistress Page? And I thank you always with my heart, la, with
  my heart.

PAGE Sir, I thank you.   65

SHALLOW Sir, I thank you; by yea and no I do.

PAGE I am glad to see you, good Master Slender.

SLENDER How does your fallow greyhound, sir? I heard say he was
  outrun on Cotsall.

PAGE It could not be judged, sir.   70

SLENDER You'll not confess, you'll not confess.

SHALLOW That he will not. [*Aside to Slender*] 'Tis your fault, 'tis your
  fault. [*To Page*] 'Tis a good dog.

PAGE A cur, sir.

SHALLOW Sir, he's a good dog and a fair dog. Can there be more said?   75
  He is good and fair. Is Sir John Falstaff here?

PAGE Sir, he is within; and I would I could do a good office between
  you.

EVANS It is spoke as a Christians ought to speak.

SHALLOW He hath wronged me, Master Page.   80

PAGE Sir, he doth in some sort confess it.

SHALLOW If it be confessed, it is not redressed. Is not that so, Master

---

72 SD] *Craik; not in* F   73 SD] *Oxford; not in* F

62 I . . . killed Craik notes that it is not clear
why Shallow has sent the venison to Page 'who has
only just been proposed, by Evans, as Slender's
father-in-law'. I incline to Hart's view that the deer
was 'ill killed' because illicitly killed by Falstaff (see
87). Oliver's suggestion that the deer had been
clumsily killed, in a way that made it less good to eat
(clearly implied by 'I wished your venison better'),
fits neatly with the assumption that it was Falstaff's
kill. A raiding party would hardly kill the deer in the
best possible way.

63 la indeed

66 by yea and no certainly. Shallow's speech
is full of repetition and almost meaningless intensi-
fication, the flaccidly fulsome and self-contented
speech of an old man.

68 fallow light brown.

69 outrun on Cotsall outrun by another dog
in a coursing match in the Cotswold hills.

70 It . . . judged It was impossible to be certain.

72–3 'Tis . . . fault You are at fault, you are at
fault. These words are said aside to Slender, reprov-
ing him for teasing Page about his greyhound. Shallow then resumes his fulsome speech to Page.

74 A cur An ordinary dog. The word 'cur' need
not have a pejorative sense at this time; and it seems
likely that Page is responding to Shallow's flattering
judgement with the pleasant modesty of saying 'he's
just an ordinary dog'.

76 good and fair Shallow is using expert
language about hounds, as NS makes clear. These
adjectives were technical terms of judgement, and
Shallow uses them to give weight to his praise.

81 in some sort to some degree.

82 If . . . redressed The proverbial expression
is 'Confession of a fault is half amends' (Tilley
c589); the more recently recorded variant, 'A fault
confessed is half redressed', may perhaps derive
from this passage.

Page? He hath wronged me, indeed he hath, at a word he hath.
Believe me. Robert Shallow, Esquire, saith he is wronged.

[*Enter* SIR JOHN FALSTAFF, PISTOL, BARDOLPH, *and* NIM]

PAGE Here comes Sir John.   85

FALSTAFF Now, Master Shallow, you'll complain of me to the King?

SHALLOW Knight, you have beaten my men, killed my deer, and broke
open my lodge.

FALSTAFF But not kissed your keeper's daughter?

SHALLOW Tut, a pin! This shall be answered.   90

FALSTAFF I will answer it straight. I have done all this. That is now
answered.

SHALLOW The Council shall know this.

FALSTAFF 'Twere better for you if it were known in counsel. You'll be
laughed at.   95

EVANS *Pauca verba*, Sir John, good worts.

FALSTAFF Good worts? Good cabbage! Slender, I broke your head.

84 SD] Q; *not in* F   86 King] F; Councell, I heare Q   91–2] *As prose, Pope; as two lines of verse, divided after* this F   94 if it
were] F; twere Q   96] F; Good vrdes sir *Iohn*, good vrdes Q   97 Good worts? Good cabbage!] F; Good vrdes, good
Cabidge. Q

83 **at a word** in a word.

84 SD NIM Craik notes that the name is derived
from the verb 'nim' (*OED v* 3), meaning 'steal, filch,
pilfer'. F spells the name both 'Nim' and 'Nym'.

86 **King** In formal terms, the play is set in the
reign of Henry V (see Introduction, pp. 4–5); but it
is plain, too, that the life of the play as it appeared
on the stage would have seemed contemporary to its
first audiences, and this explains Q's reading of
'Councell' for 'King'. An audience caught up with
the contemporaneity of the production might easily
be puzzled by an apparently anachronistic reference
to a king when a queen was on the throne.

88 **lodge** hunting lodge.

89 The line sounds metrical, and may be, as NS
suggests, from a now lost deer-stealing ballad.
Craik's reference to Greene's *Friar Bacon and Friar
Bungay* (c. 1590), where Prince Edward is 'in love
with the keeper's daughter', suggests that the amorous situation was conventional enough.

90 **Tut, a pin!** An impatiently dismissive exclamation; Falstaff's levity is not worth a pin (*OED sb*
3b).

92 **answered** Falstaff contemptuously takes
Shallow's 'answered' (which has the legal sense of
'a charge to be answered') in the reduced sense of
conversational response.

94 **'Twere . . . were** Q's reading has a more colloquial tang about it, and seems very likely what an
actor would have said if faced with the text as in F.

94 **in counsel** in private, in confidence (*OED sb*
5c), with a quibble on 'Council' at 93.

96–7 ***Pauca . . . cabbage*** The phrase *pauca
verba* was a common Latin expression meaning 'few
words' (i.e. few words are best); evidently not common enough for Q, however, where the phrase has
dropped out. It was perhaps a bit too learned and
self-conscious for the kind of play-going audience
envisaged in the performances that have given us
the text of Q. Falstaff's punning joke on Evans'
mispronunciation of 'words' would also perhaps
have been lost on this audience, so that Falstaff's
'Good cabbage!' becomes an almost meaningless
humorous expostulation. The actor playing Falstaff
might well have got his laugh, however, with a
mimicry of Evans' accent and then his dismissive
expostulation: a less sophisticated laugh than F
provides, but just as effective. In the F version, of
course, Falstaff would not mimic Evans' Welsh accent in repeating his 'worts', but would be using the
ordinary English word 'wort', meaning a plant of
the cabbage family. See Textual Analysis, p. 155.

97 **broke your head** made your head bleed
with a blow. This was probably during the deer-
stealing episode at 87–8. Oliver cautions against assuming that Falstaff refers here to the deer-stealing,
and suggests that, if Q's words telling everyone
about Slender's pocket being picked are not admitted into the text at 100–2, so that Falstaff can learn
about Pistol's misdemeanour at that point, then

What matter have you against me?

SLENDER Marry, sir, I have matter in my head against you, and against
  your cony-catching rascals, Bardolph, Nim, and Pistol. They car-   100
  ried me to the tavern and made me drunk, and afterward picked my
  pocket.

BARDOLPH You Banbury cheese!

SLENDER Ay, it is no matter.

PISTOL How now, Mephostophilus?   105

SLENDER Ay, it is no matter.

NIM Slice, I say. *Pauca, pauca.* Slice, that's my humour.

SLENDER Where's Simple, my man? Can you tell, cousin?

---

100 cony-catching] F; cogging Q   100–2 They . . . pocket] Q; *not in* F

Falstaff at 1.1.120 shows incriminating private knowledge of that escapade, and might have been present at it to break Slender's head. I share Hart's opinion, however, that whether or not Falstaff and the other characters learn at 100–2 about Pistol's thievery, 'Sir John knows his followers' doings no doubt', and so need not have been present. It seems more likely to me that he met Slender in the violent circumstances of 87–8 and there broke his head, than that he broke his head in the altogether more cunningly companionable circumstances of the pickpocketing, where Slender was lulled and gulled, not beaten. See 100–2 n.

98 matter cause of complaint. In the next line, Slender punningly uses the same word to signify '(1) matter of consequence; (2) pus' (Hibbard).

100 cony-catching cheating. A cony-catcher was a trickster who gulled the simple-minded; the term means literally a 'rabbit-catcher', and Greene's pamphlets, *A Notable Discovery of Cozenage* and *The Second Part of Cony-Catching*, both published in 1591, popularised it. It is interesting, however, that Q prefers 'cogging', the older term for cheating or underhand dealing; and it may be that this is the word the actor said, and not just a mistakenly memorised version of F. See 96–7 n.

100–2 *They . . . pocket Malone first inserted this sentence from Q, on the grounds that otherwise Falstaff could not have known of the picking of Slender's pocket at 120. I agree with Hart that this is not a sufficient reason (see 97 n.). The reason for admitting or omitting this passage is not to do with Falstaff but with the audience. It seems to me very difficult in stage terms to motivate the full degree of indignation instantly, in the following lines, expressed by Bardolph, Pistol, and Nim, unless both they and the audience have heard the whole charge made openly against them. The great cloud of in-

dignation conceals a situation which has been momentarily glimpsed with entire and telling accuracy. And indeed Slender's charge in the following lines comes to nothing under the triple onslaught of indignation. His feebly repeated words at 104 and 106 are presumably scarcely heard above the din of righteous anger from Bardolph, Pistol, and Nim. The sentence is missing from F either because omitted by scribe or compositor, or because supplied by Shakespeare or another hand at a prompt-book stage after Q's line of descent had separated from F's. See Textual Analysis, p. 159 and 109 n.

103 Banbury cheese 'As thin as Banbury cheese' was proverbial (Tilley C268); but it is the colourful rather than the commonplace quality of Bardolph's words which overwhelms the pale, thin, Banbury-cheese-like Slender.

104 This must be Slender retreating hastily from the charge he has just laid against the three rascals.

105 Mephostophilus This is Mephostophilis, the devil made popular by Marlowe's *Doctor Faustus*, in Pistol's confidently variant pronunciation. Pistol's challenge is deliberately theatrical and larger than life.

107 Slice, I . . . *pauca* 'Slice' looks like dangerous, bullying, underworld argot for sword or knife fighting. '*Pauca*' is for *pauca verba*, as at 96. Underworld slang is no doubt utterly beyond Slender, just as his grasp of Latin is shaky, too (see 7 n. 'Armigero'). Little wonder that he calls in panic for his man.

107 humour fancy. A fashionable word at this time, originally a scientific term used to indicate the four humours of the body (blood, phlegm, choler, melancholy) which in their combination made up the individual temperament or character; but used also (often by Nim) in a variety of weakened senses.

EVANS Peace, I pray you. Now let us understand. There is three umpires in this matter, as I understand: that is, Master Page (*fidelicet*   110
Master Page); and there is myself (*fidelicet* myself); and the three
party is (lastly and finally) mine host of the Garter.

PAGE We three to hear it, and end it between them.

EVANS Fery goot. I will make a prief of it in my notebook, and we will
afterwards 'ork upon the cause with as great discreetly as we can.   115

FALSTAFF Pistol!

PISTOL He hears with ears.

EVANS The tevil and his tam! What phrase is this? 'He hears with ears'?
Why, it is affectations.

FALSTAFF Pistol, did you pick Master Slender's purse?   120

SLENDER Ay, by these gloves did he, or I would I might never come
in mine own great chamber again else, of seven groats in mill-
sixpences, and two Edward shovel-boards that cost me two shilling
and twopence apiece of Yed Miller, by these gloves.

FALSTAFF Is this true, Pistol?   125

EVANS No, it is false, if it is a pickpurse.

112 Garter] Gater F   118 ears] *Daly;* eare F   123 two Edward shovel-boards] F; Two faire shouell boord shillings Q

109 **Peace, I pray you** The whole of this episode is in the form of a mock trial, with the charge
laid at 100–2, the court convened with Evans as
clerk at 109–15, and the investigation beginning
with Falstaff as attorney at 116.
  110 *fidelicet* Welsh Latin for *videlicet* (=
namely). Evans is being fussily pompous in a way
that befits the law.
  112 **host . . . Garter** As Hart indicates, there
was in fact a Garter Inn at Windsor at this time, and
this is no doubt where Slender was made drunk.
The Host is not onstage at this point, so strictly
speaking the 'court' is not fully convened when
Falstaff starts his investigation at 116. Evans, at
114–15, envisages a hearing in the near future, but
typically Falstaff hijacks the whole affair and begins
immediately.
  113 **between them** This seems to refer to
Slender, Bardolph, Pistol, and Nim, rather than to
Shallow and Falstaff. Falstaff has already dealt
ruthlessly with the charge against him, and is now
attorney and not prisoner at the bar; and it makes
good sense to have 'mine host of the Garter' as one
of the umpires if it is the tavern incident which is to
be decided upon. The Shallow/Falstaff dispute has
given way to the dispute between Slender and
Falstaff's followers.
  114 **prief** brief, summary.
  117 This Hebraic reduplicated form is no doubt

derived from the Old Testament, as previous editors have noted. With mock formality Pistol comes
verbally to attention to answer Falstaff's summons.
  118 **The . . . tam** The devil and his dam (=
mother). A common oath (Tilley D225).
  118 ***ears** As Craik notes, accepting Daly's
emendation of F, there is 'no reason why Evans
should immediately repeat Pistol's expression
inaccurately'.
  122 **great chamber** principal room of a house.
  122–3 **seven . . . mill-sixpences** A groat was
worth 4d; a mill-sixpence was a coin specially made
in a stamping mill rather than by hand, so that the
clearly defined edge made it harder to clip. As Craik
points out, 28d is not divisible by six, but perhaps
the sixpences, as Oliver suggests, were worth more
than their face value.
  123 **Edward shovel-boards** The reading of Q
is more explicit here. Hart describes these coins as
'old broad shillings of Edward VI's time, worn
smooth (not being milled), and used for the game
of shovel-board'. Slender has paid more than face
value for these coins, no doubt because they were
especially in demand for the game. See Textual
Analysis, p. 155.
  124 **Yed** Ed, for Edward.
  126 Evans takes Falstaff's words as 'Is this true
Pistol?' (= honest Pistol). This is a deliberate quibble, of the kind he is addicted to.

PISTOL   Ha, thou mountain-foreigner! Sir John and master mine,
            I combat challenge of this latten bilbo!
            Word of denial in thy *labras* here!
            Word of denial! Froth and scum, thou liest!   130
SLENDER   [*Pointing to Nim*] By these gloves, then 'twas he.
NIM   Be advised, sir, and pass good humours. I will say 'marry, trap!'
            with you, if you run the nuthook's humour on me; that is the very
            note of it.
SLENDER   By this hat, then he in the red face had it. For though I cannot   135
            remember what I did when you made me drunk, yet I am not
            altogether an ass.
FALSTAFF   What say you, Scarlet and John?

127–30] *As verse, Pope; as prose,* F   128 latten] laten Q; Latine F   129–30] F; I do retort the lie / Euen in thy gorge, thy gorge, thy gorge Q   131 SD] *Hibbard; not in* F   132–3 say . . . with you] *This edn;* say marry trap with you F; say *marry trap* with you *Johnson;* say 'marry trap with you' *Oliver;* say mary trap Q   133 the nuthook's humour] F; bace humours Q

---

127 mountain-foreigner 'foreigner from the (wild) Welsh mountains' (Oliver).

127–30 Pistol's head is stuffed full of theatrical, ranting fragments, and even when the verse feel is only approximate, as here, it seems better to print as verse because of the highly self-conscious rhythm.

127–8 Sir . . . challenge The elaborated double address to Falstaff and the inversion 'master mine' are appropriate to the pitch of rant Pistol affects here, as is the inversion 'combat challenge' by which he asserts his right to the antique chivalric practice of trial by combat to decide matters with Slender. Slender is meant to feel utterly out of his depth in this world of strange language and antique practice that Pistol conjures up in reply to the charge against him.

128 *latten bilbo 'Latten' is thin, inferior metal; 'bilbo' a sword (from the Spanish town Bilbao, famous for swords). Pistol calls Slender a 'tin sword' not only because he is thin and insubstantial but because he is unlikely to prove much of a match in combat.

129–30 Word . . . liest Craik takes *labras* as deriving from the Spanish *labios* or *labros* (= lips); earlier editors have seen it as bad Latin for *labra*, meaning the same. The general sense of Pistol's expostulation is clear, that he is throwing his word of denial ('thou liest!') back at Slender's mouth, forcing it into the very place from which the charge of theft issued. Q's reading is slacker here, but perhaps easier to understand.

131 By these gloves Slender's language is markedly poverty-stricken and tame by comparison with the language pitted against him. He has used

this oath twice before in this exchange (at 121 and 124), and manages only the variant 'By this hat' at 135. See 174–5 n.

132 Be . . . humours 'Think carefully and be agreeable' (Craik).

132–3 *say . . . with you I have taken it that the phrase 'mary trap' derives from the popular children's game of 'trap-ball' (*OED sb*¹ 3), and that it was the cry uttered when the ball was well hit. Nim is saying to Slender that, unless he is careful, he will be like the ball in a children's game. It is demeaning language Nim is using, like snapping his fingers at Slender, who is after all not much more than a boy, though he has grown-up airs. At 129–30 and 133 ('the nuthook's humour') Q has simplified the reading of F, possibly because audience or players, or both, did not readily understand. By contrast Q has the reference to 'mary trap', and in a shorter form than F's 'mary trap with you', so that I think we may suppose that the operative technical phrase consisted just of the two words 'marry trap', and that it was a well-enough known expression. See 2.3.71 n.

133 run . . . me A 'nuthook' was a hooked stick for pulling down branches to get at the nuts, and so applied to a beadle or constable who hooked in the offender; so the whole passage means 'threaten me with the constable' (Hibbard).

133–4 very note 'right tune, i.e. truth' (Craik).

138 Scarlet and John Two of Robin Hood's 'merry men' were Will Scarlet and Little John. Bardolph is given both names, the first no doubt because of his 'red face' (135).

BARDOLPH Why sir, for my part, I say the gentleman had drunk himself out of his five sentences.   140

EVANS It is 'his five senses'. Fie, what the ignorance is!

BARDOLPH And being fap, sir, was, as they say, cashiered; and so
conclusions passed the careers.

SLENDER Ay, you spake in Latin then too. But 'tis no matter. I'll ne'er
be drunk whilst I live again but in honest, civil, godly company, for   145
this trick. If I be drunk, I'll be drunk with those that have the fear
of God, and not with drunken knaves.

EVANS So Got 'udge me, that is a virtuous mind.

FALSTAFF You hear all these matters denied, gentlemen. You hear it.

[Enter Anne Page with wine]

PAGE Nay, daughter, carry the wine in; we'll drink within.   150

[Exit Anne Page]

SLENDER O heaven, this is Mistress Anne Page!

[Enter MISTRESS FORD and MISTRESS PAGE]

PAGE How now, Mistress Ford?

FALSTAFF Mistress Ford, by my troth, you are very well met. By your
leave, good mistress.

[He kisses her]

PAGE Wife, bid these gentlemen welcome. Come, we have a hot venison   155

---

143 careers] Car-eires F   149 SD] *Rowe; Enter Mistresse* Foord, *Mistresse* Page, *and her daughter* Anne. Q; *not in* F   150 SD]
Theobald; not in F   151 SD] *Rowe; not in* F   154 SD] *Syr* Iohn kisses her. Q; *not in* F

---

142 **fap** drunk.

142 **cashiered** dismissed, got rid of, turned out
of the tavern. The meaning 'deprived of cash' favoured by some previous editors seems unlikely;
Bardolph is precisely not linking the loss of
Slender's purse directly with his drunkenness in the
way that would suggest, but saying he was drunk,
then thrown out, then (in the vague phrase with
which his speech ends) 'probably . . . lost his
purse rather than was robbed of it' (Craik). See also
1.3.4.

143 **conclusions . . . careers** In horsemanship
a 'career' is a short gallop at full speed. Bardolph is
saying, deliberately vaguely, 'things ran on out of
control'. Slender in the following line supposes
Bardolph must be speaking Latin, because he can
understand so little of what he is saying. See 7 n.
'Armigero'.

147 **God** See Textual Analysis, p. 160.

149 *SD It seems best to split up Q's multiple
entrance, so that Anne Page can come in alone, to be
seen by all, including Slender, the prospective
wooer, who manages comment only after she has
left.

154 *SD 'Kissing, as Erasmus noticed with
pleasure on his first visit to England in 1499, was the
usual form of greeting between a man and a woman'
(Hibbard). Nevertheless, it is worth noting that
Falstaff kisses Mistress Ford, and not Mistress
Page, whose husband is present; we are perhaps
meant to speculate on Falstaff's intentions in the
absence of husbands.

155–6 **venison pasty** Appropriately in the
circumstances.

pasty to dinner. Come, gentlemen, I hope we shall drink down all unkindness.

[Exeunt all except Slender, Shallow, and Evans]

SLENDER I had rather than forty shillings I had my book of *Songs and Sonnets* here.

[Enter SIMPLE*]*

How now, Simple, where have you been? I must wait on myself,   160
must I? You have not the *Book of Riddles* about you, have you?

SIMPLE *Book of Riddles?* Why, did you not lend it to Alice Shortcake upon Allhallowmas last, a fortnight afore Michaelmas?

SHALLOW Come, coz; come, coz; we stay for you. A word with you, coz. Marry, this, coz: there is, as 'twere, a tender, a kind of tender,   165
made afar off by Sir Hugh here. Do you understand me?

SLENDER Ay, sir, you shall find me reasonable. If it be so, I shall do that that is reason.

SHALLOW Nay, but understand me.

SLENDER So I do, sir.   170

EVANS Give ear to his motions. Master Slender, I will description the matter to you, if you be capacity of it.

SLENDER Nay, I will do as my cousin Shallow says. I pray you pardon me. He's a justice of peace in his country, simple though I stand here.   175

---

157 SD] *As Rowe; Exit all, but* Slender *and mistresse* Anne. Q; *not in* F   159 SD] *Rowe; not in* F   163 Michaelmas] F; *Martlemas / Theobald*   171 motions. Master Slender, I] motions; (M^r. *Slender*) I F; motions, Mr. *Slender:* I *Rowe*

157 *SD Recent editors clear the stage of all except Slender at this point, and make Shallow and Evans re-enter after 163. I imagine rather that the *Exeunt* here takes some little time, and that Shallow and Evans, hanging back a little, see Slender talking to Simple, and come forward again to urge him into Page's house.

158–9 book . . . here This is no doubt the extremely popular volume of *Songs and Sonnets* by Wyatt, Surrey, and others known as Tottel's *Miscellany*, first published by Richard Tottel in 1557. In panic at the prospect of Anne Page, Slender wishes for his collection of love poems to help him, and for the *Book of Riddles* he asks Simple for.

163 Allhallowmas . . . Michaelmas Michaelmas (29 September) in fact falls a month before Allhallowmas or All Saints' Day (1 November). Theobald emended 'Michaelmas' to 'Martlemas' (i.e. St Martin's Day, which falls on 11 November); but there seems little doubt that Shakespeare intended Simple's ignorance.

164 stay are waiting.

165 tender Shallow means an offer of marriage; but in the dialogue that follows, it is plain that Slender misunderstands this at first as an offer to mediate in the dispute with Falstaff's followers.

166 afar off indirectly, circumspectly.

171 his motions what he says.

173–4 I pray . . . me Slender speaks irritably; he will follow the advice of a justice of the peace in this matter of the criminal charge. He still does not understand that Evans and Shallow are talking about the proposed marriage.

174 country county.

174–5 simple . . . here I may be a simple fellow, but I know the right thing to do. Slender's conventional expression of confident mock-modesty almost certainly derives from the fact of his man Simple standing there, and the actor playing Simple could hardly fail to stand up a little straighter at this point. Slender characteristically gathers matter for his uninventive and repetitive

EVANS But that is not the question. The question is concerning your
   marriage.

SHALLOW Ay, there's the point, sir.

EVANS Marry is it; the very point of it – to Mistress Anne Page.

SLENDER Why, if it be so, I will marry her upon any reasonable   180
   demands.

EVANS But can you affection the 'oman? Let us command to know that
   of your mouth, or of your lips; for divers philosophers hold that the
   lips is parcel of the mouth. Therefore precisely, can you carry your
   good will to the maid?   185

SHALLOW Cousin Abraham Slender, can you love her?

SLENDER I hope, sir, I will do as it shall become one that would do
   reason.

EVANS Nay, Got's lords and his ladies, you must speak possitable, if you
   can carry her your desires towards her.   190

SHALLOW That you must. Will you, upon good dowry, marry her?

SLENDER I will do a greater thing than that upon your request, cousin,
   in any reason.

SHALLOW Nay, conceive me, conceive me, sweet coz; what I do is to
   pleasure you, coz. Can you love the maid?   195

SLENDER I will marry her, sir, at your request; but if there be no great
   love in the beginning, yet heaven may decrease it upon better
   acquaintance, when we are married and have more occasion to know
   one another. I hope upon familiarity will grow more contempt. But

---

191] *As prose, Pope; as two lines of verse, divided after* must F   199 contempt] *Theobald;* content F

style of speech from rather obvious sources, unlike
Falstaff's followers. It should be noted, for instance,
that even after he has understood that it is marriage
to Anne Page that is being spoken of, he continues
to use the phraseology he had first used as appropriate to the criminal matter at 167–8, and so engages
to marry, as though coming to a settlement of griev-
ance, 'upon any reasonable demands' (180–1); and
he is still repeating his original phraseology at 187–
8 and 193, in spite of attempts by Evans and Shallow to jog him into more appropriately romantic
language.

   182 command Evans is getting a little testy;
and Shallow similarly, at 186, addresses Slender
with greater vigour and formality.

   184 parcel part.

   184–5 carry your good will feel affection towards. There is sexual inuendo here as well, since
'will' can also mean sexual desire. See 3.4.50 n.

   189 Got's . . . ladies Craik ingeniously ex-

plains Evans' nonce oath as a covert reference to the
plant called 'lords and ladies', sometimes also
'cuckoo-pintle' (pintle = penis) because of the phal-
lic shape of its spadix.

   189 possitable positively (in Evans' strange
speech).

   190 carry her . . . her extend your desire towards her (the 'her' of 'carry her' is an idiomatic
dative).

   191 upon upon the promise of.

   194 conceive understand (*OED v* 9c).

   197 decrease This is Slender's mistake for 'in-
crease', though many in the audience might have
thought him unintentionally correct.

   199 *contempt The whole drift of the absurdity of Slender's speech here demands that he follow
the foolishness of 'decrease' with the foolishness of
'contempt', thus falling into the common proverb,
'familiarity breeds contempt' (Tilley F47). Craik
adds tellingly, 'the audience will think they hear

if you say 'marry her', I will marry her; that I am freely dissolved,   200
and dissolutely.

EVANS It is a fery discretion answer, save the fall is in the 'ord 'dissolutely'. The 'ort is, according to our meaning, 'resolutely'. His
meaning is good.

SHALLOW Ay, I think my cousin meant well.   205

SLENDER Ay, or else I would I might be hanged, la!

[*Enter* ANNE PAGE]

SHALLOW Here comes fair Mistress Anne. Would I were young for
your sake, Mistress Anne.

ANNE The dinner is on the table. My father desires your worships'
company.   210

SHALLOW I will wait on him, fair Mistress Anne.

EVANS 'Od's plessèd will! I will not be absence at the grace.

[*Exeunt Shallow and Evans*]

ANNE Will't please your worship to come in, sir?

SLENDER No, I thank you, forsooth, heartily; I am very well.

ANNE The dinner attends you, sir.   215

SLENDER I am not a-hungry, I thank you, forsooth. [*To Simple*] Go,
sirrah, for all you are my man, go wait upon my cousin Shallow.

[*Exit Simple*]

A justice of peace sometime may be beholding to his friend for a
man. I keep but three men and a boy yet, till my mother be dead.
But what though? Yet I live like a poor gentleman born.   220

ANNE I may not go in without your worship; they will not sit till you
come.

202 fall] F; faul' *Hanmer;* fault *Collier*   206 SD] *Rowe; not in* F   212 SD] *Rowe; not in* F   216 SD] *NS; not in* F   217 SD]
Theobald; not in F   220 though?] *Capell;* though, F

contempt whichever word the actor uses'. F's reading
is relatively easily explained as a mistakenly careful
correction.

200–1 dissolved, and dissolutely Meaning
'resolved' and 'resolutely'; there is another laugh in
the fact that Evans only notices one of Slender's
four mistakes in this speech.

202 fall There is some difficulty in taking 'fall'
to mean 'slip' or 'mistake' because this meaning is
not listed in *OED*. Perhaps Evans, the parson, has
a more portentous sense in mind, tinged with
theology.

205 meant well Shallow takes up the two oc-
currences of 'meaning' in Evans' last speech. The
word is slipping about amusingly between precise
lexical possibilities.

207–8 Would . . . sake Shallow's greeting be-
trays, of course, no real desire, but is, as Oliver
notes, a cliché (Tilley s68).

214 I am very well i.e. I am very well as I am,
out here in the open.

217 for all although.

217 wait upon As Hart notes, it would only be
at important banquets and functions that a gentleman would bring his own servants with him to his
host's house. Besides being vain, boastful, and self-
regarding, Slender is socially incompetent as well.

218 beholding obliged, indebted.

219 till . . . dead Slender's father is already
dead, as is evident at 3.4.35.

220 *what though? what of that?

SLENDER I'faith, I'll eat nothing; I thank you as much as though I did.

ANNE I pray you, sir, walk in.

SLENDER I had rather walk here, I thank you. I bruised my shin the   225
other day with playing at sword and dagger with a master of fence
– three veneys for a dish of stewed prunes – and, by my troth, I
cannot abide the smell of hot meat since. Why do your dogs bark so?
Be there bears i'th'town?

ANNE I think there are, sir; I heard them talked of.   230

SLENDER I love the sport well, but I shall as soon quarrel at it as any
man in England. You are afraid if you see the bear loose, are you
not?

ANNE Ay, indeed, sir.

SLENDER That's meat and drink to me, now. I have seen Sackerson   235
loose, twenty times, and have taken him by the chain. But I warrant
you, the women have so cried and shrieked at it that it passed. But
women, indeed, cannot abide 'em; they are very ill-favoured rough
things.

[*Enter* PAGE]

PAGE Come, gentle Master Slender, come; we stay for you.   240

SLENDER I'll eat nothing, I thank you, sir.

---

228 since.] F; *Collier² adds 'Dogs bark.*   239 SD] Q; *not in* F

225–8 I bruised . . . since The minimally significant point Slender is making is that he associates
'hot meat' (i.e. hot food) with the occasion involving
a hot dish of stewed prunes the other day when he
hurt himself, so he does not feel like hot food now.
The unintended *double entendre* is that he was
fighting the other day for a whore (stewed prunes in
the window was the sign of a brothel 'and so came to
be a synonym for a prostitute' (Oliver)), and hurt
himself, so that now he cannot abide the idea of a
whore ('hot meat' was another synonym for a prostitute, 'hot' here in one of its usual senses, 'lustful').
See 5.5.2; and *1H4* 3.3.112–13; *2H4* 2.4.144–7; *MM*
2.1.90.

226 sword and dagger This is to be distinguished, as Craik notes, from 'rapier and dagger'
and also from 'sword and buckler'. In the variety of
fencing mentioned here, a broader sword than a
rapier was held in the right hand and a dagger in the
left. Slender would have had to be fighting very
clumsily with his skilled teacher to bruise his own
shin, which was way out of the target area.

226 master of fence professional fencing master.

227 three veneys the best of three bouts,

or *venues* (fencing terms were largely French).

228 Why . . . so? To preface this with sudden
offstage barking, as Collier suggests should be done,
would produce a merely ludicrous stage effect as
Slender is given an abruptly contrived useful cue.
Rather there should be intermittent barking of dogs
for some little time before this question. I feel con-
strained to admit, however, that in the one production of the play I have directed, we got a cheap laugh
from a sudden barking; the thing is a comedy, after
all. See Introduction, pp. 20–2.

231 sport i.e. of bear-baiting, in which dogs
tormented a chained bear.

231 quarrel at it The phrase here must mean
that Slender will be as likely as any other (real) man
in England to quarrel with another spectator while
present at a bear-baiting, although he has gone there
for love of the sport and not to fight. We have an
example here of Slender's *machismo*, which rises to
a pitch of emphasis in his next speech.

235 That's . . . me Proverbial (Tilley M842).

235 Sackerson 'A famous bear at the Bear
Gardens on the Bankside' (Hart).

237 passed was past belief, was extraordinary.

238 ill-favoured ugly.

PAGE By cock and pie, you shall not choose, sir. Come, come.

SLENDER Nay, pray you lead the way.

PAGE Come on, sir.

SLENDER Mistress Anne, yourself shall go first.   245

ANNE Not I, sir. Pray you, keep on.

SLENDER Truly, I will not go first, truly, la! I will not do you that
wrong.

ANNE I pray you, sir.

SLENDER [*Going first*] I'll rather be unmannerly than troublesome. You   250
do yourself wrong, indeed, la!

Exeunt

1.2 *Enter* EVANS *and* SIMPLE

EVANS Go your ways, and ask of Doctor Caius' house which is the way.
And there dwells one Mistress Quickly, which is in the manner of
his nurse, or his dry nurse, or his cook, or his laundry, his washer,
and his wringer.

SIMPLE Well, sir.   5

EVANS Nay, it is petter yet. Give her this letter, for it is a 'oman that is
altogethers acquaintance with Mistress Anne Page, and the letter is
to desire and require her to solicit your master's desires to Mistress
Anne Page. I pray you be gone. I will make an end of my dinner;
there's pippins and cheese to come.   10

Exeunt

250 SD] *This edn; not in* F   **Act 1, Scene 2**   1.2] *Scena Secunda.* F   0 SD] F; *Enter sir* Hugh *and* Simple, *from dinner.* Q   1
house] F; house, the French Doctor Q   6–7 is altogethers] *Craik;* altogeathers F; *that altogether's Steevens²*, conj. Tyrwhitt

242 By ... pie A mild oath; 'cock' is a euphemism for 'God', and 'pie', according to the suggestion in *OED*, is 'the ordinal of the Roman Catholic
Church'. Craik sees no reason why 'pie' should not
be 'a *pie* of pastry, which might naturally follow
from *cock* (the fowl)', and I think I agree.

242 you ... choose 'An established phrase of
courtesy' (Hart). Page is insisting, but not in any
offensive way.

250 I'll ... troublesome Proverbial   (Tilley
U15).

Act 1, Scene 2

1 **of** concerning.

1 **Doctor Caius' house** Q supplies the information at this point that Doctor Caius is 'the
French Doctor'. It would make good sense on the
stage to identify him when he is first mentioned,

just as Mistress Quickly is identified. See Textual
Analysis, p. 155.

3 **nurse** Caius also calls Mistress Quickly his
nurse at 3.2.49, and evidently means the woman
who looks after him, his housekeeper. Evans by
specifying 'his dry nurse' allows the momentary
humorous possibility to arise of Caius having a wet
nurse employed to breast-feed him, like a baby.

3 **laundry** 'used blunderingly for LAUNDRESS'
(*OED sb* 3).

6–7 *is altogethers acquaintance Craik's
emendation, which supposes a slight and easy error
in F, gives a very Evans-like phrase meaning 'is
thoroughly acquainted'.

10 **pippins and cheese** apples and cheese, the
proper finish to a meal, as Hart notes. Welshmen
were notoriously fond of cheese. See 5.5.75.

1.3   *Enter* FALSTAFF, HOST, BARDOLPH, NIM, PISTOL [, *and Robin*]

FALSTAFF Mine host of the Garter!

HOST What says my bully rook? Speak scholarly and wisely.

FALSTAFF Truly, mine host, I must turn away some of my followers.

HOST Discard, bully Hercules, cashier. Let them wag; trot, trot.

FALSTAFF I sit at ten pounds a week.   5

HOST Thou'rt an emperor: Caesar, Kaiser, and Pheazar. I will entertain
    Bardolph; he shall draw, he shall tap. Said I well, bully Hector?

FALSTAFF Do so, good mine host.

HOST I have spoke. Let him follow. [*To Bardolph*] Let me see thee froth
    and lime. I am at a word. Follow.   [*Exit*]   10

FALSTAFF Bardolph, follow him. A tapster is a good trade. An old cloak
    makes a new jerkin; a withered servingman a fresh tapster. Go,
    adieu.

Act 1, Scene 3   1.3] *Scena Tertia.* F   0 SD *Robin*] *Rowe; Page* F; *the boy* Q   6 Kaiser] *Keiser* F   6 Pheazar] F;
Phesser Q; *Feezer Craik*   9 SD] *Cam.; not in* F   9 Let me see] F; *Bardolfe / Let me see* Q   10 lime
F   10 SD] *Exit Host.* Q; *not in* F

Act 1, Scene 3

0 SD *Robin* We learn the name of Falstaff's
page at 3.3.16.

2 bully rook 'Bully' is a word often in the
Host's mouth; it is 'a term of endearment and
familiarity . . . Often prefixed as a sort of title to the
name or designation of the person addressed' (*OED*
sb[1] 1). *OED* glosses 'bully-rook' as 'jolly comrade,
boon companion', and one may suppose that 'rook'
(which normally means 'gull, simpleton', or is used
as a general term of disparagement in Shakespeare's
time (*OED sb*[1] 2)) here undergoes the kind of transformation of an abusive into an affectionate term
that we see, for instance, in the case of 'rogue' (*OED
sb* 3). See 1.4.75 n.

3, 4 turn away . . . Discard . . . cashier get
rid of.

4 wag go, depart, be off (*OED v* 7).

4 trot bustle, move briskly.

5 sit at live here at the expense of (*OED* Sit *v*
8). A comic contrast is no doubt intended between
the brisk hustling away of Falstaff's followers
and the majestic seated immobility of the emperor
himself.

6 Kaiser emperor.

6 Pheazar i.e. Vizier, as Hart suggests. Craik
rejects this suggestion on the grounds that 'a viceroy
would be too anticlimactic a conclusion for the
Host's triad of epithets', but I think we may suppose
that Shakespeare knew the audience would have
little idea what a 'Pheazar' was (indeed Q's '*Phesser*'

suggests the players had little idea themselves), and
would react only to what seemed a steadily more
and more exotic form of the word 'emperor'. Q's
spelling of the strange word may preserve the way
the player said the line, with the repeated sound of
the second syllable of each of these three titles emphasising their synonymity as they became more
exotic. By a happy chance, retaining F's reading
'Pheazar' gives the chime on all three syllables for a
modern reader.

6 entertain employ.

7 draw; tap draw liquor from a barrel by means
of a tap, be a tapster.

9 Let me see Q's reading here almost certainly
preserves what actually happened on the stage, with
the Host turning to address Bardolph by name, after
speaking to Falstaff about him.

9 froth make the beer froth up so that it goes
further.

10 *lime add lime to wine; 'the putting in of
lime to remove the sourness was one of the tricks of
the trade' (Hart). The F reading is a possible one,
since Bardolph would then be frothing up the beer
to make a good living as a tapster; but there seems
little doubt that Q here preserves the true reading: it
is semantically sharper and allows the Host to mention 'tricks of the trade in both its aspects, ale-
selling and wine-selling' (Craik).

10 I . . . word Synonymous with 'I have spoke'.

11–12 An old . . . jerkin i.e. the good parts
of the larger garment serve as cloth for the
smaller.

BARDOLPH It is a life that I have desired. I will thrive.   [*Exit*]

PISTOL O base Hungarian wight, wilt thou the spigot wield?   15

NIM He was gotten in drink. Is not the humour conceited?

FALSTAFF I am glad I am so acquit of this tinderbox. His thefts were too
    open. His filching was like an unskilful singer, he kept not time.

NIM The good humour is to steal at a minute's rest.

PISTOL 'Convey', the wise it call. 'Steal'? Foh, a *fico* for the phrase!   20

FALSTAFF Well, sirs, I am almost out at heels.

PISTOL Why then, let kibes ensue.

FALSTAFF There is no remedy: I must cony-catch; I must shift.

PISTOL Young ravens must have food.

FALSTAFF Which of you know Ford of this town?   25

PISTOL I ken the wight. He is of substance good.

---

14 SD] *Exit Bardolfe.* Q; *not in* F   **15** Hungarian] F; gongarian Q   **16** He . . . conceited?] F; His minde is not
heroick. And theres the humor of it. Q   **17** thefts were] F; stealth was Q   **19** minute's] F, Q; minim's *Collier²*;
minim- NS

---

15 Hungarian Thievish, needy, beggarly (with
play on 'hungry') (*OED adj* 2). One can be certain
that a contemporary audience, hearing this word in
the middle of a bombast poetic line of the kind
Pistol favours, would not think of the central Euro-
pean kingdom. We have here, rather, an example of
the great theatrical usefulness of a big colourful
word designed to puzzle the hearer, to overawe him
with exotic matter. The reading of Q really achieves
Pistol's aim better, since it appears to mean nothing.
See 6 n. 'Pheazar' and Textual Analysis, p. 155.

15 wight A deliberately remote archaism for
'man'. See 26 n.

15 the spigot wield Providing the word
'spigot' (= the tap of a beer barrel) with a verb that
requires a sword as its object, and giving this
tapster's 'weapon' a grand definite article, produces
a nice piece of mock-heroic. In Q's version of Nim's
following line the anti-heroic point is made with a
simplicity and obviousness that would very much
please on the stage by contrast with the big line
Pistol has just produced. As often, what seems redundant and over-obvious in the study is just what
an actor wants on the stage. See Textual Analysis,
p. 155.

16 gotten in drink begotten while his parents
(or his father) were drunk, and so appropriately
destined for a tapster, with his red nose.

16 Is . . . conceited? Is not the joke a witty
one?

17 tinderbox 'inflammable' man (*OED sb* b).

17 thefts Q's 'stealth' is attractive. It seems a
more colourful and witty word than 'thefts', since
it not only means 'a theft' (*OED* Stealth *sb* 1b) but

also 'the action of stealing or gliding along
unperceived' (*OED* 3a), so that not only Bardolph's
thievery but his cunning furtive practice at it were a
bit too obvious.

18 kept not time did not skilfully watch for his
moment.

19 good humour 'right trick of the trade'
(Hibbard).

19 at a minute's rest in the space of a moment. Nim is developing Falstaff's music image,
though in the face of the agreement between F and Q
one cannot allow the image to go so far as 'minim's'.

20 Convey A euphemism for 'to steal' (*OED v*
6b).

20 fico (Italian) fig. 'A fig for it' was a standard
contemptuous phrase (Tilley F210), and 'to give the
fico' was to make an insulting gesture 'either by
thrusting the thumb between two of the closed
fingers or by thrusting it into the mouth' (Craik).

21 out at heels penniless, with shoes worn
through (Tilley H389).

22 kibes sores on the heels, because of worn-
out shoes. Pistol takes Falstaff's figurative phrase in
its literal sense.

23 shift live on my wits.

24 The proverbial expression is 'Small birds
must have meat' (Tilley B397), but the particular
point here is probably that young ravens are not fed
by human hands but must shift for themselves, having their food from God (cf. Job 38.41; Ps. 147.9). It
is worth noting, too, that the raven is a bird of prey.

26 ken know.

26 This is very much in Pistol's style of speech:
a blank verse line, conceivably remembered from

FALSTAFF My honest lads, I will tell you what I am about.

PISTOL Two yards and more.

FALSTAFF No quips now, Pistol. Indeed I am in the waist two yards
about, but I am now about no waste; I am about thrift. Briefly, I do   30
mean to make love to Ford's wife. I spy entertainment in her. She
discourses, she carves, she gives the leer of invitation. I can construe
the action of her familiar style; and the hardest voice of her behaviour, to be Englished rightly, is 'I am Sir John Falstaff's'.

PISTOL He hath studied her will, and translated her will – out of   35
honesty into English.

NIM The anchor is deep. Will that humour pass?

FALSTAFF Now, the report goes she has all the rule of her husband's
purse; he hath a legion of angels.

PISTOL As many devils entertain, and 'To her, boy!', say I.   40

NIM The humour rises; it is good. Humour me the angels.

---

35 studied . . . translated her will] F; studied her well Q   39 he] F; She Q   39 a legion] Rowe³; a legend F; legians Q

some old play, with archaic diction and inverted
word order.

27 about engaged in (Pistol takes the word as
meaning 'in circumference').

31 entertainment (1) welcome, (2) hospitable
provision, (3) pleasure.

32 carves *OED* (v 13) offers Schmidt's conjecture 'To show great courtesy and affability'. There
must be some association, too, with the opportunity
a hostess had to please a guest as she skilfully carved
the meat. In its figurative sense, the meaning is
clearly somewhere between the ordinary affability
with a guest of 'discourses' and the openly sexual
offer of 'gives the leer of invitation'.

32 construe interpret; but the more precisely
technical sense 'to translate from a foreign language'
(*OED* v 3) is what introduces the string of linguistic
images that follows.

33 action working.

33 familiar style courteously affable behaviour.

33 hardest most difficult to translate into plain
English.

33 voice (1) significance, (2) grammatical voice.

34 to be . . . rightly when properly translated
into English.

35 studied . . . translated her will Many of
the possible meanings of 'will' are present here,
and flicker about the line (most evidently, 'inclination', 'lust', 'sexual parts', 'last will and testament'):
the most evident meaning is perhaps that Falstaff
has 'noted her sexual attraction and translated

her ordinary good humour' into his own lewd
imaginings.

36 honesty chastity.

36 English (falsely) open and explicit terms.

37 The . . . deep Just as a deep-buried anchor
holds firm, so Falstaff's deeply held conviction that
Mistress Ford is smitten by him is unshakeable.

37 Will . . . pass The first word of the question
must surely attract some of the semantic energy that
has just been accumulated round 'will', even though
the change from noun to verb makes it formally
impossible. This link with what Pistol has just said
perhaps allows Nim to be speaking of Falstaff here
as well, so the question would mean 'Will that inclination of his gain approval, achieve anything?'
Hibbard suggests the other possibility, that Nim is
referring to his own anchor image: 'What do you
think of that for a neat phrase?'

39 *legion of angels a great quantity of gold
coins. F's reading 'legend' probably derives from a
confusion that sometimes occurred between 'legion'
and 'legend' (*OED* Legend *sb* ¶1). The word 'legion' comes to have the non-military sense 'many'
from its use at Mark 5.9, but the reference here is
also to the 'legions of angels' of Matt. 26.53, though
Falstaff's angels are the gold coins of that name, so-
called because stamped with the figure of the arch-
angel Michael.

40 As . . . entertain You for your part be sure
to have as many devils on your side (as he has
angels).

41 The humour rises Either 'the witty speech

FALSTAFF [*Showing letters*] I have writ me here a letter to her; and here
　　another to Page's wife, who even now gave me good eyes too,
　　examined my parts with most judicious œillades. Sometimes the
　　beam of her view gilded my foot, sometimes my portly belly.　　45
PISTOL Then did the sun on dunghill shine.
NIM I thank thee for that humour.
FALSTAFF O, she did so course o'er my exteriors, with such a greedy
　　intention, that the appetite of her eye did seem to scorch me up like
　　a burning-glass. Here's another letter to her. She bears the purse　　50
　　too. She is a region in Guiana, all gold and bounty. I will be cheaters
　　to them both, and they shall be exchequers to me. They shall be my
　　East and West Indies, and I will trade to them both. [*To Nim*] Go,
　　bear thou this letter to Mistress Page; [*To Pistol*] and thou this to
　　Mistress Ford. We will thrive, lads, we will thrive.　　55
PISTOL Shall I Sir Pandarus of Troy become,
　　　　And by my side wear steel? Then Lucifer take all!
　　　　[*He gives back the letter*]
NIM I will run no base humour. Here, take the humour-letter. [*He gives
　　it back*] I will keep the haviour of reputation.
FALSTAFF [*To Robin*] Hold, sirrah, bear you these letters tightly;　　60

---

42 SD] *Oxford; not in* F   44 œillades] *Hanmer, conj. Pope;* illiads F   53 SD] *Furnivall; to Pistol / NS; not in* F   54 SD] *Furnivall; to Nym / NS; not in* F   57 SD] *Craik; not in* F   58–9 SD] *Craik; not in* F   60 SD] *Theobald (after 61); not in* F

gets cleverer' or 'the energy of Falstaff's inclination is growing' (this would correspond neatly with the sense for 'humour' I suggest at 37, and would lead in to Nim's next use of the word).

41 Humour . . . angels Use your inclination towards Mistress Ford to conjure the money out of her. Nim's use of 'humour' becomes ever more capacious, as Shakespeare satirises the vogue for this word. See 1.1.107 n.

44 œillades (French) amorous glances. F's reading here is not an error but a spelling that represents the Elizabethan pronunciation.

46 Then . . . shine Compare the proverb 'The sun is never the worse for shining on a dunghill' (Tilley s982).

48 course o'er run her eye over.

49 intention intent observation (*OED sb* 1).

50 burning-glass a lense for magnifying the intensity of the sun's rays.

51 Guiana Sir Walter Raleigh made an expedition to this South American country in 1595, in the hope of finding the 'golden city' of Eldorado. Like the Indies of 53, Guiana was legendary in contemporary belief for its wealth.

51 cheaters 'Cheater' was the common abbre-

viated form of 'escheater', an official of the Exchequer who supervised in his district the 'escheats', the estates that came to be forfeit to the crown. The pun with the sense 'swindler' was common. The plural form is presumably because Falstaff thinks of himself as acting in a separate official capacity for each woman, and because the plural chimes well with 'exchequers'.

53 SD *To Nim Nim is given the first letter because it is he who warns Page about Falstaff's designs on his wife in 2.1. See 73 n.

56–7 i.e. Shall I who wear a sword like a soldier stoop to become like Pandarus of Troy (the 'pander' or go-between who brought Troilus and Cressida together). If I do, then the devil take everything into his power!

58 humour-letter The word 'humour' in Nim's usage almost ceases here to have any semantic charge. It has perhaps temporarily come to adopt the meaning 'Falstaff's humour (or inclination) to attempt seduction', so that this letter becomes the 'seduction-letter'. See 41 nn.

59 keep . . . reputation continue to behave honourably.

60 tightly properly, well.

I pray thee, go to the casement and see if you can see my master,
Master Doctor Caius, coming. If he do, i'faith, and find anybody in
the house, here will be an old abusing of God's patience and the
King's English.   5

RUGBY I'll go watch.

MISTRESS QUICKLY Go; and we'll have a posset for't soon at night, in
faith, at the latter end of a sea-coal fire.

                                                                    [*Exit Rugby*]

An honest, willing, kind fellow as ever servant shall come in house
withal; and, I warrant you, no tell-tale, nor no breed-bate. His worst   10
fault is that he is given to prayer. He is something peevish that way,
but nobody but has his fault. But let that pass. Peter Simple you say
your name is?

SIMPLE Ay, for fault of a better.

MISTRESS QUICKLY And Master Slender's your master?   15

SIMPLE Ay, forsooth.

MISTRESS QUICKLY Does he not wear a great round beard like a
glover's paring-knife?

SIMPLE No, forsooth. He hath but a little wee face, with a little yellow
beard, a Cain-coloured beard.   20

---

8 SD] *Rowe; not in* F   19 wee] wee- F; whey- *Capell*   20 Cain-coloured] Caine coulourd F; kane colored Q; Cane-colour'd *Rowe³*

Act 1, Scene 4

4 **old** plentiful, abundant (*OED adj*¹ 6).

4 **God** See Textual Analysis, p. 160.

5 **King's English** This proverbial expression (Tilley K80) was in use during Elizabeth's reign, as Hart demonstrates, and so cannot be used as evidence for a revision of the play in the reign of James I, which would in any case mean setting aside the fact that the action allegedly takes place in the reign of Henry V. See Introduction, pp. 4–6.

7 **posset** 'a drink composed of hot milk curdled with ale, wine, or other liquid, often with sugar, spices, or other ingredients' (*OED*).

7 **for't** as a reward for our trouble now.

7 **soon at night** before the night is much advanced (*OED* Soon *adv* 3).

8 **at . . . fire** over the embers of a fire of good coal (i.e. brought in by sea from areas like Newcastle upon Tyne where there were coal mines; as distinct from the notably inferior charcoal).

9–10 **as . . . withal** as any servant you will have in a house.

10 **breed-bate** breeder of discord, trouble maker (*OED* Bate *sb*¹ 2).

11 **peevish** 'Usually glossed as "silly, foolish"

(*OED adj* 1), but the more frequent sense in Shakespeare is "perverse, refractory" (*OED adj* 4)' (Craik).

12 **nobody . . . fault** A proverbial phrase (Tilley M116).

14 **for . . . better** Again proverbial (Tilley F106).

18 **glover's paring-knife** 'Shakespeare should have known what such a knife looked like, for his father was a glover (one who worked in leather, not only to make gloves)' (Oliver).

19 **wee** tiny. Some editors have been uneasy about 'wee' on the grounds that it seems to be a distinctively northern word at this time and is not found elsewhere in Shakespeare. Q's reading 'whay coloured' at about this point, as Mistress Quickly attempts to describe Slender's beard, has encouraged 'whey-face' for F's 'wee-face'.

20 **Cain-coloured** Yellow. There can be no doubt of the colour intended here, in spite of *OED*'s slightly puzzling gloss, which cites this passage as its only instance of the term: 'of the reputed colour of the hair of Cain, to whom, as to Judas Iscariot, a "red" or reddish-yellow beard was attributed' (Cain² 2).

MISTRESS QUICKLY A softly-sprighted man, is he not?

SIMPLE Ay, forsooth. But he is as tall a man of his hands as any is
between this and his head. He hath fought with a warrener.

MISTRESS QUICKLY How say you? – O, I should remember him. Does
he not hold up his head, as it were, and strut in his gait?   25

SIMPLE Yes, indeed does he.

MISTRESS QUICKLY Well, heaven send Anne Page no worse fortune!
Tell Master Parson Evans I will do what I can for your master.
Anne is a good girl, and I wish –

RUGBY [*Within*] Out, alas! Here comes my master.   30

MISTRESS QUICKLY We shall all be shent. Run in here, good young
man; go into this closet. He will not stay long.

                [*He steps into the closet*]

What, John Rugby! John! What, John, I say!

                [*Enter* RUGBY]

[*Speaking loudly*] Go, John, go enquire for my master. I doubt he be
not well, that he comes not home.   35

                           [*Exit Rugby*]

[*Sings*] And down, down, adown-a, etc.

                [*Enter* DOCTOR CAIUS]

CAIUS Vat is you sing? I do not like dese toys. Pray you go and vetch me
in my closet *une boîte en vert* – a box, a green-a box. Do intend vat
I speak? A green-a box.

---

30 SD] *Craik; Enter Rugby. / Rowe; not in* F   **32** SD] *This edn; He steps into the Counting-house.* Q; *Shuts Simple in the closet.
/ Rowe (after* He*); not in* F   **33** SD] *Oxford; not in* F   **34** SD] *Oxford; not in* F   **35** SD] *Oxford; not in* F   **36** SD.1] *As Theobald;
not in* F   **36** SD.2] *Rowe; And she opens the doore.* Q; *not in* F   **37** dese toys] *Theobald;* des-toyes F   **38** *une boîte en] Hart;*
vnboyteene F; *un boitier / Rowe; une boitine / Irving/Marshall*   **38** vert] *Cam.;* verd F

---

21 softly-sprighted soft-spirited, of a mild
disposition.

22 Ay, forsooth Simple gets stuck in linguistic
grooves just as his master does. See 16 and 19.

22 as tall . . . hands as brave a man in fighting
(with his hands). See *WT* 5.2.167–8.

23 between . . . head 'in these parts'
(Hibbard).

23 warrener gamekeeper in charge of a rabbit
warren. The combat does not sound heroic.

24 I . . . him 'Now I can call him to mind'
(Craik).

30 Out, alas! An expression of alarm.

31 shent blamed, scolded.

32 closet small private room. That it is a room
to step into and not a cupboard to be shut in is made

clear by Mistress Quickly's 'Run in here' at 31,
and by Q's description of the hiding place (throughout the scene) as a 'counting-house'. See Textual
Analysis, p. 156.

34–5 'Mistress Quickly says this in a loud voice
in order to prevent Caius from suspecting that she
knows of his return' (Craik).

34 doubt fear.

36 etc. 'The implication of *etc.* would seem to be
that Mistress Quickly goes on repeating the refrain
until Caius interrupts her' (Hibbard).

38 ***une boîte en vert*** We know that F's
'vnboyteene verd' has got to mean a green box, since
Caius translates his phrase; and we may presume
from Q's valuably alternative account of the reason
for Caius' hasty return ('*I begar I be forget my*

MISTRESS QUICKLY Ay, forsooth. I'll fetch it you. [*Aside*] I am glad he   40
went not in himself. If he had found the young man, he would have
been horn-mad.

                         [*She goes into the closet*]

CAIUS *Fe, fe, fe, fe! Ma foi, il fait fort chaud. Je m'en vais voir à le* court
la grande affaire.

                    [*Returning, she shows him the box*]

MISTRESS QUICKLY Is it this, sir?   45

CAIUS *Oui, mette-le au mon* pocket. *Dépêche*, quickly. Vere is dat knave
Rugby?

MISTRESS QUICKLY What, John Rugby! John!

                         [*Enter* RUGBY]

RUGBY Here, sir.

---

40 Ay . . . you] *As prose, Capell; as a verse line,* F   40 SD] *Pope; not in* F   42 SD] *As NS; not in* F   43 *Ma . . . chaud*] *Rowe;
mai foy, il fait for ehando* F   43–4 *Je . . . affaire*] *This edn; Je m'en vais voir à la court la grande affaire / Oliver; Ie man voi
a le Court la grand affaires* F; *je m'en vais à la Cour – la grande Affaire / Rowe³*   44 SD] *This edn; She shows him the box / Craik
(after 45); not in* F   46–7] *As prose, Pope; as two lines of verse, divided after* quickly F   46 mette] F; *mettez / Theobald*   46
Dépêche] *NS; de-peech* F; *Depêch / Rowe; depêchez / Theobald*   48 SD] *Wheatley; not in* F

oyntment') that the actors onstage knew that the
box in question was a small ointment box. This
rules out Rowe's 'boitier' (a box of surgical instru-
ments) which would in any case not go into Caius'
pocket at 46; and 'boitine' (though it should mean a
small box) can be rejected perhaps on the grounds
that Caius translates 'box' not 'small box', and that
it is not actually a French word, though it is formed
in a French way with the '-ine' diminutive ending,
and Shakespeare may have thought it was French
(see Textual Analysis, p. 162). '*En vert*', as Craik
points out, is not very good French either, but nothing more can be done with it. All in all, the reconstruction of the phrase as '*une boîte en vert*' (a box in
green) seems correct.

38 Do intend Do you hear ('intend' for French
entendre).

42 horn-mad A proverbial phrase (Tilley
H628) meaning 'fighting-mad with rage, like a
horned beast in mating season' (Craik).

43 *chaud F's '*ehando*', probably written in the
copy in italic script, as Oliver suggests, like most of
Caius' French, since the compositor set it in italic,
would be an easy compositorial misreading for
'chaude' (or 'chaud' with a final flourish misinterpreted as an extra letter, like F's 'mai' for 'Ma' earlier in this line). The mistaken letters 'e' and 'n'
could also easily be the result of foul-case error.

43–4 *Je . . . affaire Oliver's suggested version, which I accept, of F's French here would mean

'I'm going to see the great affair at court' (probably
the Garter ceremony; see Introduction, p. 1). Oliver
supposes that F's '*voi*' stands for either '*vais*' or
'*voir*' and that the compositor omitted the companion word because of the similarity in appearance
between the two as written. This seems to make
easier sense to me than Rowe's ellipsis, made necessary by reading simply '*Je m'en vais à la Cour*'. I
print 'court' unitalicised on the assumption that,
like 'pocket' and 'quickly' at 46 (both, like 'court',
italicised in F), this is an English word put in either
for the audience's benefit or because Shakespeare
could not recall the French word.

46 mette . . . pocket The phrase is grammati-
cally inaccurate, and eked out with an English word
(perhaps for the benefit of the audience) but there is
no piece of puzzling nonsense like 'vnboyteene' (F's
reading at 38). The level of inaccuracy here seems to
me more what one would expect of an English play-
wright who had pretty much enough French to give
verisimilitude to a French character in his play,
than what would be likely from a compositor knowing no French and faced with an indecipherable
word: 'vnboyteene' seems to me to fall into this
latter category, and '*mette-le*', for instance, into the
former.

46 quickly This is plainly to help an audience
by translating 'Dépêche' (which in its turn is spelt
phonetically in F to help the actor).

CAIUS You are John Rugby, and you are jack Rugby. Come, take-a your   50
rapier, and come after my heel to the court.

RUGBY 'Tis ready, sir, here in the porch.

CAIUS By my trot, I tarry too long. 'Od's me! *Que ai-je oublié?* Dere is
some simples in my closet, dat I vill not for the varld I shall leave
behind.   55

[*He goes into the closet*]

MISTRESS QUICKLY Ay me, he'll find the young man there, and be
mad.

CAIUS [*Within*] O, *diable, diable*! Vat is in my closet? Villainy! *Larron*!

[*He pulls Simple out of the closet*]

Rugby, my rapier!

MISTRESS QUICKLY Good master, be content.   60

CAIUS Wherefore shall I be content-a?

MISTRESS QUICKLY The young man is an honest man.

CAIUS What shall de honest man do in my closet? Dere is no honest man
dat shall come in my closet.

MISTRESS QUICKLY I beseech you, be not so phlegmatic. Hear the   65
truth of it. He came of an errand to me from Parson Hugh.

CAIUS Vell?

SIMPLE Ay, forsooth, to desire her to –

MISTRESS QUICKLY Peace, I pray you.

---

50 jack] *Iacke* F   53 *Que . . . oublié*] *que ay ie oublie* F   55 SD] *As Craik; not in* F   58 SD.1] *This edn; not in* F   58–9] *As prose, Pope; as two lines of verse, divided after* closet F   58 Villainy] *Villanie* F; *Villaine* Q3   58 *Larron*] *Rowe;* La-roone F   58 SD.2] *As Theobald; not in* F   67 Vell?] *Neilson; Vell.* F

50 **jack** knave (*OED sb*[1] 2). There is, of course, a glance here at the proper noun 'Jack'; we see at 3.1.68 that Caius is aware of the verbal quibble. I print the word as a common noun here on the grounds that Caius has just referred to Rugby as 'dat knave Rugby' (46–7) and on the grounds that Caius' habitually choleric and testy disposition in the rest of the play leads him to use the word freely in the undoubted sense 'knave' (F always capitalising, as here). It is true, as Craik notes, that in 2.3 and 3.1 Caius consistently refers to his servant as 'jack' (or 'Jack'). I take it that we have here an instance of his ingrained and institutionalised hostility, and that his use of this form of address to his servant (whose name, he knows perfectly well, is John) would have contributed to his unpopularity with the audience (who already, no doubt, hated a Frenchman). I print the word as a common noun whenever Caius uses it, to remind the modern audience of his unpleasantness. See 90 n. and 2.3.3 n.

51 **after my heel** There is a notably peremptory and even contemptuous tone here. It is not a form of address to a servant used elsewhere in Shakespeare.

53 **trot** troth (in a French accent).

53 **'Od's me** God's me (i.e. God save me) (*OED* God *sb* 8b).

54 **simples** medicines 'composed or concocted of only one constituent, *esp.* of one herb or plant' (*OED* Simple *sb* 6). Of course, there is Simple in the closet as well as simples. See 1.1.174–5 n.

58 **Villainy!** Both here and at 2.3.12 it is tempting to emend to 'villain'; but unnecessary, because the abstract term in each case makes a perfectly good Gallic exclamation. Here the general sense 'villainy afoot!' sufficiently glosses the following French word.

58 ***Larron*** (French) thief.

65 **phlegmatic** phlegmatic (cold and moist) is Mistress Quickly's error for 'choleric' (hot and dry). See 1.1.107 n.

CAIUS Peace-a your tongue. [*To Simple*] Speak-a your tale.   70

SIMPLE To desire this honest gentlewoman, your maid, to speak a good
    word to Mistress Anne Page for my master in the way of marriage.

MISTRESS QUICKLY This is all indeed, la! But I'll ne'er put my finger
    in the fire, and need not.

CAIUS Sir Hugh send-a you? Rugby, *baillez* me some paper. [*To Simple*]   75
    Tarry you a little-a while.

        [*Rugby brings paper from the closet. Caius writes*]

MISTRESS QUICKLY [*Aside to Simple*] I am glad he is so quiet. If he had
    been throughly moved, you should have heard him so loud and so
    melancholy. But notwithstanding, man, I'll do your master what
    good I can. And the very yea and the no is, the French doctor, my   80
    master – I may call him my master, look you, for I keep his house,
    and I wash, wring, brew, bake, scour, dress meat and drink, make
    the beds, and do all myself –

SIMPLE 'Tis a great charge to come under one body's hand.

MISTRESS QUICKLY Are you advised o'that? You shall find it a great   85
    charge; and to be up early and down late. But notwithstanding – to
    tell you in your ear; I would have no words of it – my master himself
    is in love with Mistress Anne Page. But notwithstanding that, I
    know Anne's mind. That's neither here nor there.

---

70 SD] *Oliver, as Steevens; not in* F   74 and] F; an't *Craik*   75 *baillez*] *Theobald;* ballow F   75 SD] *Hibbard; not in* F   76
SD] *Craik, as Oxford; The Doctor writes.* Q; *not in* F   77 SD] *Hibbard; not in* F   79 do your] *Capell;* doe yoe your F

73–4 I'll … not A proverbial expression
(Tilley F230) meaning 'I'll not meddle with a risky
business if I don't have to.' Craik's emendation of
F's 'and' seems to me unnecessary because Mistress
Quickly's speech, as well as being narrowly
repetitious in the way of Slender and Simple (see
'notwithstanding' at 79, 86, and 88), is in general a
very loose weave. She is approximate about difficult
words, as at 65 and 79, she strays from her main
topic easily, as at 81–3, and here she leaves out the
pronoun 'it' or 'I' ('and' meaning 'if').

75 *baillez (French) bring. Craik suggests convincingly that F's 'ballow' is some sort of attempt at
a phonetic spelling of the French word, and cites Q's
reading at 2.3.10 (where it precedes the beginning
of Caius' speech in F) 'Bully moy, mon rapier *Iohn
Rugabie*'; here '*Baillez-moi*' is clearly intended, and
indeed the particular phonetic attempt at the
French verb at that point in Q brings on an avalanche of the Host's favourite (and very English)
word 'bully' (see 1.3.2 n.). There seems little doubt
that the players in the performances behind the Q
text found the Host's seizing and transmogrifying

of the French into his joyously abundant English
word went down very well on the stage. Perhaps
'ballow' was, in fact, the more accurate attempt at
phonetic representation, and Q's 'bully' a phonetic
version designed to lead into the English 'bully'.
See Textual Analysis, pp. 155–6.

76 *SD Caius will have his pen and inkhorn already about his person, and Q's stage direction im-
plies that there is a table and chair already on the
stage. In Q Caius also asks for pen and ink to be
brought to him.

78 throughly thoroughly.

79 melancholy Mistress Quickly's second attempt at 'choleric'. See 65 n.

79 *do your Jowett argues convincingly for
Capell's emendation, that the compositor of F originally set 'doe yoe' wrongly for 'doe your' and then
mistakenly took the proof reader's correction to
'your' as an additional word to include.

82 dress prepare.

85–6 Are … charge 'You think so, do you?
Yes, I can tell you, it is a real load' (Craik).

CAIUS [*Giving a letter to Simple*] You, jack'nape, give-a this letter to Sir   90
Hugh. By gar, it is a shallenge. I will cut his troat in de Park, and I
will teach a scurvy jackanape priest to meddle or make. You may be
gone. It is not good you tarry here.

[*Exit Simple*]

By gar, I will cut all his two stones. By gar, he shall not have a stone
to throw at his dog.   95

MISTRESS QUICKLY Alas, he speaks but for his friend.

CAIUS It is no matter-a ver dat. Do not you tell-a me dat I shall have
Anne Page for myself? By gar, I vill kill de jack priest; and I have
appointed mine host of de Jarteer to measure our weapon. By gar, I
will myself have Anne Page.   100

MISTRESS QUICKLY Sir, the maid loves you, and all shall be well. We
must give folks leave to prate. What the good-year!

CAIUS Rugby, come to the court with me. [*To Mistress Quickly*] By gar,
if I have not Anne Page, I shall turn your head out of my door. –
Follow my heels, Rugby.   105

MISTRESS QUICKLY You shall have An –

[*Exeunt Caius and Rugby*]

---

90 SD] *Oxford; not in* F   90 jack'nape] Iack 'Nape F   93 SD] *As NS; not in* F   102 good-year] good year *Capell;* good-ier
F   103 SD] *Wheatley, as Steevens; not in* F   106–7 An – – fool's head] *An-*fooles head F; Anne – – ass-head *Oxford*   106
SD] *Irving/Marshall, conj. Daniel; Rowe (after 105); Exit Doctor.* Q *(after line corresponding to 105); not in* F

---

90 **jack'nape** (1) jackanapes, monkey (2) fool.
OED suggests that the original form was Jack
Napes, perhaps a pet name for an ape, and F prints
the word almost in this form, reminding us of Jack
Rugby.

91 **By gar** By God.

91 **Park** i.e. Windsor Park.

92 **meddle or make** interfere (Tilley M852).

94 **stones** testicles.

94–5 **stone . . . dog** The proverbial phrase
(Tilley s880) accommodates a pun on 'stone'.

97 **ver** for (in Caius' French accent).

99 **Jarteer** Garter; with a glance at the French
equivalent '*jarretière*'.

99 **to . . . weapon** 'to act as umpire in our duel'
(Hibbard). The weapons would be measured before
a duel to make sure neither combatant had an unfair
advantage. The audience would no doubt have
picked up the unconscious sexual connotation of
'weapon' (singular for plural in Caius' odd speech).

101 **all . . . well** 'All shall be well and Jack shall
have Jill' (Tilley A164).

102 **give . . . prate** Mistress Quickly's speech
is full of proverbial and common expressions; this
derives from 'Give losers leave to prate' (Tilley

L458), and is meant to give Caius the sense that he is
a winner in the contest for Anne Page.

102 **What the good-year!** An expletive of
uncertain origin, meaning something like 'What
the devil!'. Mistress Quickly uses it twice at *2H4*
2.4.58–9 and 177.

106–7 **An – fool's head** There is no need for
emendation here. Craik accepts the emendation to
'ass-head' from Oxford, on the grounds that if F's
'*An*' was going to serve suddenly as the indefinite
article upon Caius' abrupt departure (and F makes
quite clear that this was intended by spelling '*Anne*'
as '*An*' in the rest of this speech, by contrast with its
usual '*Anne*'), then the word which triggered the
switch from proper noun to indefinite article would
have to be one which required 'an' and not 'a'. Thus
the linguistic mechanism which assured Caius that
he would get Anne, and the audience that he would
not, would move smoothly and correctly. Craik admits, however, that F's 'fooles head' is hard to explain as an error for 'ass-head', and it is for this
reason that I feel unable to accept the emendation.
Instead it seems possible to explain why F should
read 'fooles head' if we consider the circumstances
of the stage and not the study. In the study, the

– fool's head of your own. No, I know Anne's mind for that. Never
a woman in Windsor knows more of Anne's mind than I do, nor can
do more than I do with her, I thank heaven.

FENTON [*Within*] Who's within there, ho?   110

MISTRESS QUICKLY Who's there, I trow? Come near the house, I pray
you.

[*Enter* FENTON]

FENTON How now, good woman, how dost thou?

MISTRESS QUICKLY The better that it pleases your good worship to
ask.   115

FENTON What news? How does pretty Mistress Anne?

MISTRESS QUICKLY In truth, sir, and she is pretty, and honest, and
gentle, and one that is your friend – I can tell you that by the way,
I praise heaven for it.

FENTON Shall I do any good, think'st thou? Shall I not lose my suit?   120

MISTRESS QUICKLY Troth, sir, all is in His hands above. But notwithstanding, Master Fenton, I'll be sworn on a book she loves you.
Have not your worship a wart above your eye?

110 SD] *Rowe; not in* F   110 ho] hoa F   111 I trow] I troa F; trow *conj. Hart*   112 SD] *Rowe; not in* F

linguistic joke works clearly and precisely: the
sound 'an' can be written '*An*' to signal a quibbling
use of the proper noun, and Caius can exit in a flash
to enable the sentence to run on past the point of
fracture rapidly enough to take up the indefinite
article smoothly. Not so on the stage. Here the
player must say '*An*' as 'Anne' (with no possibility
of an indeterminate stressing that could be either
indefinite article or proper noun) because he is cut
off not by another speech sound but by Caius' exit,
which takes longer than a speech interruption and
must allow the sound of the word to emerge fully.
On the stage, then, the word Mistress Quickly says
is at this point not the indefinite article at all; it is
wrenched suddenly, after a pause for the exit, into
being the indefinite article by the common nouns
that follow. There is no longer, then, any particular
merit in the smooth fit between '*An*' and the following word; indeed, the very roughness of the transformation, together with the energy that could be
got into the initial 'f' sound to carry the contemptuous change of tone, may have been what decided for
'fool' rather than the equally available 'ass'. If this
piece of business worked well onstage, it would
surely have been memorable, so that the fact that Q
has nothing of it may suggest that it was difficult to
do clearly enough for the audience to react, so that

it was dropped from the acting version behind Q. It
might be noted that Falstaff, not Caius, wears a
fool's head near the end of the play, when he appears as a stag.

107 for that on that matter.

111 I trow I wonder. F's spelling is unusual
here, as it is at 2.1.50. Oliver suggests that Mistress
Quickly 'completes a rhyme here' with F's 'hoa' at
110.

111 Come ... house Come into the house.
Hart shows that 'near' often meant 'in' or 'into' in
contexts of this kind.

117 honest virtuous.

122 on a book on the Bible.

123 Have Strictly the third person and not the
second is required here, but in Mistress Quickly's
speech the 'your' of 'your worship' does duty for a
second person pronoun. This kind of formulation
was probably fairly ordinary colloquial practice, as
well as being part of the texture of Mistress Quickly's speech. Professor Craik draws my attention to
the better educated Marrall in Massinger's *A New
Way to Pay Old Debts* 2.1: 'Your worship have the
way on't.'

123 wart Craik quotes from Lyly's *Euphues*:
'Venus had her mole in her cheek which made her
more amiable, Helen her scar in her chin which

FENTON Yes, marry, have I. What of that?

MISTRESS QUICKLY Well, thereby hangs a tale. Good faith, it is such   125
another Nan! But, I detest, an honest maid as ever broke bread. We
had an hour's talk of that wart. I shall never laugh but in that maid's
company. But, indeed, she is given too much to allicholy and
musing. But for you – well – go to –

FENTON Well, I shall see her today. Hold, there's money for thee: 130
let me have thy voice in my behalf. If thou seest her before me,
commend me –

MISTRESS QUICKLY Will I? I'faith, that we will. And I will tell your
worship more of the wart the next time we have confidence, and of
other wooers.   135

FENTON Well, farewell; I am in great haste now.   [*Exit*]

MISTRESS QUICKLY Farewell to your worship. Truly an honest
gentleman. But Anne loves him not, for I know Anne's mind as well
as another does. – Out upon't! What have I forgot!   [*Exit*]

2.1 [*Enter* MISTRESS PAGE, *with a letter*]

MISTRESS PAGE What, have I 'scaped love-letters in the holiday time
of my beauty, and am I now a subject for them? Let me see.
[*She reads*]

---

133 we] F; I Hanmer   136 SD] Rowe; not in F   Act 2, Scene 1   2.1] Actus Secundus, Scæna Prima. F   0 SD] Rowe; Enter
Mistris Page, Mistris Ford, Master Page, Master Ford, Pistoll, Nim, Quickly, Host, Shallow. F; Enter Mistresse Page, reading
of a Letter. Q   1 I] Q3; not in F   2 SD] Capell; not in F

Paris called *cos amoris* the whetstone of love.
Aristippus his wart, Lycurgus his wen' (Lyly
1.185). It is clear from 134 that the audience is
expected to react less solemnly to Fenton's wart.

125 thereby ... tale A cliché, then as now
(Tilley T48).

125–6 it ... Nan 'she is such an extraordinary
Nan' (Craik).

126 detest Mistress Quickly means 'protest'.

126 an ... bread Proverbial (Tilley M68).

128 allicholy Mistress Quickly's approximation for 'melancholy', a word she has successfully
used at 79 to mean 'choleric'.

129 go to enough of that.

133 we will I am reluctant to accept Hanmer's
reading. It must be confessed that there is not very
much evidence, outside the use of the royal 'we', for
switching of this kind between the singular and plural pronoun as a speech habit, but in view of Mis-

tress Quickly's otherwise loosely assembled speech,
it seems rash to emend. Compare, perhaps, Bertram
in *All's Well*: 'it is / A charge too heavy for my
strength, but yet / We'll strive to bear it' (3.3.3–5).

136 *SD Recent editors place Rowe's stage direction after 'worship' at 137, but since the point is
made that Fenton is in haste as he goes, it seems
better that he should already be gone by the time
Mistress Quickly responds.

138–9 But ... does 'There are no grounds for
Mistress Quickly's statement that Anne does not
love Fenton, which presumably is just her way of
laying claim to a special understanding of Anne's
feelings' (Craik).

139 Out ... forgot! Mistress Quickly bustles
offstage about some task.

Act 2, Scene 1

1 holiday time best, most festive time.

'Ask me no reason why I love you, for though Love use Reason for
his precisian, he admits him not for his counsellor. You are not
young, no more am I. Go to, then, there's sympathy. You are   5
merry, so am I. Ha, ha, then, there's more sympathy. You love sack,
and so do I. Would you desire better sympathy? Let it suffice thee,
Mistress Page – at the least if the love of soldier can suffice – that I
love thee. I will not say, pity me – 'tis not a soldier-like phrase – but
I say, love me. By me,   10
   Thine own true knight,
   By day or night,
   Or any kind of light,
   With all his might,
   For thee to fight,   15
     John Falstaff.'
What a Herod of Jewry is this! O, wicked, wicked world! One that
is well-nigh worn to pieces with age to show himself a young
gallant! What an unweighed behaviour hath this Flemish drunkard
picked – with the devil's name – out of my conversation, that he   20
dares in this manner assay me? Why, he hath not been thrice in my
company. What should I say to him? I was then frugal of my mirth.
Heaven forgive me! Why, I'll exhibit a bill in the parliament for the

---

4 precisian] F; physician *Collier²*, *conj. Johnson*   8 soldier] F; a soldier F3   10–16 By . . . Falstaff] *Capell; as two and a half lines of verse, divided after* night *and* might, *the third line filled out with the signature,* F   17–20 What . . . with] *As prose, Pope; as four lines of verse, divided after* world, age *and* unweighed F (*thereafter as prose but each line beginning with a capital until after* putting down *at 24)*   19 an unweighed] F; unwayed F3   20 with the] with / The F; i'th' F3

---

3 Love use Reason Falstaff affects the
Petrarchan mode with these personifications.

4 precisian puritanical spiritual guide.

4 counsellor sympathetic confidant. 'Love lets
reason preach, but he has no intention that he
should dictate the ministry of his affairs' (Hart).

5 sympathy affinity.

6 sack wine (usually white) from Spain or the
Canaries.

8 if . . . suffice Henry V similarly woos the
French princess 'plain soldier' (5.2.149). See Introduction, pp. 4–5.

17 Herod of Jewry Boastful ranting villain.
King Herod was usually represented as not only
wicked but absurdly boastful in mediaeval plays.

19 What . . . behaviour The reading of F3
need not be preferred here. Craik accepts F3's reading on the grounds that it is interrogative as against
F's exclamatory mode, and better suits Mistress
Page's uncertainty as to what it might have been

about her behaviour that was so unconsidered (=
'unweighed' (*OED* Weigh *v*¹ 11)) as to have set on
Falstaff. Both here and at 8 (with 'a soldier') F3
normalises a slightly strange usage relating to the
indefinite article, inserting in the first case and
omitting in the second. In each case I am inclined to
retain the more strenuous reading of F; and to suggest here that we are to understand the phrase as
meaning 'What instance of unweighed behaviour'.
See Textual Analysis, p. 151.

19 Flemish drunkard The inhabitants of the
Low Countries were traditionally thought of as
pot-bellied drunkards.

20 with . . . name in the devil's name. Again,
as at 19, F3 prefers the more conventional usage.

20 conversation conduct.

22 What . . . say What was it that I could have
said (Abbott 325).

23 exhibit The technical term for introducing
or submitting a bill to parliament (*OED v* 5a).

putting down of men. How shall I be revenged on him? For revenged I will be, as sure as his guts are made of puddings. [*She puts*   25
away the letter]

[*Enter* MISTRESS FORD]

MISTRESS FORD Mistress Page! Trust me, I was going to your house.

MISTRESS PAGE And, trust me, I was coming to you. You look very ill.

MISTRESS FORD Nay, I'll ne'er believe that. I have to show to the
contrary.

MISTRESS PAGE Faith, but you do, in my mind.   30

MISTRESS FORD Well, I do, then. Yet I say I could show you to the
contrary. O Mistress Page, give me some counsel!

MISTRESS PAGE What's the matter, woman?

MISTRESS FORD O woman, if it were not for one trifling respect, I
could come to such honour!   35

MISTRESS PAGE Hang the trifle, woman, take the honour. What is it?
Dispense with trifles. What is it?

MISTRESS FORD If I would but go to hell for an eternal moment or so,
I could be knighted.

MISTRESS PAGE What? Thou liest! Sir Alice Ford? These knights will   40
hack, and so thou shouldst not alter the article of thy gentry.

---

25 SD.1] *As Craik (after 25 SD.2)*   25 SD.2] Q; *not in* F   40 What? Thou liest!] *Johnson;* What thou liest? F

24 **putting down** suppression.

25 **puddings** 'The stomach or one of the entrails of a pig, sheep, or other animal, stuffed with a
mixture of minced meat, suet, oatmeal, seasoning,
etc., boiled and kept till needed'; in the plural the
word was also used to mean 'guts' (*OED*). As Oliver
remarks, 'guts' and 'puddings' here are almost
tautologous, and Falstaff's guts are much more like
a sixteenth-century pudding than the modern
variety.

25 *SD In Q, Mistress Ford enters and sees Mistress Page reading her letter: 'How now Mistris
Page, are you reading Loue Letters?' Mistress Ford
probably surmises that it is a love-letter because
Mistress Page tries to put it away hurriedly as she
sees her friend. This is a good piece of stage business, but F will not allow it, because there is no
mention of a letter at the beginning of the conversation between the two women.

27 **ill** 'Mistress Ford is probably looking pale
with anger . . . Mistress Page thinks that she looks
sick. Mistress Ford's reply is a denial that she looks
ill, i.e. ugly' (Craik).

28–9 **I . . . contrary** I have something to show
you (i.e. the love-letter from Falstaff) to prove the
contrary, that I am not ugly.

30 **do** do look ill.

40 **These knights** 'The derogatory generaliza-
tion would amuse the original audience if the first
performance of the play was at a Garter Feast'
(Craik).

41 **hack** go whoring, fuck. The noun 'hackney',
often abbreviated to 'hack', means 'whore' (*OED*
Hack *sb*³ 4b; Hackney *sb* 4). *OED* records the abbreviation from the eighteenth century, but we may
easily suppose it could be much earlier. The verb 'to
hack' (for 'to hackney'), in the sense 'to make common, vulgar, or stale [by] indiscriminate or promis-
cuous use' (*OED* Hack *v*³) is again only recorded
from the eighteenth century, but it seems a small
supposition that one undisputed sixteenth-century
sense of the noun 'hackney' (used by Shakespeare in
this sense of prostitute at *LLL* 3.1.32) could have
been accompanied by a verb (on the analogy of the
verb 'to whore') meaning 'to have to do with a hack'
or 'to make a woman a hack'. The other occurrence

MISTRESS FORD We burn daylight. Here, read, read. Perceive how I
     might be knighted.
          [*She produces a letter and gives it to Mistress Page, who reads it*]
     I shall think the worse of fat men as long as I have an eye to make
     difference of men's liking. And yet he would not swear, praised   45
     women's modesty, and gave such orderly and well-behaved reproof
     to all uncomeliness that I would have sworn his disposition would
     have gone to the truth of his words. But they do no more adhere
     and keep place together than the Hundredth Psalm to the tune of
     'Greensleeves'. What tempest, I trow, threw this whale, with so   50
     many tuns of oil in his belly, ashore at Windsor? How shall I be
     revenged on him? I think the best way were to entertain him with
     hope till the wicked fire of lust have melted him in his own grease.
     Did you ever hear the like?
MISTRESS PAGE Letter for letter, but that the name of Page and Ford   55
     differs.
          [*She holds up her own letter from Falstaff*]
     To thy great comfort in this mystery of ill opinions, here's the twin-

---

43 SD] *Craik, not in* F   45 praised] *Theobald;* praise F   49 place] F; pace *Rann, conj. Capell*   49 Hundredth Psalm] *Rowe;*
hundred Psalms F; hundred and fifty psalms *Oxford*   50 trow] *Rowe;* troa F   56 SD] *As Craik, not in* F

---

of the verb in *Wiv.*, at 4.1.57, seems to have an
undoubted sexual sense.

41 alter . . . gentry change the matter of your
social rank (*OED* Article *sb* 10b). As Craik remarks,
a rather oddly elaborate formulation for the sense it
bears. His suggestion, that there is some sexual innuendo connected with the primary sense of 'article' ('a joint connecting two parts of the body', *OED*
sb 1), seems interesting. Mistress Page has just taken
Mistress Ford's remark that she could be knighted,
not in her evidently supposed sense of 'become a
knight's mistress', but in the literal sense 'become a
(male) knight', and here it may be that she goes on
to advise against acquiring male sexual equipment.

42 burn daylight Proverbial for 'waste time'
(Tilley D123).

44–5 make . . . liking differentiate between
men's bodily condition (*OED* Liking *sb* 6).

45 *praised F's 'praise' would be an easy error
for 'praised', which makes evident syntactic sense
here.

47 uncomeliness unseemly behaviour.

48 gone . . . of accorded truly with.

48–9 adhere . . . together agree and correspond together.

49 *Hundredth Psalm It seems clear that the

text here should read either 'Hundredth Psalm' or
(as in the Oxford text) 'hundred and fifty psalms'.
The text of F as it stands falls between these
two satisfactorily unitary possibilities; 'the hundred
Psalms' makes no greater rhetorical sense than 'the
fifty sonnets' of Shakespeare. The reading adopted
here not only involves less radical interference with
F, it also yields a neater one-to-one comparison between a very well-known psalm and an equally well-
known and wholly incongruous tune. As Craik
notes, the error in F is easy to explain: 'it is only
necessary to suppose that the scribe or the compositor misread "hundredth" as "hundreth" (a widely-
current spelling of "hundred") and regularized
accordingly, at the same time altering "psalm" to
"psalms" to correct the sense'.

50 *I trow I wonder.

51 tuns barrels.

52 entertain him occupy his attention (*OED*
vb 9).

53 wicked . . . grease The proverbial torment
is 'to fry in one's own grease' (Tilley G433), or in the
more modern version 'to stew in one's own juice'.

57 mystery . . . opinions 'puzzle about the
bad characters or reputations we seem to have'
(Hart).

brother of thy letter. But let thine inherit first, for I protest mine never shall.

[She gives the two letters to Mistress Ford, who compares them]

I warrant he hath a thousand of these letters, writ with blank space   60
for different names – sure, more, and these are of the second edition. He will print them, out of doubt; for he cares not what he puts into the press when he would put us two. I had rather be a giantess and lie under Mount Pelion. Well, I will find you twenty lascivious turtles ere one chaste man.   65

MISTRESS FORD Why, this is the very same: the very hand, the very words. What doth he think of us?

MISTRESS PAGE Nay, I know not. It makes me almost ready to wrangle with mine own honesty. I'll entertain myself like one that I am not acquainted withal; for, sure, unless he know some strain in me that   70
I know not myself, he would never have boarded me in this fury.

MISTRESS FORD 'Boarding' call you it? I'll be sure to keep him above deck.

MISTRESS PAGE So will I. If he come under my hatches, I'll never to sea again. Let's be revenged on him. Let's appoint him a meeting,   75
give him a show of comfort in his suit, and lead him on with a fine-baited delay till he hath pawned his horses to mine host of the Garter.

MISTRESS FORD Nay, I will consent to act any villainy against him that

---

59 SD] *Craik; not in* F   **70** strain] F; stain *Pope*

---

58 inherit first Mistress Page jokingly disclaims any right to the legacy of Falstaff's favours which might be due to the first-born of the twin letters, the first, as it were, to appear on the stage, at the beginning of this scene.

61–2 second edition second batch of a thousand copies.

62 print The notion that Falstaff is into his second batch of love-letters, and calling this his 'second edition', allows in the further idea that he will get them publicly printed off, no doubt to save the labour of writing. The quibble on 'press' follows easily.

63–4 I . . . Pelion In the Greek myth, the giants in their war against the gods piled Pelion on Mount Ossa in order to climb to Olympus. As punishment Zeus imprisoned some of them under mountains. Mistress Page makes the giants giantesses to suit the present context.

65 lascivious turtles Turtle-doves were pro-

verbial for their fidelity (Tilley T624), so it would be inconceivable that a turtle could be lascivious.

68–9 wrangle . . . honesty call into question my own virtue (for not being evident enough to have prevented Falstaff's advances).

69 entertain behave towards.

70 strain tendency, quality.

71 boarded accosted, assailed. The metaphor is from one ship coming up alongside another. It was commonly used at this time for sexual approach. The nautical metaphor, with its sexual innuendo, is carried on in the next speeches.

71 fury tempest of emotion.

76 show of comfort outward appearance of encouragement (*OED* Comfort *sb* 1).

76–7 fine-baited skilfully alluring, like a delicate bait on a fishhook.

77 pawned . . . horses i.e. to pay for the expenses they will oblige him to in his courtship. See 5.5.106 n.

may not sully the chariness of our honesty. O that my husband saw   80
this letter! It would give eternal food to his jealousy.

[*Enter* FORD *with* PISTOL, *and* PAGE *with* NIM]

MISTRESS PAGE Why, look where he comes, and my goodman too.
He's as far from jealousy as I am from giving him cause, and that, I
hope, is an unmeasurable distance.
MISTRESS FORD You are the happier woman.   85
MISTRESS PAGE Let's consult together against this greasy knight.
Come hither.
                          [*They withdraw*]
FORD Well, I hope it be not so.
PISTOL Hope is a curtal dog in some affairs.
        Sir John affects thy wife.   90
FORD Why, sir, my wife is not young.
PISTOL He woos both high and low, both rich and poor,
        Both young and old, one with another, Ford.
        He loves the gallimaufry. Ford, perpend.
FORD Love my wife?   95
PISTOL With liver burning hot. Prevent,
        Or go thou, like Sir Actaeon he,

---

81 SD] *Rowe; Enter Ford, Page, Pistoll and Nym.* Q; *not in* F   82 goodman] *Bowers;* good/man F   87 SD] *Craik, as Theobald; not in* F   92–4] *As verse, Pope; as prose,* F   94 gallimaufry. Ford, perpend] *Capell;* Gally-mawfry (*Ford*) perpend F   96–9] *Oliver; as three lines of verse, divided after* prevent *and* with F; *as three lines of verse, divided after* thou *and* heels *Capell*

---

80 chariness . . . honesty our scrupulously guarded virtue.

82 *goodman husband. In F the word is split between two lines, with no hyphen, so that F actually reads 'good man'. Mistress Page's immediately following comment on Page makes it clear that he is indeed a good man; but on the other hand Mistress Ford has just been speaking about her own husband, Mistress Page than notes that Mistress Ford's husband is coming ('look where he comes'), together with her own 'good/man' – the change of tone needed to make 'good/man' mean anything more than 'husband' would be difficult, especially since the subject of his goodness is only clearly introduced in the following sentence. It seems very likely that 'goodman' only becomes 'good man' in Mistress Page's mind as she speaks this following sentence. See 2.2.27 n.

89 curtal dog dog with its tail docked; hope is unnaturally cut short like the dog.

90 affects loves.

94 gallimaufry 'whole lot' (Hibbard). This is

primarily a cooking term, meaning 'a hodge-podge, a ragout' into which any available odds and ends of food were put (*OED sb* 1). No doubt, however, Shakespeare uses it here because of its salacious, mouth-filling quality.

94 perpend consider. This word seems to have had an archaic, theatrical quality for Shakespeare, perhaps especially when occurring, as here, after a vocative. Craik cites Thomas Preston's *Cambises* (an old play, c. 1570), very much Pistol's kind of ranting piece, at line 1018: 'My queen, perpend.'

96 liver Usually thought of as the seat of the passion of love.

96 Prevent Take preventive measures.

97 like . . . he like that Sir Actaeon. The prefix 'sir' was not uncommonly added to the names of mythical characters, but together with the archaic use of the pronoun here, it gives the whole phrase an antique quality of the kind Pistol favours. Actaeon was killed by his own hounds when he had been changed into a stag by Diana after he had seen the naked goddess bathing.

With Ringwood at thy heels.
O, odious is the name!
FORD What name, sir?   100
PISTOL The horn, I say. Farewell.
Take heed, have open eye, for thieves do foot by night.
Take heed, ere summer comes, or cuckoo-birds do sing.
Away, Sir Corporal Nim!
Believe it, Page; he speaks sense.   [*Exit*]   105
FORD I will be patient. I will find out this.
NIM [*To Page*] And this is true. I like not the humour of lying. He hath
wronged me in some humours. I should have borne the humoured
letter to her, but I have a sword and it shall bite upon my necessity.
He loves your wife. There's the short and the long. My name is   110
Corporal Nim. I speak and I avouch. 'Tis true. My name is Nim,
and Falstaff loves your wife. Adieu. I love not the humour of bread
and cheese. Adieu.   [*Exit*]
PAGE The humour of it, quoth'a! Here's a fellow frights English out of
his wits.   115

104–5] F; *Page* believe him what he ses. Away sir Corporall *Nym*. Q   **105** SD] *Exit Pistoll:* Q; *not in* F   **107** SD] *As Hanmer;*
not in F   **110–12** My . . . wife] *As prose,* F; *as two lines of verse, divided after* avouch NS   **111** avouch. 'Tis] auouch; 'tis F;
auouch tis Q   **113** cheese. Adieu] cheese: adieu F; *cheese;* / *And theres the humor of it* Q   **113** SD] *Exit Nym.* Q; *not in* F
114 English] F; humor Q

98 Ringwood This was a popular name for a
hunting dog, and Golding in his translation of
the story from Ovid's *Metamorphoses* calls one of
Actaeon's hounds Ringwood.

99 name the name of cuckold, which Pistol, as
it were, cannot bring himself to say directly. Although not himself a cuckold, Actaeon seems often
to have been alluded to where cuckoldry was hinted
at, because of his stag's horns. See 3.2.32 n.

102 foot walk.

103 cuckoo-birds The word 'cuckold' is derived from 'cuckoo', a bird which sings in the spring
and deceives other birds by laying its eggs in their
nests. The song of the cuckoo was the derisive
warning to the deceived husband.

105 Some editors have assigned this line to Nim,
but the Q reading discourages such an emendation,
and it makes good sense to suppose that Pistol calls
across to Page as he leaves.

106 find out find out the truth of.

109 bite . . . necessity reach its mark when I
need it to.

110 the short . . . long Proverbial for 'the
whole truth of the thing' both in this ordering of the
phrase and in the reverse ordering with which we
are more familiar (Tilley L419).

111 avouch. 'Tis I feel inclined to preserve the
unusual absolute sense for 'avouch' that the punctuation of F indicates, on the grounds that the

rhetorical abruptness of 'I speak and I avouch' then
fits into a pattern of short and forceful phrases with
'My name is Corporal Nim' and ''Tis true'. I would
not go so far as the NS editors and print
'My . . . wife' (110–12) as two lines of verse divided
after 'avouch' because this would seem to emphasise
too much the touch of a Pistol-like style in Nim's
speech here.

112–13 humour . . . cheese style of life reduced to the bare necessities. Nim uses 'humour' in
his usual loosely capacious sense; and 'bread and
cheese' is proverbially a description of minimal ra-
tions. The corporal is no doubt describing his very
basic form of life in Falstaff's service and means
Page to understand that he looks for better things,
'that he is a respectable man, a corporal, not a needy
or cast-off serving-man' (Craik).

114–21 Page and Ford pursue independent lines
of thought in these lines, but they are not in the
formal sense 'asides'.

114 The . . . it As both Oliver and Craik remark, this need not be a repetition of Nim's immediately preceding words in Q, so that there is no
need to admit the phrase from Q into the text at 113.
What Q introduces at 113 is Nim's favourite phrase
in *H5* which he is not found using at all in the F text
of *Wiv.* See Introduction, p. 67. Page's 'of it' is
simply a reference to the 'bread and cheese'.

115 his its.

FORD I will seek out Falstaff.

PAGE I never heard such a drawling, affecting rogue.

FORD If I do find it – well.

PAGE I will not believe such a Cataian, though the priest o'th'town
commended him for a true man.   120

FORD 'Twas a good sensible fellow – well.

[Mistress Page and Mistress Ford come forward]

PAGE How now, Meg?

MISTRESS PAGE Whither go you, George? Hark you.

[They withdraw and talk]

MISTRESS FORD How now, sweet Frank, why art thou melancholy?

FORD I melancholy? I am not melancholy. Get you home, go.   125

MISTRESS FORD Faith, thou hast some crotchets in thy head now. –
Will you go, Mistress Page?

MISTRESS PAGE Have with you. – You'll come to dinner, George?

[Enter MISTRESS QUICKLY]

[Aside to Mistress Ford] Look who comes yonder. She shall be our
messenger to this paltry knight.   130

MISTRESS FORD Trust me, I thought on her. She'll fit it.

MISTRESS PAGE You are come to see my daughter Anne?

MISTRESS QUICKLY Ay, forsooth; and I pray how does good Mistress
Anne?

MISTRESS PAGE Go in with us and see. We have an hour's talk with   135
you.

[Exeunt Mistress Page, Mistress Ford, and Mistress Quickly]

PAGE How now, Master Ford?

---

121 SD] *Theobald; not in* F   123 SD] *Craik, as Hibbard; not in* F   125] *As prose, Pope; as two lines of verse, divided after* not
melancholy FQ   126–7] *As prose, Pope; as two lines of verse, divided after* head F   126–7 head now. – Will] *Hanmer;* head,
/ Now: will F   128 come] F; come home *Craik*   128 SD] Q *(after line corresponding to 123); not in* F   129 SD] *Johnson; not
in* F   135 We have] F; we would have *conj. Walker*   136 SD] *Exit Mistresse* Ford, Mis. Page, *and* Quickly. Q; *not in* F

---

117 **drawling, affecting** affectedly repetitious.
OED cites this passage and defines 'drawling' as to
'prolong or lengthen out the words of speech in an
indolent or affected manner' (Drawl *v* 2), but as
Craik notes, 'this is not the impression that Nim's
clipped style gives'. I accept Craik's suggestion that
Page is here rather describing Nim's unnecessary
lengthening of his speech by constant rhetorical
repetition.

119 **Cataian** i.e. Cathaian, inhabitant of
Cathay, or China. OED suggests that, among other
things, the word was used to mean a scoundrel, and
that seems the appropriate sense here.

123 **Whither . . . George?** 'Not an indication
that Page is moving towards an exit . . . Mistress
Page is asking her husband where he is going because she wants to know whether he is coming home
to dinner' (Craik). See 128.

126 **crotchets** absurd fancies. The phrase is
proverbial (Tilley c843).

128 **Have . . . you** I'll come with you.

135–6 **We . . . you** Craik notes the same idiomatic use in Beaumont and Fletcher, *The Maid's
Tragedy* 3.1.147: 'I have some speech with you'.

FORD You heard what this knave told me, did you not?

PAGE Yes, and you heard what the other told me?

FORD Do you think there is truth in them?   140

PAGE Hang 'em, slaves! I do not think the knight would offer it. But
these that accuse him in his intent towards our wives are a yoke of
his discarded men: very rogues, now they be out of service.

FORD Were they his men?

PAGE Marry, were they.   145

FORD I like it never the better for that. Does he lie at the Garter?

PAGE I, marry, does he. If he should intend this voyage toward my wife,
I would turn her loose to him; and what he gets more of her than
sharp words, let it lie on my head.

FORD I do not misdoubt my wife, but I would be loath to turn them   150
together. A man may be too confident. I would have nothing lie on
my head. I cannot be thus satisfied.

[Enter HOST]

PAGE Look where my ranting host of the Garter comes. There is either
liquor in his pate or money in his purse when he looks so merrily.
How now, mine host?   155

HOST How now, bully rook? Thou'rt a gentleman. – Cavaliero justice,
I say!

[Enter SHALLOW]

SHALLOW I follow, mine host, I follow. Good even and twenty, good
Master Page. Master Page, will you go with us? We have sport in
hand.   160

146] *As prose, Pope; as two lines of verse, divided after* that F   152 SD] *Dyce; Enter Host and Shallow* Q; *not in* F   153 ranting]
F; *ramping* Q   157 SD] *Dyce; not in* F

141 **I do not think** ... The sensible Page is, of
course, quite wrong in his suggestion about Falstaff.

141 **offer** attempt.

142 **yoke** pair.

147 **voyage** It may be, as Hart suggests, that
Nim has repeated to Page the words Falstaff uses
about the East and West Indies at 1.3.53, but we do
not need to suppose this. The word is used in this
figurative sense elsewhere by Shakespeare.

148 **turn** ... **him** offer her to his sexual advances. The phrase would be used of offering a cow
to a bull, and so is nakedly sexual.

149 **lie** ... **head** be upon my head, be my fault.
Ford uses the same phrase at 151–2 to refer to the
cuckold's horns.

153 **ranting** bombastic, verbally larger than
life.

156 **Cavaliero** Courtly gentleman, swaggering
gallant. A fanciful title bestowed on Shallow by the
Host in this scene and on Slender at 2.3.59.

158 **Good** ... **twenty** Good afternoon, many
times repeated. There is a difficulty with the timing
of events here, because, although 'even' could mean
any time after noon, Falstaff's first assignation,
which is fixed for between 10 and 11 a.m. (2.2.66–
7), has not yet happened, neither has the midday
meal, dinner, mentioned at 128.

HOST Tell him, cavaliero justice; tell him, bully rook.

SHALLOW Sir, there is a fray to be fought between Sir Hugh the Welsh priest and Caius the French doctor.

FORD Good mine host o'th'Garter, a word with you.

HOST What sayst thou, my bully rook?   165

[They withdraw and talk]

SHALLOW *[To Page]* Will you go with us to behold it? My merry host hath had the measuring of their weapons, and, I think, hath appointed them contrary places; for, believe me, I hear the parson is no jester. Hark, I will tell you what our sport shall be.

[They withdraw and talk]

HOST *[Coming forward with Ford]* Hast thou no suit against my knight,   170 my guest cavalier?

FORD None, I protest. But I'll give you a pottle of burnt sack to give me recourse to him, and tell him my name is Brook – only for a jest.

HOST My hand, bully. Thou shalt have egress and regress – said I well? – and thy name shall be Brook. It is a merry knight. *[Speaks to all]*   175 Will you go, ameers?

SHALLOW Have with you, mine host.

PAGE I have heard the Frenchman hath good skill in his rapier.

---

165 SD] *Craik;* Ford *and the Host talkes.* Q; *not in* F   166 SD] *Johnson; not in* F   169 SD] *Craik, as Capell; not in* F   170 SD] *As Craik; not in* F   171 cavalier] -Caualeire F; -cavaleiro *Kittredge;* cauellira Q   172 SH FORD] Q; *Shal.* F   173 Brook] *Rrooke* Q *(thereafter Brooke); Broome* F *(and so thereafter)*   175 SD] *This edn; To Shallow and Page / Oxford; not in* F   176 ameers] *NS, conj. Hart;* An-heires F; *mynheers Hanmer, conj. Theobald;* mijnheers *Oxford*

171 guest cavalier i.e. Falstaff. F's spelling changes from 'Caueleiro' at 156 and 161 to 'Caualeire' here. Craik suggests that the spelling here 'is probably an error caused by misreading' and so prints 'cavaliero' in his text as on the two previous occasions. But I think it likely that a distinction is made between the Host's use of the noun in a vocative role (where it has the extended 'o' ending) and in ordinary circumstances.

172 pottle vessel holding half a gallon.

172 burnt sack mulled white wine.

173 *Brook Q preserves the true reading here. See Introduction, pp. 3–4 and Textual Analysis, p. 158.

174 egress and regress The Host plays with these legal terms, which simply mean the freedom to come and go.

176 *ameers This is a variant spelling of 'emirs'. F's reading is unintelligible as it stands, and the most plausible suggestions have been either that the Host is using the Dutch term for gentlemen (in partially anglicised forms = mynheers, mijnheers) or that he is using an exotic oriental title, meaning in this context much the same as 'sirs', rather as he

seems to have done at 1.3.6. F's word here, 'Anheires', is unemended in the later Folios, which may mean that it was understood, was a term in use, or that it was not understood but that no satisfactory correction suggested itself. The word has often been seen as related to the equally puzzling term used at *1H4* 2.1.76, where Gadshill claims that he keeps company with 'nobility and tranquility, burgomasters and great oney'rs' (the early Qq read 'Oneyres' and F1 and the later Qq have the variant 'Oneyers'). It is difficult to believe that 'mynheers' can have been misspelt as either the term here or in *1H4*, even though 'burgomasters' would suggest an appropriately Dutch context in the latter case; and in addition the word 'mynheer' is not recorded in ordinary English use elsewhere until the mid-seventeenth century. By contrast, 'ameer' is found in various variant spellings as early as 1614 (*OED*, Hart quotes an occurrence in 1592), and as Hart points out, was thought at this time (correctly) to be the word behind 'admiral'. The spelling 'Anheires' could relatively easily be for 'Amheeres', and this somewhat domesticated but still exotic term seems not inconceivable in the Host's colourful speech.

SHALLOW Tut, sir, I could have told you more. In these times you
    stand on distance, your passes, stoccadoes, and I know not what.   180
    'Tis the heart, Master Page; 'tis here, 'tis here. I have seen the time,
    with my long sword, I would have made you four tall fellows skip
    like rats.
HOST Here, boys, here, here! Shall we wag?
PAGE Have with you. I had rather hear them scold than fight.   185
                              [*Exeunt Host, Shallow, and Page*]
FORD Though Page be a secure fool and stands so firmly on his wife's
    frailty, yet I cannot put off my opinion so easily. She was in his
    company at Page's house, and what they made there I know not.
    Well, I will look further into't, and I have a disguise to sound
    Falstaff. If I find her honest, I lose not my labour. If she be other-   190
    wise, 'tis labour well bestowed.   [*Exit*]

2.2 [*Enter* FALSTAFF *and* PISTOL]

FALSTAFF I will not lend thee a penny.
PISTOL Why then, the world's mine oyster,
    Which I with sword will open.

182 long sword] F; two hand sword Q   185 hear] F; have *Hanmer*   185 than] then F; than see them *Collier*²   185 SD] *Rowe*;
Exit Host and Shallow. Q; *not in* F   191 SD] *Exeunt.* F; *Exit omnes.* Q   Act 2, Scene 2   2.2] *Scæna Secunda.* F   0 SD] *Enter
Syr Iohn, and* Pistoll. Q; *Enter* Falstaffe, Pistoll, Robin, Quickly, Bardolffe, Ford. F   1–4 FALSTAFF . . . penny] *As* F; *Fal.
I*le not lend thee a peny. / *Pis. I* will retort the sum in equipage. / *Fal.* Not a pennie Q   2–3] *As verse, Steevens*³; *as
prose*, F

179 **Tut . . . more** As Craik notes, the implication of Shallow's words here is 'You may have heard
that, but let me tell you that all this fighting with
rapiers is a silly modern fashion.' Shallow is sighing
for the good old custom of fighting with sword and
buckler, now replaced by a fancy foreign fashion.
179–80 **you stand on distance** Importance is
attached to the duellists standing well apart from
each other.
180 **passes, stoccadoes** Kinds of thrust in
fencing.
181 **'Tis . . . here.** Whereas what is really important is the heart a man has for the fight (Shallow
resting a hand on his own heart).
182 **long sword** As the reading of Q makes
clear, Shallow is referring to the good old heavy
sword of his youth, by contrast with the fashionable
modern rapier, a lightweight weapon.
182 **you . . . skip** four valiant fellows skip for
you.
184 **wag** go, as at 1.3.4.
186 **secure** over-confident.

186–7 **stands . . . frailty** puts such trust in
what must in reality be his wife's moral weakness.
188 **made** 'did, got up to' (Hibbard).
189 **disguise** He has just arranged to be presented to Falstaff as Brook, perhaps actually wearing a disguise. See 2.2.124 SD n.

Act 2, Scene 2

1–4 FALSTAFF . . . **penny** Some editors make
room here for Q's line '*I* will retort the sum in
equipage', which it is very tempting to think of as
genuinely Shakespeare's. The use of 'equipage' as 'a
fantastic equivalent for "equity"' (Greg) suits Pistol's usual linguistic style very well. However, there
is no difficulty at this point in the F text which
would justify emendation, and we may suppose perhaps that Q represents Shakespeare's own later revision, possibly at one of the two prompt-book stages
in Q's line of descent. See Textual Analysis, p. 156.
2 **the . . . oyster** 'i.e. from which I will extract
the pearl' (Craik).

FALSTAFF Not a penny. I have been content, sir, you should lay my
    countenance to pawn. I have grated upon my good friends for three   5
    reprieves for you and your coach-fellow Nim, or else you had
    looked through the grate, like a gemini of baboons. I am damned in
    hell for swearing to gentlemen my friends you were good soldiers
    and tall fellows. And when Mistress Bridget lost the handle of her
    fan, I took't upon mine honour thou hadst it not.   10
PISTOL Didst not thou share? Hadst thou not fifteen pence?
FALSTAFF Reason, you rogue, reason. Think'st thou I'll endanger my
    soul gratis? At a word, hang no more about me; I am no gibbet for
    you. Go – a short knife and a throng – to your manor of Pickt-hatch,
    go! You'll not bear a letter for me, you rogue? You stand upon your   15
    honour? Why, thou unconfinable baseness, it is as much as I can do
    to keep the terms of my honour precise. I, I, I myself sometimes,
    leaving the fear of God on the left hand and hiding mine honour in
    my necessity, am fain to shuffle, to hedge, and to lurch; and yet you,

---

11] *As verse*, Q; *as prose*, F   17 I, I, I] F; I, I Q   18 God] Q; heauen F   19–20 yet you, you rogue] *Collier²*; yet, you Rogue
F; yet you, rogue *Pope*

4–5 lay . . . pawn 'borrow money on the
strength of my patronage of you' (Hibbard).

5 grated upon importuned.

6 coach-fellow horse yoked with another to
the same coach.

7 grate prison bars.

7 gemini pair (from the Latin 'gemini' =
twins). Dr Neil Rhodes, commenting on the phrase
'gemini of baboons', suggests to me that Shakespeare may have seen either the original or some
sort of copy of Pieter Bruegel's painting, the *Dulle
Griet*, on the right of which 'is a depiction of hell,
where from a tower with a barred window two mon-
keys draw up a bucket from a stream below'.

9 tall brave.

9–10 handle . . . fan Fan-handles were often
valuable, being made of silver or some other costly
material. We gather from line 11 that this particular
handle was sold for 30d, an appreciable sum.

10 took't . . . honour engaged my honour that.

12 Reason i.e. it was the reasonable thing to do.
He had endangered his soul by lying, so the least he
could do was have this modest reward for it.

13 hang . . . me be a burden to me no longer.
The following gibbet metaphor begins with a quibble on 'hang'.

14 a short . . . throng i.e. live your life as a
cutpurse, with a short knife to cut open purses in a
crowd.

14 manor of Pickt-hatch Falstaff ironically
describes a gentlemanly residence (manor) for Pistol, suitably named for a pickpocket. Not only is
there the quibble with 'Pickt' but the name 'Pickt-
hatch', literally meaning a 'half door, surmounted
by a row of pikes or spikes', seems to have been the
popular name for an unsavoury district of London
(*OED* Picked-hatch).

16 unconfinable limitless.

17 terms . . . precise my honour clearly defined and uncompromised.

18 *God See Textual Analysis, p. 160.

18 on . . . hand aside.

19 shuffle . . . lurch The three verbs are more
or less synonymous, though they derive a good deal
of their dramatic force from seeming like three mys-
teriously distinct technical terms. Their common
meaning is 'to depart from the plain and forthright
way' for dishonest gain.

19–20 *you, you rogue F's reading can be
made to make sense by a change of punctuation, as
in Oliver's text ('you, rogue'); but, as Hibbard
notes, the use of 'you rogue' as a form of address
twice before in this speech supports Collier's emendation, as indeed does Falstaff's shortly preceding
triple emphasis of the first person pronoun to match
the double emphasis here of the second person pronoun. The use of first and second person pronouns
makes an interestingly developing rhetorical shape

you rogue, will ensconce your rags, your cat-a-mountain looks, your   20
red-lattice phrases, and your bold beating oaths, under the shelter
of your honour! You will not do it! You!
PISTOL I do relent. What would thou more of man?

[*Enter* ROBIN]

ROBIN Sir, here's a woman would speak with you.
FALSTAFF Let her approach.   25

[*Enter* MISTRESS QUICKLY]

MISTRESS QUICKLY Give your worship good morrow.
FALSTAFF Good morrow, good wife.
MISTRESS QUICKLY Not so, an't please your worship.
FALSTAFF Good maid, then.
MISTRESS QUICKLY   I'll be sworn,
     As my mother was the first hour I was born.   30
FALSTAFF I do believe the swearer. What with me?
MISTRESS QUICKLY Shall I vouchsafe your worship a word or two?

---

21 bold beating oaths] bold-beating-oathes F; bull-baiting oaths *Hanmer*; bowl-beating oaths *conj. NS*   23 relent] F; recant Q   23 would] F; woulst Q   23 SD] *Rowe; not in* F   25 SD] Q; *not in* F   27 good wife] F4; good-wife F; faire wife Q   29 I'll] F; That I am Ile Q

---

in this speech, which ends with a fivefold repetition of the possessive pronoun 'your' and a final double emphasis of 'you'.

20 **ensconce** 'find protective covering for' (Hibbard); a sconce is a small fortification.

20 **cat-a-mountain** wild cat.

21 **red-lattice** ale-house. A tavern would generally have red-painted wooden lattices instead of glazed windows.

21 **bold beating** The phrase has caused difficulty, but if we discount in F what are no doubt the scribe's hyphens (Ralph Crane was very fond of hyphens, and has had legitimate use for them with the two previous epithets), then we can see that the two previous compound adjectives lead into a dramatically slowed and weightier pair of adjectives here, with the word 'beating' indicating that the oaths strike repeated rhetorical blows.

23 **relent** yield, give way (*OED v*[1] 2b). Q's 'recant' here, in the sense 'renounce, withdraw, retract', persuades me against Craik's glossing of 'relent' as 'repent' (*OED v*[1] 5). Public recantation, in any case, seems more Pistol's style.

23 **man** Robin's 'here's a woman' in the following line chimes smartly against Pistol's last word.

27 ***good wife** I take this as two words (with F4) and not as the style or title 'goodwife', noting that if

F hyphenates here, then it does the same with 'Good morrow', and that both Q's reading and the following little debate about wife or maid treat the 'wife' element as independent. Indeed, the steady repetition of 'good' in 26–9, as Falstaff plays teasingly with Mistress Quickly's conventional address, gives the adjective its own independent status as well, so that it gains its maximum semantic force just at the moment, in 29, when this is most inappropriate, for Mistress Quickly is surely not a maid, as the following lines confirm. See Textual Analysis, p. 151.

29 **I'll be sworn** Craik prefaces these words with 'That I am' from Q, as seeming 'necessary to the sense', and he notes that the phrase 'I'll be sworn' 'normally either follows or introduces a statement by the speaker'. I think, however, we may imagine Mistress Quickly here taking over Falstaff's immediately preceding words and making them her own with this exclamation.

30 As Oliver notes, this is 'a delightful "Freudian" conflation of the proverbs "as good a maid as her mother" and "as innocent as a new-born babe" (Tilley M14, B4)'. Mistress Quickly succeeds in saying the reverse of what she intended, and Falstaff indicates that he believes what the words actually say, that Mistress Quickly is as much a maid as her mother was in childbirth.

FALSTAFF Two thousand, fair woman, and I'll vouchsafe thee the hearing.

MISTRESS QUICKLY There is one Mistress Ford, sir – I pray come a   35
little nearer this ways – I myself dwell with Master Doctor Caius –

FALSTAFF Well, on. Mistress Ford, you say –

MISTRESS QUICKLY Your worship says very true. I pray your worship,
come a little nearer this ways.

FALSTAFF I warrant thee nobody hears – [*Indicating Pistol and Robin*]   40
mine own people, mine own people.

MISTRESS QUICKLY Are they so? God bless them and make them his
servants!

FALSTAFF Well, Mistress Ford – what of her?

MISTRESS QUICKLY Why, sir, she's a good creature. Lord, Lord, your   45
worship's a wanton! Well, heaven forgive you, and all of us, I pray!

FALSTAFF Mistress Ford – come, Mistress Ford –

MISTRESS QUICKLY Marry, this is the short and the long of it: you
have brought her into such a canaries as 'tis wonderful. The best
courtier of them all, when the court lay at Windsor, could never   50
have brought her to such a canary. Yet there has been knights, and
lords, and gentlemen, with their coaches, I warrant you, coach after
coach, letter after letter, gift after gift, smelling so sweetly, all musk,
and so rushling, I warrant you, in silk and gold, and in such alligant
terms, and in such wine and sugar of the best and the fairest, that   55
would have won any woman's heart, and, I warrant you, they could
never get an eye-wink of her. I had myself twenty angels given me

---

37 on. Mistress] on; Mistresse F   40 SD] *Craik, as NS; not in* F   42 God] Q; heauen F   46 pray!] *Cam.;* pray – F   47]
Cam.; Mistresse *Ford:* come, Mistresse *Ford.* F   54 rushling] F; rustling *Oxford*

33 **vouchsafe** entreat (in Quickly-speech). The
word actually means 'grant', as it does in Falstaff's
reply as he toys with Mistress Quickly's strange
English.
36 **this ways** this way.
37 **on** go on.
41 **mine . . . people.** The breach between Pistol and Falstaff has been healed at 23, and so both
Robin and Pistol (the only other characters on the
stage) are in Falstaff's confidence, his 'own people'.
42 ***God** See Textual Analysis, p. 161.
49 **canaries** quandary (and so at 51). The word
'quandary' was usually accented on the second syllable (*OED*), so Mistress Quickly's approximation
chimes quite well with the word she intends. Properly speaking, 'canary' at this time could either
mean white wine, or a Spanish dance (*OED sb* 1, 2).
50 **when . . . Windsor** We can read 'when' as

meaning 'at times when'. As Craik notes, this clause
'does not necessarily mean that the court is not at
Windsor now'.
54 **rushling** This perhaps archaic variant pronunciation of 'rustling' is clearly part of Mistress
Quickly's idiom. It is perhaps not fanciful to think
of her preference for the less sharply defined sound
as of a piece with her semantic and syntactic loose-
ness. Her language fits her comfortably like an old
slipper.
54 **alligant** elegant. *OED* describes this as an
improper form of 'elegant' and also as at this time a
current variant form of 'alicant(e)', 'a kind of wine
made at Alicante in Spain' (*OED* Alicant). As Craik
remarks, Mistress Quickly's 'immediately following
mention of *wine and sugar*' ensures that her errone-
ous pronunciation does not go unnoticed.
57 **eye-wink** wink or motion of the eye, look,

this morning, but I defy all angels in any such sort, as they say, but
in the way of honesty. And, I warrant you, they could never get her
so much as sip on a cup with the proudest of them all, and yet there   60
has been earls – nay, which is more, pensioners – but, I warrant you,
all is one with her.

FALSTAFF But what says she to me? Be brief, my good she-Mercury.

MISTRESS QUICKLY Marry, she hath received your letter, for the
which she thanks you a thousand times, and she gives you to notify   65
that her husband will be absence from his house between ten and
eleven.

FALSTAFF Ten and eleven.

MISTRESS QUICKLY Ay, forsooth; and then you may come and see the
picture, she says, that you wot of. Master Ford, her husband, will be   70
from home. Alas, the sweet woman leads an ill life with him; he's a
very jealousy man; she leads a very frampold life with him, good
heart.

FALSTAFF Ten and eleven. Woman, commend me to her. I will not fail
her.   75

MISTRESS QUICKLY Why, you say well. But I have another messenger
to your worship. Mistress Page hath her hearty commendations to
you too; and let me tell you in your ear, she's as fartuous a civil
modest wife, and one, I tell you, that will not miss you morning nor
evening prayer, as any is in Windsor, whoe'er be the other. And she   80
bade me tell your worship that her husband is seldom from home,
but she hopes there will come a time. I never knew a woman so dote
upon a man. Surely, I think you have charms, la! Yes, in truth.

FALSTAFF Not I, I assure thee. Setting the attraction of my good parts
aside, I have no other charms.   85

74–5] *As prose, Pope; as two lines of verse, divided after* eleven F

glance. *OED* records this instance and then nothing
until the nineteenth century, so perhaps it is Shakespeare's own coinage to suit Mistress Quickly's
style.

58 defy reject.

58 angels See 1.3.39.

58 in . . . sort of any such kind.

60 sip to sip.

61 which . . . pensioners The comic suggestion here is that pensioners (gentlemen who acted as
'a bodyguard to the sovereign within the royal palace' – *OED sb* 2) are even more important than earls.

63 Mercury The messenger of the gods.

65 notify understand (in Quickly-speech).

66 absence absent. See 1.1.212.

70 wot know.

72 jealousy jealous. Compare 'simplicity' at
4.1.25.

72 frampold disagreeable.

72–3 good heart i.e. poor thing.

76 messenger for 'message'.

78 fartuous for 'virtuous'.

79 miss you miss ('you' is a redundant dative
pronoun: see Abbott 220).

83 charms enchantments, magic spells (as in Q:
'*I* think you work by *I*nchantments').

84 parts (1) qualities, (2) looks.

MISTRESS QUICKLY Blessing on your heart for't!

FALSTAFF But I pray thee tell me this: has Ford's wife and Page's wife
acquainted each other how they love me?

MISTRESS QUICKLY That were a jest indeed! They have not so little
grace, I hope. That were a trick indeed! But Mistress Page would   90
desire you to send her your little page, of all loves. Her husband has
a marvellous infection to the little page; and truly, Master Page is an
honest man. Never a wife in Windsor leads a better life than she
does. Do what she will, say what she will, take all, pay all, go to bed
when she list, rise when she list, all is as she will. And, truly, she   95
deserves it; for if there be a kind woman in Windsor, she is one. You
must send her your page, no remedy.

FALSTAFF Why, I will.

MISTRESS QUICKLY Nay, but do so, then; and, look you, he may come
and go between you both. And in any case have a nay-word, that   100
you may know one another's mind, and the boy never need to
understand anything; for 'tis not good that children should know
any wickedness. Old folks, you know, have discretion, as they say,
and know the world.

FALSTAFF Fare thee well; commend me to them both. There's my   105
purse; I am yet thy debtor. Boy, go along with this woman.
                    [*Exeunt Mistress Quickly and Robin*]
        This news distracts me.

PISTOL This punk is one of Cupid's carriers.

---

89 That . . . indeed] F; O God no sir: there were a iest indeed Q   106 SD] *Rowe; Exit Mistresse Quickly.* Q; *not in* F   108
punk] Puncke F; pink *Warburton*

---

89 **That . . . indeed** See Textual Analysis, p.
161.
91 **of . . . loves** for dear love's sake ('phr. of
strong adjuration or entreaty' Onions).
92 **infection** for 'affection'.
92 **Master Page** The proliferation of pages in
this speech cannot be accidental on Shakespeare's
part: Mistress Page . . . little page . . . little page
. . . Master Page.
94 **take all, pay all** She has as much money
as she needs, to spend as she thinks fit (for this
proverbial phraseology, see Tilley A203).
97 **no remedy** there's no help for it.
100 **nay-word** password.
108–10 With this speech Pistol disappears from
the play (see 5.5.29 SD n.), and we hear no more of
his pursuit of Mistress Quickly; his relationship
with her in *2H4* and *H5* has no strict connection

with the circumstances of this play (see Introduction, pp. 5, 9). Both Pistol and Falstaff's other two
companions, Bardolph and Nim, are intended as
elaborations of Falstaff's own stage presence in
Wiv., and as the mechanism of the plot begins to
draw Falstaff in, so that he is no longer a static
presence in the midst of his own linguistically energetic world, but rather a character carried along by
forces now beyond him, he loses his superfluities
of stage presence (though not of body) without
ceremony.
108 **punk** prostitute. Warburton's emendation
'pink' (meaning a small sailing vessel – *OED sb¹*)
certainly leads into the nautical language of the next
two lines, but is not necessary; 'punk' leads us well
enough to Cupid.
108 **carriers** messengers.

Clap on more sails; pursue; up with your fights;

Give fire; she is my prize, or ocean whelm them all!   [*Exit*]   110

FALSTAFF Sayst thou so, old Jack? Go thy ways, I'll make more of thy
old body than I have done. Will they yet look after thee? Wilt thou,
after the expense of so much money, be now a gainer? Good body,
I thank thee. Let them say 'tis grossly done; so it be fairly done, no
matter.   115

[*Enter* BARDOLPH *with a goblet of sack*]

BARDOLPH Sir John, there's one Master Brook below would fain speak
with you, and be acquainted with you, and hath sent your worship
a morning's draught of sack.

FALSTAFF Brook is his name?

BARDOLPH Ay, sir.   120

FALSTAFF Call him in.

[*Exit Bardolph*]

Such brooks are welcome to me, that o'erflows such liquor. Aha!
Mistress Ford and Mistress Page, have I encompassed you? Go to,
via!

[*Enter* BARDOLPH, *with* FORD *disguised as Brook*]

FORD God bless you, sir.   125

FALSTAFF And you, sir. Would you speak with me?

FORD I make bold to press with so little preparation upon you.

FALSTAFF You're welcome. What's your will? – Give us leave, drawer.

[*Exit Bardolph*]

---

110 SD] *Rowe; not in* F   115 SD] *Craik, as Oxford; Enter Bardolfe.* Q; *not in* F   121 SD] *Theobald; not in* F   124 SD] *Craik,
as Theobald; Enter* Foord *disguised like* Brooke. Q; *not in* F   125 God bless] *Oxford;* 'Blesse F; God saue Q   128 SD]
Theobald; not in F

---

109 **fights** 'screens used during a naval engage-
ment to conceal and protect the crew of the vessel'
(*OED sb* 5).

110 **Give fire** Fire.

110 **ocean whelm** let the ocean overwhelm.

111 **Sayst . . . so** 'Is that how matters stand?'
(Craik).

111 **make . . . of** think better of.

112 **look after** look with desire at.

112–13 **Wilt . . . gainer** Falstaff has spent large
sums on food and drink (so that his body has gained
size), but it is only now that this large body truly
brings him gain.

114 **grossly** clumsily (with an allusion also to
the grossness of his body).

114 **fairly** properly and completely (with an allusion also to the fairness of his handsome body).

122 **o'erflows** overflow with (Abbott 333).

123 **encompassed** got possession of
(Schmidt).

124 **via** (Italian) 'an adverb of encouraging
much used by commanders, as also by riders to their
horses' (Florio, quoted by Schmidt).

124 *SD Craik observes that Ford did not mention actual disguise, only a false name, in 2.1; but
that the introduction of disguise in Q's stage direction 'is dramatically appropriate to Ford's new
identity'. See Textual Analysis, p. 156.

125 *God bless See Textual Analysis, p. 161.

128 **Give . . . drawer** Falstaff dismisses Bar-

FORD Sir, I am a gentleman that have spent much. My name is Brook.

FALSTAFF Good Master Brook, I desire more acquaintance of you.   130

FORD Good Sir John, I sue for yours: not to charge you, for I must let
  you understand I think myself in better plight for a lender than you
  are, the which hath something emboldened me to this unseasoned
  intrusion; for they say, if money go before, all ways do lie open.

FALSTAFF Money is a good soldier, sir, and will on.   135

FORD Troth, and I have a bag of money here troubles me. [*He sets it
  down*] If you will help to bear it, Sir John, take half, or all, for easing
  me of the carriage.

FALSTAFF Sir, I know not how I may deserve to be your porter.

FORD I will tell you, sir, if you will give me the hearing.   140

FALSTAFF Speak, good Master Brook. I shall be glad to be your servant.

FORD Sir, I hear you are a scholar – I will be brief with you – and you
  have been a man long known to me, though I had never so good
  means as desire to make myself acquainted with you. I shall discover
  a thing to you wherein I must very much lay open mine own   145
  imperfection. But, good Sir John, as you have one eye upon my
  follies as you hear them unfolded, turn another into the register of
  your own, that I may pass with a reproof the easier, sith you yourself
  know how easy it is to be such an offender.

FALSTAFF Very well, sir. Proceed.   150

FORD There is a gentlewoman in this town – her husband's name is
  Ford.

FALSTAFF Well, sir.

FORD I have long loved her, and, I protest to you, bestowed much on
  her, followed her with a doting observance, engrossed opportunities 155
  to meet her, fee'd every slight occasion that could but niggardly give

136–7 SD] *Craik; not in* F   137 half, or all] *Collier²;* all, or halfe F   139 Sir . . . may] F; *O Lord, would I could tell how to* Q

dolph with a customary phrase, affecting while in Ford's company not to know his name. There is a contrast here with the treatment of Pistol at 40–1 because Pistol at that point was still in Falstaff's service.

131 charge you burden you (with expense).

133 unseasoned unseasonable, untimely.

134 if . . . open A proverbial saying (Tilley M1050).

135 will on will march bravely forward.

137 *half, or all Craik is surely right to argue that F's reading here is an accidental transposition, and to contrast Ford's wittily polite escalating offer with Evans' clumsy mistake at 3.3.173.

139 Sir . . . may See Textual Analysis, p. 161.

142 scholar See 1.3.2, 2.2.180n. 'warlike . . . learned'.

144 discover reveal.

147 register catalogue.

148 pass . . . easier 'get off with an easier reproof' (Craik).

148 sith since.

155 observance respectful attention, dutiful service.

155 engrossed collected together.

156 fee'd employed, made use of (as in paying a servant).

me sight of her, not only bought many presents to give her, but have
given largely to many to know what she would have given. Briefly,
I have pursued her as love hath pursued me, which hath been on the
wing of all occasions. But whatsoever I have merited, either in my   160
mind or in my means, meed I am sure I have received none, unless
experience be a jewel; that I have purchased at an infinite rate, and
that hath taught me to say this:

> 'Love like a shadow flies when substance love pursues,
> Pursuing that that flies, and flying what pursues.'   165

FALSTAFF Have you received no promise of satisfaction at her hands?

FORD Never.

FALSTAFF Have you importuned her to such a purpose?

FORD Never.

FALSTAFF Of what quality was your love, then?   170

FORD Like a fair house built on another man's ground, so that I have
  lost my edifice by mistaking the place where I erected it.

FALSTAFF To what purpose have you unfolded this to me?

FORD When I have told you that, I have told you all. Some say that
  though she appear honest to me, yet in other places she enlargeth   175

---

162 jewel; that] *Theobald;* Iewell, that F

158 would have given would wish to have
given her.

159–60 on ... occasions i.e. every occasion
has given love wings.

161 meed recompense, reward.

162 *; that ... purchased i.e. experience I
have purchased. The punctuation of F, which I do
not follow here, makes relative clauses of this and
the following formulation introduced by 'that'; the
antecedent for both these relative clauses would be
'jewel', and the meaning could be paraphrased thus:
'unless it is true that experience itself is a jewel, a
jewel that I have bought dearly, a jewel that has
taught me to say this'. Theobald's repunctuation
makes 'that' on both occasions a demonstrative pronoun, and the demonstrative pronoun can refer to
the double antecedent 'experience, the jewel', so
that the meaning could be paraphrased thus: 'unless
it is true that experience itself is a jewel. That jewel,
experience, I have bought dearly; and that experience has taught me to say this.' I prefer Theobald's
emendation on the grounds that Ford is taught by
experience and not a jewel; and on the grounds that,
with F's punctuation, the merely conditional identification of experience as a jewel extends to the two
relative clauses and sits uneasily with Ford's very
non-conditional affirmation that experience has

taught him, whereas in Theobald's reading the conditional force of the identification expires at the
semicolon. We should note, as well, that with
Theobald's punctuation the second 'that' has to be
emphatically pronounced, and that emphasis is
taken up by the emphatic 'this' just before the con-
cluding proverbial quotation.

164–5 Oliver compares this epigrammatic or
sententious couplet with the proverb 'Love, like a
shadow, flies one following and pursues one fleeing'
(Tilley L518).

164 when ... pursues when wealth pursues
love (with a quibble on substance and shadow).
Falstaff is pursuing love in order to acquire wealth,
and Ford represents himself as wealth in pursuit of
love. Although he is jealous of some suspected intimacy of love between Falstaff and his wife, he does
in fact realise in his enticing of Falstaff in this scene
that money is for Falstaff the bewitching bait.

170 quality kind.

171–2 The law was that a building erected on
ground not one's own belonged to the owner of the
ground; hence the proverb 'Who builds upon another's ground loses both mortar and stones' (Tilley
G470).

175 appear ... me gives the appearance of
chastity in her dealings with me.

her mirth so far that there is shrewd construction made of her.
Now, Sir John, here is the heart of my purpose: you are a gentleman
of excellent breeding, admirable discourse, of great admittance,
authentic in your place and person, generally allowed for your many
warlike, courtlike, and learned preparations.   180
FALSTAFF O, sir!
FORD Believe it, for you know it. [*Pointing to the bag*] There is money.
Spend it, spend it; spend more; spend all I have. Only give me so
much of your time in exchange of it as to lay an amiable siege to
the honesty of this Ford's wife. Use your art of wooing, win her to   185
consent to you. If any man may, you may as soon as any.
FALSTAFF Would it apply well to the vehemency of your affection that
I should win what you would enjoy? Methinks you prescribe to
yourself very preposterously.
FORD O, understand my drift. She dwells so securely on the excellency   190
of her honour that the folly of my soul dares not present itself. She
is too bright to be looked against. Now, could I come to her with any
detection in my hand, my desires had instance and argument to
commend themselves. I could drive her then from the ward of her
purity, her reputation, her marriage vow, and a thousand other her   195
defences, which now are too too strongly embattled against me.
What say you to't, Sir John?
FALSTAFF Master Brook, I will first make bold with your money; [*He*

182 SD] *Craik; not in* F   184 exchange] Q3; enchange F   198–9 SD] *Craik, as Oxford; not in* F

175–6 enlargeth . . . far to such an extent
gives rein to her merriment.
176 there . . . her people come to malicious
conclusions about her.
178 of . . . admittance admitted to the houses
of the great.
179 authentic entitled to respect (*OED adj*
1).
179 generally allowed universally approved
of.
180 warlike . . . learned This is Falstaff as
soldier, courtier, and scholar, the 'complete man' of
the Renaissance. See 2.3.26 n.
180 preparations accomplishments (*OED sb*
4). *OED* cites only this passage from *Wiv.* for this
sense of 'preparation'; Craik suggests that the 'unusual sense of the word suits the exaggeratedly complimentary style used by Ford as Brook'.
184 *exchange F's reading is plainly a slip, the
compositor perhaps thinking of the n. sound later in
the word.

184 amiable siege siege of love, amorous
siege.
185 art of wooing skill as a wooer; 'with an
indirect allusion to Ovid's *Ars Amatoria*, the handbook of the polished seducer' (Craik).
187 apply well to be appropriate to.
189 preposterously perversely, against the
natural order of things.
190 my drift what I am driving at.
190 dwells . . . on is so well settled in.
191 folly wantonness.
192 looked against looked directly at (as one
would not look straight at the sun).
193 detection exposure, accusation.
193 had . . . argument would have example
and reason. 'Instance' and 'argument' are terms
used in scholastic logic.
194 ward of defence afforded by ('ward' is a
fencing term).
195–6 other her defences other defences of
hers.

takes the bag] next, give me your hand; and last, as I am a gentleman,
you shall, if you will, enjoy Ford's wife.   200

FORD O good sir!

FALSTAFF I say you shall.

FORD Want no money, Sir John; you shall want none.

FALSTAFF Want no Mistress Ford, Master Brook; you shall want none.
I shall be with her, I may tell you, by her own appointment. Even as   205
you came in to me, her assistant or go-between parted from me. I
say I shall be with her between ten and eleven, for at that time the
jealous rascally knave her husband will be forth. Come you to me at
night; you shall know how I speed.

FORD I am blest in your acquaintance. Do you know Ford, sir?   210

FALSTAFF Hang him, poor cuckoldy knave! I know him not. Yet I
wrong him to call him poor. They say the jealous wittolly knave
hath masses of money, for the which his wife seems to me well-
favoured. I will use her as the key of the cuckoldy rogue's coffer,
and there's my harvest-home.   215

FORD I would you knew Ford, sir, that you might avoid him if you saw
him.

FALSTAFF Hang him, mechanical salt-butter rogue! I will stare him out
of his wits. I will awe him with my cudgel; it shall hang like a meteor
o'er the cuckold's horns. Master Brook, thou shalt know I will   220
predominate over the peasant, and thou shalt lie with his wife.
Come to me soon at night. Ford's a knave, and I will aggravate his
style: thou, Master Brook, shalt know him for knave and cuckold.
Come to me soon at night.   [*Exit*]

---

206 assistant] F; spokes mate Q   224 SD] *Exit Falstaffe.* Q; *not in* F

206 assistant Craik accepts Q's reading here,
on the grounds that 'spokesmate' (=mouthpiece) is
both an appropriate and a rare word, and so likely to
be Shakespeare's. There seems, however, no evident difficulty in F which would justify emendation, or prevent our supposing that at one time or
another Shakespeare wrote both 'assistant' and
'spokesmate'.

212 wittolly cuckoldy. A 'wittol' is strictly
speaking an uncomplaining cuckold, but the adjective is plainly used here as a simple synonym for
'cuckoldy'.

213–14 for . . . well-favoured i.e. the wife
seems good-looking because the husband is rich.

215 my harvest-home the bringing in of my
harvest (Falstaff's corn is Ford's gold).

218 mechanical base, vulgar (the original
meaning is 'engaged in a manual occupation').

218 salt-butter 'cheap-living, cheese-paring
(salt-butter, imported from Flanders, being cheaper
than English butter)' (Hibbard).

219 like a meteor 'i.e. ready to fall, and also as
a portentous sign' (Craik).

220 thou shalt Craik notes that Falstaff's sudden switch from 'you' to 'thou' in his last words
here to Ford 'displays his familiarity and self-
confidence'.

221 predominate have   ascendancy   (like
a planet). This astrological use goes well with
'meteor'.

221 peasant rogue.

222 soon at night See 1.4.7 n.

222–3 aggravate his style i.e. call him cuckold
in addition to knave.

FORD   What a damned epicurean rascal is this! My heart is ready to crack   225
with impatience. Who says this is improvident jealousy? My wife
hath sent to him, the hour is fixed, the match is made. Would any
man have thought this? See the hell of having a false woman! My
bed shall be abused, my coffers ransacked, my reputation gnawn at;
and I shall not only receive this villainous wrong, but stand under   230
the adoption of abominable terms, and by him that does me this
wrong. Terms! Names! Amaimon sounds well; Lucifer, well;
Barbason, well; yet they are devils' additions, the names of fiends:
but Cuckold! Wittol! – Cuckold? the devil himself hath not such a
name. Page is an ass, a secure ass. He will trust his wife, he will not   235
be jealous. I will rather trust a Fleming with my butter, Parson
Hugh the Welshman with my cheese, an Irishman with my
aquavitae bottle, or a thief to walk my ambling gelding, than my
wife with herself. Then she plots, then she ruminates, then she
devises. And what they think in their hearts they may effect, they   240
will break their hearts but they will effect. God be praised for my
jealousy! Eleven o'clock the hour: I will prevent this, detect my
wife, be revenged on Falstaff, and laugh at Page. I will about it.
Better three hours too soon than a minute too late. Fie, fie, fie!
Cuckold, cuckold, cuckold!   [*Exit*]   245

2.3 [*Enter* CAIUS *and* RUGBY, *with rapiers*]

CAIUS   Jack Rugby!
RUGBY   Sir?

---

234 Cuckold! Wittol! – Cuckold?] *This edn;* Cuckold, Wittoll, Cuckold? F   241 God] Q; Heauen F   **Act 2, Scene 3**   2.3]
Scena Tertia. F   0 SD] *Oxford; Enter the Doctor and his man.* Q; *Enter Caius, Rugby, Page, Shallow, Slender, Host.* F

225 epicurean sensual.
226 improvident rash, heedless.
230–1 stand . . . terms suffer being called
detestable names' (Hibbard).
232–3 Amaimon; Lucifer; Barbason At this
time devils often had personal names, sometimes
curiously derived, since the demonic was a more
intimate part of people's experience. Shakespeare
uses these names elsewhere, the first two together at
1H4 2.4.336–7, the third at *H5* 2.1.54.
233 additions titles.
234 *Cuckold! Wittol! – Cuckold? It seems
natural to capitalise these names since they are contrasted with the proper names of devils which by
comparison sound well. Modification of F's punctuation is not normally a matter for note, but differ-

ent editors have punctuated differently here, as
though hearing different kinds of dramatic delivery.
I suppose that Ford exclaims the names aloud first,
and then holds up for inspection and query before
his eyes the name of cuckold.
   235 secure over-confident.
   238 aquavitae whisky, strong spirits.
   238 walk 'exercise gently, either by leading or
riding' (Craik).
   238 ambling gentle, easy to ride.
   240 effect do as deeds, put into effect.
   241 *God See Textual Analysis, p. 161.
   242 hour i.e. the (approximate) hour of
Falstaff's assignation.
   244 Better . . . late A proverbial saying (Tilley
H745).

CAIUS Vat is the clock, jack?

RUGBY 'Tis past the hour, sir, that Sir Hugh promised to meet.

CAIUS By gar, he has save his soul dat he is no come. He has pray his   5
Pible well dat he is no come. By gar, jack Rugby, he is dead already
if he be come.

RUGBY He is wise, sir. He knew your worship would kill him if he came.

CAIUS By gar, de herring is no dead so as I vill kill him. [*He draws his
rapier*] Take your rapier, jack. I vill tell you how I vill kill him.   10

RUGBY Alas, sir, I cannot fence.

CAIUS Villainy! Take your rapier.

RUGBY Forbear. Here's company.

[*Caius sheathes his rapier*]

[*Enter* HOST, SHALLOW, SLENDER, *and* PAGE]

HOST God bless thee, bully doctor!

SHALLOW God save you, Master Doctor Caius!   15

PAGE Now, good Master Doctor!

SLENDER Give you good morrow, sir.

CAIUS Vat be all you, one, two, tree, four, come for?

HOST To see thee fight, to see thee foin, to see thee traverse; to see thee
here, to see thee there; to see thy pass, thy punto, thy stock, thy   20

9–10 SD] *Craik (at beginning of Caius' speech / Oxford); not in* F   12 Villainy] Villanie F   13 SD.1] *Oxford; not in* F   13 SD.2] *Enter Shallow, Page, my Host, and Slender.* Q; *not in* F   14 God bless] Q; 'Blesse F   15 God save] Q *(attributed to Page);* 'Saue F   17 Give] 'Giue F; God give *conj. Oxford*   20 thy pass, thy punto,] *Craik;* thee passe thy puncto, F; thee passe the punto. Q

Act 2, Scene 3

3 jack See 1.4.50 n. In Q throughout this scene, Caius calls his servant John and reserves the contemptuous 'jack' for Sir Hugh; in F the distinction is not made.

9 de herring ... him the herring is not so dead as he will be when I kill him (the phrase 'dead as a herring' was proverbial – Tilley H446).

10 tell you i.e. show you. Caius wants to give Rugby a practical demonstration of the deadly tactics he intends to employ against Sir Hugh.

12 Villainy See 1.4.58 n.

14–17 *On two occasions within these lines Q seems to preserve the unexpurgated text, which is restored here. In the lines as they now stand, we can see a careful variation of greeting, from the hearty intimacy of the Host ('God'; 'thee'; 'bully doctor') to the full and hearty formality of Shallow ('God'; 'you'; 'Master Doctor Caius'), the less elaborate and emphatic tone of Page ('Now'; 'Master Doctor') and the feebler civility of Slender ('Give'; 'you'; 'sir').

Slender's 'Give' is prefaced in F by an apostrophe, in the same way as 'Bless' and 'Save', and there is no equivalent in Q of Slender's greeting to supply 'God'. It seems unlikely, however, that God would have been intended as prefixed to this entirely ordinary formula of greeting; the compositor of F no doubt made an automatic mistake with his apostrophe here. See Textual Analysis, p. 160 and 1.3.2 n.

18 Caius responds to the rich variety of greeting with a surly and monochrome incivility (one, two, tree, four). The whole of this little scene of greeting would be a gift to the players on the stage.

19 foin thrust.

19 traverse move from side to side in fencing.

20 *thy pass thy thrust. Craik is surely right to emend here, even against the united testimony of F and Q. The emended text allows the rhetorical shape of the whole speech to move smoothly from verbs (fight; foin; traverse) to adverbs (here; there) and then to nouns (pass; punto; stock; reverse; distance; montant). The changes from 'thee' to 'thy' required to introduce the nouns would be one that a com-

reverse, thy distance, thy montant. Is he dead, my Ethiopian? Is he
dead, my Francisco? Ha, bully? What says my Aesculapius, my
Galen, my heart of elder, ha? Is he dead, bully stale? Is he dead?
CAIUS By gar, he is de coward jack priest of de vorld. He is not show his
face.   25
HOST Thou art a Castalion king-urinal! Hector of Greece, my boy!
CAIUS I pray you bear witness that me have stay six or seven, two, tree
hours for him, and he is no come.

22 Francisco] F; francoyes Q   23 Galen] *Rowe; Galien* F; gallon Q   23 bully stale] F; bullies taile Q   26 Castalion . . . boy!]
This edn; Castalion-king-Vrinall: *Hector* of *Greece* (my Boy). F; castallian king vrinall. *Hector* of *Greece* my boy. Q;
Castillian, king urinal; *Hector* of *Greece*, my boy. *Capell*; Castalion King Urinal Hector of Greece, my boy! *Craik*

positor might easily miss, being mesmerised by the
repeated form 'to see thee'; and the emended form
of the text does not require 'pass' to be a transitive,
verb (and it is normally intransitive in its fencing
sense, meaning 'to thrust') governing a rather unlikely series of objects. As Craik notes, 'OED gives
only one example (this passage) of *pass* used transi-
tively in fencing to mean "to make or execute (a
thrust)" (*pass v.* 53); even if this meaning is accepted, *pass* can hardly govern *thy distance*, which is
not a thrust.' It should be said that Q makes better
sense of 'pass' as a transitive verb than F, by putting
a stop after 'punto' and obliging the verb to govern
only one object. Q is then left, however, with a string
of nouns drifting in syntactic limbo and making
equivocal contact with the next verb, 'is', which in
F's text begins the next sentence: 'The stock, the
reuerse, the distance: the montnce is a dead my
francoyes?'
   20–1 punto; stock; reverse All these are kinds
of thrust.
   21 distance i.e. the distance you skilfully keep
from your opponent.
   21 montant upward thrust.
   21 Ethiopian i.e. dark, swarthy fellow (like all
Frenchmen, as we know). The Host turns from his
avalanche of fencing terms, intended to mock Caius
in a way that the Frenchman can hardly pick up, to
a series of epithets for him as a Frenchman, a doctor, and a (not very) brave man.
   22 Francisco i.e. Frenchman (Q understands
the term in this sense). See 20 n.
   22 Aesculapius The Greek god of medicine.
   23 *Galen Celebrated Greek physician of the
second century AD, born in Asia Minor.
   23 heart of elder 'Heart of oak' would be the
complimentary epithet, meaning brave man, because oak is a wood solid and firm at its centre; elder
by contrast has a pithy, soft centre. The Host frequently relies on the fact that the Frenchman will
not understand his real meaning.

23 bully stale my dear old urine-sniffer. The
Host began this exchange with 'bully doctor' at 14,
and proceeds here to an even less respectful title
(stale = urine; and doctors often diagnosed by inspecting urine). It is clear that the Frenchman can
have had no chance of understanding what the Host
was saying, because even the Englishman responsible for the reading of Q, clearly recording what he
heard, makes of it 'bullies taile'. See Textual Analysis, p. 153.
   24 he . . . vorld i.e. 'he is the most cowardly
knave of a priest in the world' (Craik).
   26 *You are a Castiglione-like king of urine-
sniffers! You are Hector of Greece, my boy! Both F
and Q agree about the heavy punctuation after 'urinal' and about the second vowel of 'Castalion'. This
gives some guidance on how to interpret the run
of 'Castalion king urinal Hector'. As Craik notes,
'Castalion' is 'a contemporary spelling of
Castiglione' and refers to Castiglione's *The Courtier*
(*Il cortegiano* 1528, translated 1561), the popular
sixteenth-century handbook of courtesy which
presented the ideal of the 'complete man' of the
Renaissance, soldier, scholar, and courtier. I agree
with Craik that the 'agreement of Q and F about the
middle vowel makes it unlikely that both print in-
correct versions of "Castilian"' (= Spanish); that
there is no reference here to the unpopular Philip II
of Spain. The next two words seem to be a rhetori-
cally inflated version of 'bully stale', which in its
turn goes back to 'bully doctor' at 14. Caius by this
point, in the Host's deliberately barely intelligible
speech, has become the very Renaissance ideal of a
king of quacks; and goes on to be epic in his gran-
deur before the fight, with the reference to the Ho-
meric champion of the Trojans (here, again no
doubt deliberately, associated with the wrong side
by the Host, so that the epic allusion is nicely
shoddy).
   27 bear witness i.e. bear witness to my asser-
tion that.

SHALLOW He is the wiser man, Master Doctor. He is a curer of souls,
and you a curer of bodies. If you should fight, you go against the   30
hair of your professions. Is it not true, Master Page?

PAGE Master Shallow, you have yourself been a great fighter, though
now a man of peace.

SHALLOW Bodykins, Master Page, though I now be old and of the
peace, if I see a sword out, my finger itches to make one. Though   35
we are justices and doctors and churchmen, Master Page, we have
some salt of our youth in us. We are the sons of women, Master
Page.

PAGE 'Tis true, Master Shallow.

SHALLOW It will be found so, Master Page. – Master Doctor Caius, I   40
am come to fetch you home. I am sworn of the peace. You have
showed yourself a wise physician, and Sir Hugh hath shown himself
a wise and patient churchman. You must go with me, Master
Doctor.

HOST Pardon, guest justice. – [To Caius] A word, Monsieur   45
Mockwater.

CAIUS Mockvater? Vat is dat?

HOST Mockwater, in our English tongue, is valour, bully.

CAIUS By gar, then I have as much mockvater as de Englishman. Scurvy
jack-dog priest! By gar, me vill cut his ears.   50

HOST He will clapper-claw thee tightly, bully.

CAIUS Clapper-de-claw? Vat is dat?

HOST That is, he will make thee amends.

---

45 SD] *Craik; not in* F   45 A word] Q; a F

30–1 **against . . . of** contrary to, against the
grain of (proverbial, Tilley H18, a 'saying taken
from rubbing an animal's fur the wrong way'
(Hart)).

33 **man of peace** Shallow is a justice of the
peace in his old age and perhaps an unreliable re-
porter of his youthful valour.

34 **Bodykins** a mild form of the oath 'by God's
body'.

35 **make one** join in.

37 **salt** savour, piquancy.

37 **the . . . women** men like other men.

45 **guest justice** Shallow is a guest at the Garter Inn, like Falstaff. See 2.1.171.

45 ***A word** F's reading here looks very much
like a simple compositorial error.

46 **Mockwater** ?Urine-sniffing   quack.   As

Schmidt suggests, the meaning of this word, which
occurs only in this passage from *Wiv.*, probably has
to do with the Host's previous description of Caius
as 'king-urinal'. The 'mock' element suggests the
quackery of diagnosing by inspecting urine, and
'water' as urine goes with 'urinal' and 'stale' at 26
and 23.

49 **de Englishman** my English opponent. Sir
Hugh is, of course, Welsh: foreigner against
foreigner.

50 **jack-dog priest** knavish dog of a priest.

50 **cut** cut off.

51 **clapper-claw** maul, thrash. 'Formed by
some process from clap (strike) and claw (scratch)'
(Hart).

51 **tightly** soundly.

CAIUS By gar, me do look he shall clapper-de-claw me, for, by gar, me
vill have it.   55

HOST And I will provoke him to't, or let him wag.

CAIUS Me tank you for dat.

HOST And moreover, bully – but first, Master guest, and Master Page,
and eke Cavaliero Slender, [*Aside*] go you through the town to
Frogmore.   60

PAGE [*Aside to Host*] Sir Hugh is there, is he?

HOST [*Aside to Page*] He is there. See what humour he is in; and I will
bring the doctor about by the fields. Will it do well?

SHALLOW [*Aside to Host*] We will do it.

PAGE, SHALLOW, *and* SLENDER Adieu, good Master Doctor.   65

[*Exeunt Page, Shallow, and Slender*]

CAIUS By gar, me vill kill de priest, for he speak for a jackanape to Anne
Page.

HOST Let him die. Sheathe thy impatience; throw cold water on thy
choler. Go about the fields with me through Frogmore. I will bring
thee where Mistress Anne Page is, at a farmhouse a-feasting; and   70
thou shalt woo her. 'Cried game!' Said I well?

CAIUS By gar, me dank you vor dat. By gar, I love you, and I shall
procure-a you de good guest: de earl, de knight, de lords, de gentlemen, my patients.

HOST For the which I will be thy adversary toward Anne Page. Said I   75
well?

CAIUS By gar, 'tis good. Vell said.

HOST Let us wag, then.

CAIUS Come at my heels, jack Rugby.

[*Exeunt*]

---

59 SD] *Clarke; not in* F   **61** SD] *Craik; not in* F   **62** SD] *Craik; not in* F   **64** SD] *Craik; not in* F   **65** SH PAGE, SHALLOW, *and* SLENDER] *Malone; All.* F   **65** SD] *Exit all but the Host and Doctor.* Q; *not in* F   **68** die. Sheathe] die: sheath F; die, but first sheth Q   **71** her. 'Cried game!'] her: Cride-game, F; hir cried game: Q   **74** my patients] F; mon patinces Q; my patiences *Oxford*

---

56 wag depart, 'i.e. go to the devil' (Craik).

59 SD *Aside* Some editors place the aside after 'bully' at 58, but Craik argues convincingly that this is dramatically awkward, that the Host would hardly begin whispering aside immediately after engaging Caius's attention.

66 jackanape i.e. Slender, who has just left.

68 Let him die i.e. Well, I agree, kill him when you can; but for now . . .

70 at . . . a-feasting McKerrow comments in his edition of Nashe (*Works* IV, 262) that it was

common to go on excursions to eat at farms just outside London. Anne Page, similarly, has gone out to eat beyond the village of Frogmore.

71 Cried game! This seems like a cry in the midst of a game, or more probably a sporting cry. The Host is perhaps enticing Caius onwards with visions of victory. See 1.1.132–3 n.

75 adversary 'The Host invites Caius to understand this in the sense of "advocate" while enjoying his private joke' (Craik).

79 at my heels See 1.4.51 n.

3.1 [*Enter* EVANS *with a book in one hand and a drawn rapier in the other and* SIMPLE *carrying Evans' gown*]

EVANS   I pray you now, good Master Slender's serving-man, and friend
    Simple by your name, which way have you looked for Master Caius,
    that calls himself Doctor of Physic?
SIMPLE   Marry, sir, the Petty-ward, the Park-ward, every way; Old
    Windsor way, and every way but the town way.   5
EVANS   I most fehemently desire you you will also look that way.
SIMPLE   I will, sir.   [*Going aside*]
EVANS   Pless my soul, how full of cholers I am, and trempling of mind!
    I shall be glad if he have deceived me. How melancholies I am! I will
    knog his urinals about his knave's costard when I have good oppor-   10
    tunities for the 'ork. Pless my soul!
        [*Sings*] To shallow rivers, to whose falls

Act 3, Scene 1   3.1] *Actus Tertius. Scæna Prima.* F   0 SD] *This edn, as Craik;* Enter Euans, Simple, Page, Shallow, Slender, Host, Caius, Rugby. *F;* Enter Syr Hugh and Simple. Q   4 Petty-ward] petty-ward *Collier;* pittie-ward F   7 SD] *Oliver; not in* F   8 Pless my soul] 'Plesse my soule F; *Ieshu ples mee* Q*; Jeshu pless my soul* Riverside   11 Pless] 'Plesse F   12, 18, 24 SDS] *As Pope; not in* F   12–16] *As verse, Pope; as italicised prose,* F

Act 3, Scene 1

0 SD *book* Shallow's mentions of 'book' and 'word' at 30 and 35 indicate either that Evans has brought a copy of the Scriptures with him, or that Shallow supposes it must be the Scriptures and not, for example, a book of songs. See also 28 and n.

4 *the Petty-ward towards Windsor Little Park ('Petty' from the French *petit*, and probably pronounced as F spells it). Compare the street names Petty France and Petty Cury.

4 the Park-ward towards Windsor Great Park.

4–5 Old Windsor A village outside Windsor proper, south of Frogmore.

7 SD *Going aside* It is clear that Simple does not leave the stage here, because at 22 and 26 his form of words indicates that he sees the people coming from a vantage point on the stage.

8 Pless my soul The Riverside reading here, which assumes that Q preserves a version of the unexpurgated text, is attractive. See Textual Analysis, p. 161.

8 cholers choler, anger. Craik assumes that Evans uses the wrong word here, that the association of it with 'trempling of mind' shows he meant to say 'melancholies'; but there seems to be no difficulty in supposing that Evans is in a complicated state of mind, full of anger and at the same time full of trepidation. The following lines certainly support

this supposition. The two moods are interwoven together in the first passage of his speech, which passes from anger to fear to anger again.

10 urinals genitals. A doctor's urinal was a glass vessel used for the collection of urine for medical examination, and Evans, with his characteristic plural for singular, could intend this meaning; but it seems more likely that the association between urine and the sexual organs leads Evans to a nonce-word for the sexual organs that focuses rather on their evacuative than their generative function. It would be a more direct and vivid threat to the doctor to wish, as it were, to tie him up in his testicles than strangle him with his stethoscope.

10 costard head (the sense humorously derived from the word's main meaning, a large apple).

11 Pless See Textual Analysis, p. 161.

12–21 Evans sings fragments of two consecutive stanzas of Marlowe's famous love poem: 'Come live with me and be my love', interrupted at 19 by the first line of the metrical version of Ps. 137. Evans' cause is love and he sings no doubt to hearten himself, but cannot prevent the melancholy note of the Psalmist's lament over the exile of Israel from creeping in. Q records F's psalm line as being a line from the distinctly unmelancholic *Ballad of Constant Susanna* that Sir Toby Belch also begins to sing at *TN* 2.3.78–9. It may well have been difficult on the stage to convey sudden change of mood in

Melodious birds sings madrigals.
There will we make our peds of roses
And a thousand fragrant posies.   15
To shallow –
Mercy on me! I have a great dispositions to cry.
[*Sings*] Melodious birds sing madrigals –
Whenas I sat in Pabylon –
And a thousand vagrom posies.   20
To shallow, etc.
SIMPLE Yonder he is coming, this way, Sir Hugh.
EVANS He's welcome.
[*Sings*] To shallow rivers, to whose falls –
Heaven prosper the right! What weapons is he?   25
SIMPLE No weapons, sir. There comes my master, Master Shallow, and
another gentleman, from Frogmore, over the stile, this way.
EVANS Pray you, give me my gown – or else keep it in your arms.

[*Enter* PAGE, SHALLOW, *and* SLENDER]

SHALLOW How now, Master Parson? Good morrow, good Sir Hugh.
Keep a gamester from the dice, and a good student from his book,   30
and it is wonderful.
SLENDER Ah, sweet Anne Page!
PAGE God save you, good Sir Hugh!
EVANS God pless you from his mercy sake, all of you!

---

17 Mercy] 'Mercie F 18–21] *As verse, Pope; as italicised prose,* F 19] F; There dwelt a man in *Babylon* Q 24] *As verse, Pope; as italicised prose,* F 25 Heaven] F; God *Oxford* 28 SD] Q; *not in* F 33 God save] Q; 'Saue F 34 God pless] Q; 'Plesse F

the midst of the parson's song, so that the player instead used the whole of the first snatch of song at 12–16 to express Evans' combative mood at 10–11, and contrasted that with a block of song at 18–21 sung in quavering fashion (and petering out uncertainly at 'etc.') to express the mood swing at 17.

12 **falls** cascades.

17 **Mercy** See Textual Analysis, p. 161.

20 **vagrom** vagrant (Evans' version of 'fragrant', which he manages well enough at 15; perhaps the failure to get the word out correctly the second time is evidence of his sudden apprehension).

22 **he** Caius, who is coming by the long way, as planned at 2.3.62–3.

25 **Heaven** See Textual Analysis, p. 161.

26 **No weapons** It is plain when Caius arrives

that he is armed, so this must mean he is not actually carrying a drawn rapier here as Evans is.

26 **There comes** Simple sees Slender, Shallow, and Page coming from another direction by the quicker route, as planned at 2.3.59–60.

28 **give . . . arms** Evans is embarrassed to be stripped ready for combat, with his gown off, as the spectators and his opponent arrive fully dressed, but since he has a book in one hand and a drawn sword in the other, there is little he can immediately do about putting it on. It is clear that Evans has a drawn sword in his hand: his state of readiness contrasts with Caius' appearance (see 26 n.), and in Q Evans' instant response to Simple's announcing of Page and Shallow is 'it is verie necessary *I* put vp my sword, / Pray giue me my cowne too'.

33, 34 **God** See Textual Analysis, p. 161.

SHALLOW What, the sword and the word? Do you study them both,   35
   Master Parson?

PAGE And youthful still, in your doublet and hose this raw rheumatic
   day?

EVANS There is reasons and causes for it.

PAGE We are come to you to do a good office, Master Parson.   40

EVANS Fery well. What is it?

PAGE Yonder is a most reverend gentleman who, belike having received
   wrong by some person, is at most odds with his own gravity and
   patience that ever you saw.

SHALLOW I have lived fourscore years and upward. I never heard a man   45
   of his place, gravity, and learning so wide of his own respect.

EVANS What is he?

PAGE I think you know him: Master Doctor Caius, the renowned
   French physician.

EVANS Got's will and his passion of my heart! I had as lief you would tell   50
   me of a mess of porridge.

PAGE Why?

EVANS He has no more knowledge in Hibbocrates and Galen – and he
   is a knave besides, a cowardly knave as you would desires to be
   acquainted withal.   55

PAGE [*To Shallow*] I warrant you, he's the man should fight with him.

SLENDER O sweet Anne Page!

SHALLOW It appears so by his weapons. Keep them asunder; here
   comes Doctor Caius.

[*Enter* CAIUS, HOST, *and* RUGBY. *Evans and Caius offer to fight.*]

35–6] *As prose, Pope; as two lines of verse, divided after* word F   53 Galen –] *Hibbard; Galen,* F   56 SD] *Oxford; not in* F   59
SD] *Enter Doctor and the Host, they offer to fight.* Q *(before* Keep *at 58; Rowe adds Rugby's entrance); not in* F

35 word scripture. Evans must be carrying the
book, perhaps unopened, in his one hand (he could
no more easily open it than receive his gown). Shallow assumes that it is the Bible that Evans has with
him for study, as he has the sword ready for combat.
  42 reverend respectable.
  46 wide . . . respect far from a proper esteem-
ing of himself.
  51 mess of porridge dish of thick soup (soup
being the merely preparatory course before the
meat). In the Geneva Bible, Esau sold his birthright
for a 'mess of pottage' (Gen. 25), and the parson is
probably remembering this, though he uses an alternative form of the word.

53 no . . . Galen – Evans breaks off because
he cannot instantly think of a scornful enough
comparison.
  53 Hibbocrates and Galen Hippocrates,
famous Greek physician of the fifth century BC,
and thought of as the founding father of medicine.
See 2.3.23 n.
  54 a cowardly . . . as as cowardly a knave as.
  56 he's . . . him he's a man in a state of mind to
fight with him. Page and Shallow, of course, already
know that Evans *is* the man who is to fight Caius,
but the remark is not superfluous because Evans
does not know that they know.

PAGE Nay, good Master Parson, keep in your weapon.   60

SHALLOW So do you, good Master Doctor.

HOST Disarm them, and let them question. Let them keep their limbs
whole and hack our English.

   [Shallow and Page take Caius' and Evans' rapiers]

CAIUS I pray you let-a me speak a word with your ear. Verefore vill you
not meet-a me?   65

EVANS *[Aside to Caius]* Pray you, use your patience. *[Aloud]* In good
time.

CAIUS By gar, you are de coward, de jack dog, John ape.

EVANS *[Aside to Caius]* Pray you, let us not be laughing-stocks to other
men's humours. I desire you in friendship, and I will one way or   70
other make you amends. *[Aloud]* I will knog your urinal about your
knave's cogscomb.

CAIUS *Diable!* Jack Rugby, mine host de Jarteer, have I not stay for him
to kill him? Have I not, at de place I did appoint?

EVANS As I am a Christians soul, now look you, this is the place ap-   75
pointed. I'll be judgement by mine host of the Garter.

HOST Peace, I say, Gallia and Gaul, French and Welsh, soul-curer and
body-curer.

CAIUS Ay, dat is very good, *excellent*.

HOST Peace, I say. Hear mine host of the Garter. Am I politic? Am I   80

62–3 Let . . . English] F; Q *assigns this second sentence of the Host's speech to Shallow*   63 SD] *Oxford; not in* F   66 SD *Aside
to Caius]* Cam.; *not in* F   66 patience. In] *Johnson; patience in* F   66 SD *Aloud]* Bowers; *not in* F   69 SD] *Staunton; not in*
F   71 SD] *Staunton; not in* F   71 I will] F; By Ieshu *I* will Q   71 urinal] F; vrinalls Q   72 cogscomb] F; cockcomes, for
missing your meetings and appointments Q   77 Gallia and Gaul] F; gawle and gawlia Q; *Gallia* and *Wallia / Hanmer;*
Gwallia and Gaul *Rann, conj. Farmer*   79 *excellent]* excellant F; excellent Q   80–1 Peace . . . Machiavel] *As prose, Pope; as
two lines of verse, divided after* Garter FQ

---

62 question debate the matter, talk over the
matter.

62–3 Let . . . English Let these two foreigners
make mincemeat of our English tongue, but not of
each other.

66–7 In good time Very well, I will. Evans
publicly carries on his quarrel with Caius while pri-
vately trying to come to terms with him.

68 jack . . . ape See 1.4.50 n.

71 I will See Textual Analysis, p. 161.

71 urinal See 10 n.

72 cogscomb coxscomb, i.e. head (the sense
'head' humorously derived from the word's main
meaning, a fool's cap); see 10.

77 Gallia and Gaul Wales and France. There

are difficulties here because elsewhere Shakespeare
always uses 'Gallia' to mean France, hence the
various attempts at emendation. Craik notes that
Shakespeare nowhere else uses the word 'Gaul', and
so supposes that this must be the word that should
mean Wales; but if we suppose that Gallia is a
latinising of the French *Galles* (= Wales), then the
three doublets here are arranged in a neat contrapuntal order, referring to Evans Caius/Caius
Evans/Evans Caius.

79 Caius' line may be an angry reply to Evans,
not an appreciative comment on the Host's last
words. F's spelling 'excellant' is unusual and probably indicates that Caius pronounces the word in
the French way.

subtle? Am I a Machiavel? Shall I lose my doctor? No; he gives me
the potions and the motions. Shall I lose my parson, my priest, my
Sir Hugh? No; he gives me the proverbs and the no-verbs. [*To
Caius*] Give me thy hand, terrestrial; so. [*To Evans*] Give me thy
hand, celestial; so. Boys of art, I have deceived you both. I have   85
directed you to wrong places. Your hearts are mighty, your skins are
whole, and let burnt sack be the issue. [*To Page and Shallow*] Come,
lay their swords to pawn. [*To Caius and Evans*] Follow me, lads of
peace; follow, follow, follow.   [*Exit*]

SHALLOW Trust me, a mad host. Follow, gentlemen, follow.   90
SLENDER O sweet Anne Page!
                            [*Exeunt Shallow, Slender, and Page*]
CAIUS Ha, do I perceive dat? Have you make-a de sot of us, ha, ha?
EVANS This is well. He has made us his vlouting-stog. I desire you that
we may be friends, and let us knog our prains together to be revenge
on this same scall, scurvy, cogging companion, the host of the   95
Garter.
CAIUS By gar, with all my heart. He promise to bring me where is Anne
Page. By gar, he deceive me too.
EVANS Well, I will smite his noddles. Pray you follow.
                                                      [*Exeunt*]

---

81 a Machiavel] a Machiuell F; Matchauil Q   83–4 SD] *Oxford; not in* F   84–5 Give me thy hand, terrestrial . . . Boys]
Theobald; Giue me thy hand (Celestiall) so: Boyes F; Giue me thy hand terestiall, / So giue me thy hand celestiall: / So
boyes Q   84 SD] *Oxford; not in* F   87 SD] *NS; not in* F   88 SD] *Oxford; not in* F   88 lads] Q; Lad F   89 SD] *Exit Host.* Q;
not in F   90] F; *Afore God a mad host, come let vs goe* Q   91 SD] *Neilson; not in* F   99 SD] *Exit omnes.* Q; *not in* F

81 **Machiavel** subtle intriguer. Machiavelli's
The Prince (1532) was understood in England at this
time as recommending unscrupulously skilful
political practices, and the term Machiavel (pronounced as in the spelling of Q here) came popularly
to mean a sinister and unscrupulous politician.
82 **potions . . . motions** medicines that relieve
my constipation.
83 **proverbs . . . no-verbs** words of wisdom
and words of warning. It may be that 'no-verbs'
means non-existent words, but such a jokingly
scornful reference to Evans' Welsh English seems
out of place here; there is no equivalent reference to
Caius' English, and the Host is in a friendly way
calling to mind what each of these would-be duellists does to profit him.
84–5 *****Give me thy hand, terrestrial
. . . Boys** The reading of Q is plainly correct here.

It is easy to explain how the copyist or compositor of
F could have accidentally overlooked part of this
neatly balanced contrapuntal shape, with its antith-
esis of 'terrestrial' for the body-curer and 'celestial'
for the soul-curer.
85 **art** learning.
87 **burnt sack** See 2.1.172 n.
88 **lay . . . pawn** i.e. because no longer
needed.
90 See Textual Analysis, p. 161.
92 **sot** fool (*OED sb*[1] 1).
93 **vlouting-stog** flouting-stock, object of
mockery.
95 **scall** afflicted with scall, a scabby disease of
the skin.
95 **cogging companion** cheating rogue.
99 **noddles** head.

3.2 [*Enter* ROBIN, *followed by* MISTRESS PAGE]

MISTRESS PAGE Nay, keep your way, little gallant. You were wont to
    be a follower, but now you are a leader. Whether had you rather,
    lead mine eyes, or eye your master's heels?

ROBIN I had rather, forsooth, go before you like a man than follow him
    like a dwarf.   5

MISTRESS PAGE O, you are a flattering boy: now I see you'll be a
    courtier.

[*Enter* FORD]

FORD Well met, Mistress Page. Whither go you?

MISTRESS PAGE Truly, sir, to see your wife. Is she at home?

FORD Ay, and as idle as she may hang together, for want of company. I   10
    think if your husbands were dead you two would marry.

MISTRESS PAGE Be sure of that – two other husbands.

FORD Where had you this pretty weathercock?

MISTRESS PAGE I cannot tell what the dickens his name is my husband
    had him of. What do you call your knight's name, sirrah?   15

ROBIN Sir John Falstaff.

FORD Sir John Falstaff!

MISTRESS PAGE He, he. I can never hit on's name. There is such a
    league between my goodman and he! Is your wife at home indeed?

FORD Indeed she is.   20

MISTRESS PAGE By your leave, sir. I am sick till I see her.

[*Exeunt Robin and Mistress Page*]

FORD Has Page any brains? Hath he any eyes? Hath he any thinking?
    Sure, they sleep: he hath no use of them. Why, this boy will carry
    a letter twenty mile as easy as a cannon will shoot point-blank
    twelve score. He pieces out his wife's inclination. He gives her folly   25

Act 3, Scene 2   3.2] *Scena Secunda.* F   0 SD] *As Oliver; Mist. Page, Robin, Ford, Page, Shallow, Slender, Host, Euans, Caius.* F   6–7] *As prose,* F4; *as a single line of verse, with the last word turned up,* F   7 SD] Q; *not in* F   19 goodman] F; good man F4   21 SD] *Oxford; not in* F

Act 3, Scene 2

1 **keep your way** keep on going ahead.

10 **as idle . . . together** as bored as she can be
without falling completely to pieces' (Hibbard).

13 **weathercock** This is perhaps an allusion
to feathers in the boy's cap; or to the fact that he is
the small ornament completing Mistress Page's
presence, in which case he would be the reverse of

the dwarf at 5, but alas still not the man he hopes
he is.

19 **league** bond of friendship.

19 **goodman** See 2.1.82 n.

24–5 **point-blank . . . score** on a horizontal
line a distance of twelve score, or 240 paces.

25 **pieces out** adds to.

25–6 **folly . . . advantage** wantonness encouragement and opportunity.

motion and advantage. And now she's going to my wife, and
Falstaff's boy with her. A man may hear this shower sing in the
wind. And Falstaff's boy with her! Good plots they are laid, and our
revolted wives share damnation together. Well, I will take him, then
torture my wife, pluck the borrowed veil of modesty from the so-   30
seeming Mistress Page, divulge Page himself for a secure and wilful
Actaeon; and to these violent proceedings all my neighbours shall
cry aim. [*Clock strikes*] The clock gives me my cue, and my assur-
ance bids me search. There I shall find Falstaff. I shall be rather
praised for this than mocked, for it is as positive as the earth is firm   35
that Falstaff is there. I will go.

[*Enter* SHALLOW, PAGE, HOST, SLENDER, CAIUS, EVANS, *and Rugby*]

SHALLOW, PAGE, etc. Well met, Master Ford.
FORD   Trust me, a good knot. I have good cheer at home, and I pray you
    all go with me.
SHALLOW   I must excuse myself, Master Ford.   40
SLENDER   And so must I, sir. We have appointed to dine with Mistress
    Anne, and I would not break with her for more money than I'll
    speak of.
SHALLOW   We have lingered about a match between Anne Page and my
    cousin Slender, and this day we shall have our answer.   45
SLENDER   I hope I have your good will, father Page.
PAGE   You have, son Slender. I stand wholly for you. But my wife,
    Master Doctor, is for you altogether.

28 Good . . . laid,] good plots, they are laide, F; Good plots! They are laid; *Oliver*   33 SD] *As Capell; not in* F   33 cue] Qu
F   36 SD] *Enter Shallow, Page, host, Slender, Doctor, and sir Hugh.* Q *(Capell adds Rugby's entrance); not in* F   37 SH
SHALLOW, PAGE, etc.] *Shal. Page, &c.* F   38 FORD . . . knot] F; *Ford. [Aside]* . . . *knot Oliver*   38 a good knot] F; a knot
well met Q   41–3] *As prose, Pope; as four lines of verse, divided after* sir, Anne, *and* money F   47 son] Q; Mr F   47–8
You . . . altogether] *As prose,* F3; *as two lines of verse, divided after* wholly for you F

27–8 hear . . . wind anticipate trouble here, as
a shower of rain may sometimes be felt on the wind
before it arrives.
28 Good . . . laid Those are good plots which
have been laid.
29 revolted i.e. from their duty as wives.
29 take trap, catch.
30 torture tormentingly punish.
30–1 so-seeming apparently seeming modest.
31 divulge proclaim (*OED v* 1b).
32 Actaeon cuckold (Actaeon, who was turned
into a stag, is associated with the horned cuckold).
See 2.1.97 n.
33 cry aim give encouragement as applauding
spectators (from the encouraging spectators' shout
of 'Aim!' at an archery contest).
38 a good knot a pleasant company. In spite of

the derogatory use of the word at 4.2.98, there are
no grounds for making Ford say this ironically aside
here, as Oliver does; Q's reading emphasises Ford's
friendly manner.
42 break break my appointment.
44 lingered . . . match been waiting to see
whether a match was possible.
47 *son Slender Q's reading seems attractive
here, and emphasises Page's approval of Slender as
his future son-in-law (as does Page's later use of the
same form of address to Slender, at 3.4.68, contrast-
ing here with the more formal 'Master' for Fenton,
whom he does not approve of). 'F's "Mr *Slender*"
seems to have been caught from "Mr Doctor" in the
line below' (Craik).
47 stand wholly for wholly support.

CAIUS Ay, by gar, and de maid is love-a me; my nursh-a Quickly tell me
    so mush.   50

HOST [*To Page*] What say you to young Master Fenton? He capers, he
    dances, he has eyes of youth, he writes verses, he speaks holiday, he
    smells April and May. He will carry't, he will carry't; 'tis in his
    buttons, he will carry't.

PAGE Not by my consent, I promise you. The gentleman is of no   55
    having. He kept company with the wild Prince and Poins. He is of
    too high a region; he knows too much. No, he shall not knit a knot
    in his fortunes with the finger of my substance. If he take her, let
    him take her simply. The wealth I have waits on my consent, and
    my consent goes not that way.   60

FORD I beseech you heartily, some of you go home with me to dinner.
    Besides your cheer, you shall have sport: I will show you a monster.
    Master Doctor, you shall go. So shall you, Master Page, and you,
    Sir Hugh.

SHALLOW Well, fare you well. [*Aside to Slender*] We shall have the freer 65
    wooing at Master Page's.
                                                    [*Exeunt Shallow and Slender*]

CAIUS Go home, John Rugby. I come anon.
                                                                    [*Exit Rugby*]

HOST Farewell, my hearts. I will to my honest knight Falstaff, and drink
    canary with him.   [*Exit*]

---

51 SD] *Oxford; not in* F 53 smells April] F; smelles / All April Q 54 buttons, he] F; *betmes he* Q; talons – he *conj. NS;*
fortunes, he *Sisson;* buttons he *Oliver* 65–6] *As prose, Pope; as two lines of verse, divided after* well F 65 SD] *Oxford; not*
in F 65 freer] F; fairer Q 66 SD] Q; *not in* F 67 SD] *Capell; not in* F 69 SD] *Exit host.* Q; *not in* F

52 **speaks holiday** speaks delightfully.

53 **carry't** carry it off, succeed.

53–4 **'tis . . . carry't** he will succeed with Anne
because of the body he carries about buttoned inside
his clothes (he relies on no extrinsic attractions, like
money, which is what Caius and Slender can offer).
The phrase 'in his buttons' is a difficult one, and
plainly is not understood in Q, which prints
nonsense here. Hart, however, quotes a phrase from
Marston's *The Fawne* (1606) ('within the buttons of
the prince' 2.1) which gives the sense of 'in the
confidence of' for a similar formulation, and allows
us to interpret the image as of clothing enclosing an
inner reality; and the host is very much emphasising
here Fenton's bodily attractiveness, what is 'inside'
his buttons.

55–6 **of no having** without fortune.

56 **He . . . Poins** See Introduction, p. 5.

57 **region** social sphere.

57 **he knows too much** i.e. of fine manners
and the way the aristocratic world goes.

57–8 **knit . . . substance** secure his own fortune with the aid of my wealth. The image is, as
Craik suggests, of a friend helping with the tying of
a knot by putting his finger on it while it is made
secure.

59 **simply** by herself, i.e. without a dowry.

62 **monster** i.e. Falstaff, whom Ford thinks of
as both morally and physically monstrous for his
attempt upon Mistress Ford, and so fit to be shown
at a fair, as 'monsters' of all kinds commonly were at
this time.

65–6 **We . . . Page's** Caius, who is also a suitor
for the hand of Anne Page, needs not to hear this
remark.

67 **John Rugby** Caius drops his usual, bad-
tempered 'jack Rugby'; his tempest of anger has
passed.

FORD [*Aside*] I think I shall drink in pipe-wine first with him; I'll make   70
    him dance. – Will you go, gentles?
PAGE, CAIUS, *and* EVANS Have with you to see this monster.

                                                               Exeunt

3.3 [*Enter* MISTRESS FORD *and* MISTRESS PAGE]

MISTRESS FORD What John! What, Robert!

    [*Enter John and Robert with a great buck-basket*]

MISTRESS PAGE Quickly, quickly! Is the buck-basket –
MISTRESS FORD I warrant. What, Robin, I say!
MISTRESS PAGE Come, come, come.
MISTRESS FORD Here, set it down.   5
MISTRESS PAGE Give your men the charge. We must be brief.
MISTRESS FORD Marry, as I told you before, John and Robert, be ready
    here hard by in the brew-house, and when I suddenly call you, come
    forth, and without any pause or staggering take this basket on your
    shoulders. That done, trudge with it in all haste, and carry it among   10
    the whitsters in Datchet Mead, and there empty it in the muddy
    ditch close by the Thames side.
MISTRESS PAGE [*To John and Robert*] You will do it?

70 SD] *Johnson; not in* F   72 SH PAGE, CAIUS, *and* EVANS] *Oxford; All.* F   *Act 3, Scene 3   3.3*] *Scena Tertia.* F   0 SD]
Capell; Enter M. Ford, M. Page, Seruants, Robin, Falstaffe, Ford, Page, Caius, Euans. F; *Enter Mistresse Ford, with two of her
men, and a great buck busket.* Q   1 SD] *as* Q *(at 0 SD); not in* F   3 Robin] F; *Robert Bowers*   11 Datchet] *Rowe; Dotchet* F   13
SD] *Oxford; not in* F

70–1 **I shall . . . dance** I shall meet him first
and do my kind of drinking with him, not canary the
wine but canary the dance (see 2.2.49 n.); it will be
pipe-wine (wine from the pipe, or cask; *OED* Pipe
*sb*² 3) in the true sense, since I'll pipe him a tune and
make him dance, that is, beat him till he struggles to
escape.
   70 **drink in** drink.
   71 **gentles** gentlemen.

Act 3, Scene 3
   1 SD Editors normally place the entrance of
John and Robert after 3, and that strengthens the
case for emending F's Robin to Robert. We may
suppose, however, that Mistress Ford first calls for
her two servants, and then as they are coming in
calls also for Falstaff's boy, who enters at 15. This

double summons adds to the excited bustle at the
beginning of this scene.
   2 **buck-basket** dirty linen basket (buck = wash
clothes). If, as I suggest, the basket is already
onstage at this point, then Mistress Page is not asking whether it is available in her truncated question
here, but perhaps whether it is empty: that is, with
room in it for Falstaff.
   9 **staggering** In conjunction with 'pause' this
must mean primarily 'hesitating'; but of course the
servants will undoubtedly stagger in the more usual
sense under the weight of Falstaff.
   10 **trudge** walk off sturdily (*OED* v^1 1 a, c).
   11 **whitsters** whiteners, bleachers of clothes.
   11 **Datchet Mead** The meadow between
Windsor Little Park and the Thames.

MISTRESS FORD I ha' told them over and over, they lack no direction.
– Be gone, and come when you are called.   15

[*Exeunt John and Robert*]

[*Enter* ROBIN]

MISTRESS PAGE Here comes little Robin.

MISTRESS FORD How now, my eyas-musket, what news with you?

ROBIN My master, Sir John, is come in at your back door, Mistress
Ford, and requests your company.

MISTRESS PAGE You little Jack-a-Lent, have you been true to us?   20

ROBIN Ay, I'll be sworn. My master knows not of your being here, and
hath threatened to put me into everlasting liberty if I tell you of it;
for he swears he'll turn me away.

MISTRESS PAGE Thou'rt a good boy. This secrecy of thine shall be a
tailor to thee and shall make thee a new doublet and hose. – I'll go   25
hide me.

MISTRESS FORD Do so. – Go tell thy master I am alone.

[*Exit Robin*]

Mistress Page, remember you your cue.

MISTRESS PAGE I warrant thee. If I do not act it, hiss me.   [*Exit*]

MISTRESS FORD Go to, then. – We'll use this unwholesome humidity,   30
this gross watery pumpkin. We'll teach him to know turtles from
jays.

[*Enter* FALSTAFF]

FALSTAFF Have I caught thee, my heavenly jewel? Why now let me die,

14] *As prose, Pope; as a single line of verse, with the last word turned up,* F   15 SD.1] *As Johnson; Exit seruant.* Q; *not in* F   15
SD.2] *Rowe; not in* F   17] *As prose,* F4; *as a single line of verse, with the last two words turned up,* F   18–19] *As prose,* F3; *as
two lines of verse, divided after* door F   27 SD] *As NS; Rowe (after 28); not in* F   28 cue] *Qu* F   29 SD] *Rowe; NS (after 32);
Craik (after* Do so *at 27); not in* F   31 pumpkin] Pumpion F   32 SD] *Enter Sir Iohn.* Q; *not in* F   33 Have . . . jewel?] F;
Haue I caught my heauenlie Iewel? Q

15 SD.2 *Enter* ROBIN We need not necessarily
suppose that Robin enters here in response to Mistress Ford's call at 3. He seems to have come independently when he had news to bring of Falstaff's
arrival.

17 eyas-musket fledgling sparrow-hawk (eyas
= young hawk taken from the nest for training;
musket = male sparrow-hawk).

18 back door An undignified, conspiratorial
entrance.

20 Jack-a-Lent Puppet set up to be pelted during Lent, a kind of 'Aunt Sally' (*OED sb* 1). Here
affectionately referring to Robin's small, vividly
dressed figure. See 3.2.13 n.

22 put . . . liberty This has the authentic ring
of Falstaff's wit about it; Robin is repeating his
master's words.

30 use turn to our use, i.e. deal with.

31–2 turtles from jays faithful spouses (turtle-doves were proverbially faithful) from brightly
tricked out whores (jays are noisy and predatory and
have bright plumage, and so stand for morally suspect painted women). See 2.1.65 n.

33 Have . . . jewel Q preserves the accurate
text of this adapted line from the beginning of the
Second Song in Sidney's *Astrophel and Stella*.

for I have lived long enough. This is the period of my ambition. O
this blessèd hour!   35
MISTRESS FORD O sweet Sir John!
FALSTAFF Mistress Ford, I cannot cog; I cannot prate, Mistress Ford.
Now shall I sin in my wish: I would thy husband were dead. I'll
speak it before the best lord, I would make thee my lady.
MISTRESS FORD I your lady, Sir John? Alas, I should be a pitiful lady.   40
FALSTAFF Let the court of France show me such another. I see how
thine eye would emulate the diamond. Thou hast the right arched
beauty of the brow that becomes the ship-tire, the tire-valiant, or
any tire of Venetian admittance.
MISTRESS FORD A plain kerchief, Sir John. My brows become nothing   45
else, nor that well neither.
FALSTAFF Thou art a tyrant to say so. Thou wouldst make an absolute
courtier, and the firm fixture of thy foot would give an excellent
motion to thy gait in a semicircled farthingale. I see what thou wert
if Fortune (thy foe) were – not Nature – thy friend. Come, thou   50
canst not hide it.
MISTRESS FORD Believe me, there's no such thing in me.
FALSTAFF What made me love thee? Let that persuade thee. There's

---

43 tire-valiant] Tyre-valiant F; tire vellet Q   **45–6**] *As prose*, Pope; *as two lines of verse, divided after* John F   **47** Thou art]
F; By the Lord thou art Q   **47** tyrant] F; traitor Q   **50** if . . . friend] *Oliver*; if Fortune this, were not Nature thy friend
F; if Fortune thy foe were not, Nature thy friend F2; if Fortune thy foe, were but nature thy friend *conj.* Staunton; if Fortune
thy foe were, not Nature, thy friend *Alexander*; if fortune, thy foe, were, with nature, thy friend *Oxford*; if Fortune thy foe
were Nature thy friend *Craik*   **53** thee. There's] F; thee / Ther's Q

---

34 period full extent, conclusion.

37 cog fawn, wheedle (*OED v*³ 5).

37 prate speak braggingly (*OED v* 1).

42 emulate challenge comparison with.

43 becomes suits.

43 ship-tire ornamental head-dress (*OED* Tire *sb*¹ 3) made in the form of a ship.

43 tire-valiant fanciful head-dress (the word is not otherwise recorded, so that perhaps the real meaning is more precise and technical).

44 of . . . admittance accepted as fashionable in Venice, i.e. in the very height of fashion.

47 Thou See Textual Analysis, p. 161.

47 tyrant i.e. cruel. Q's reading is perhaps easier, with Falstaff saying Mistress Ford is a traitor to herself, but the pun on 'tire' noted by NS seems typically Falstaffian and explains F.

47 absolute perfect, complete.

48 firm . . . foot confident walk. Falstaff describes in elaborate language the no-nonsense gait of his beloved.

49 semicircled farthingale hooped skirt projecting only at the back and not in a complete circle.

50 *if . . . friend if Fortune who is your foe (because of your modest social status) were instead to be your friend, rather than Nature being your friend, as she is (by making you so handsome). Alexander's reading keeps the words of F by repunctuating to make likely sense of them, but Oliver's punctuation seems clearer. There was a popular song at this time which began 'Fortune my foe, why dost thou frown on me?', and no doubt Falstaff is echoing this.

53 thee. There's Editors generally adopt Q's punctuation here, but there is something a little less ordinary about F's version, with the clear emphasis it allows on the three times repeated 'thee' (Falstaff when wooing often affects a manly brevity of phrase). Interestingly, Q includes an extra 'Goe too *I loue* thee' at 54, as though to give the effect of an emphatic triple 'thee' because the second of the four

something extraordinary in thee. Come, I cannot cog and say thou
art this and that, like a many of these lisping hawthorn-buds that   55
come like women in men's apparel and smell like Bucklersbury in
simple-time. I cannot. But I love thee, none but thee; and thou
deserv'st it.

MISTRESS FORD Do not betray me, sir. I fear you love Mistress Page.

FALSTAFF Thou mightst as well say I love to walk by the Counter gate,   60
which is as hateful to me as the reek of a lime-kiln.

MISTRESS FORD Well, heaven knows how I love you, and you shall one
day find it.

FALSTAFF Keep in that mind. I'll deserve it.

MISTRESS FORD Nay, I must tell you, so you do; or else I could not be   65
in that mind.

[Enter ROBIN]

ROBIN Mistress Ford, Mistress Ford! Here's Mistress Page at the door,
sweating and blowing and looking wildly, and would needs speak
with you presently.

FALSTAFF She shall not see me. I will ensconce me behind the arras.   70

MISTRESS FORD Pray you, do so; she's a very tattling woman.
[Falstaff stands behind the arras]

[Enter MISTRESS PAGE]

What's the matter? How now?

MISTRESS PAGE O Mistress Ford, what have you done? You're
shamed, you're overthrown, you're undone for ever.

MISTRESS FORD What's the matter, good Mistress Page?   75

---

54 in thee.] F; in thee: Goe too *I* loue thee Q   61 lime-kiln] Lime-kill F; lime kill Q   62–3] *As prose,* F3; *as two lines of verse, divided after* loue you F   65–6] *As prose,* F3; *as two lines of verse, divided after* do F   66 SD] *Capell; not in* F   71 SD.1–2] Q *(Mistress Page's entrance shortly precedes Falstaff's hiding); not in* F   73–4] *As prose, Pope; as two lines of verse, divided after* done F

that appear in Q has been swallowed by the continuous syntax of 'thee there's'.

55 a many many (Abbott 87).

55 hawthorn-buds i.e. affected young dandies (the budding of the hawthorn is a sign of spring).

56 Bucklersbury a street off Cheapside in the City of London where medicinal herbs (simples) were sold.

57 simple-time high summer, when there would be greatest abundance of fragrant herbs.

59 betray deceive.

60 Counter a debtors' prison in Southwark, south of the Thames, a foul-smelling place (as prisons are) across the river from the sweet-smelling Bucklersbury; Falstaff choosing to identify with neither.

61 reek smoke, stench.

69 presently immediately.

70 ensconce me hide myself, take shelter.

70 arras woven tapestry hung in front of a wall.

71 tattling woman Falstaff wishes to conceal himself, of course, because he has also made advances to Mistress Page; but Mistress Ford pretends to understand that his reason is simply to avoid Mistress Page gossiping about the liaison with Mistress Ford.

MISTRESS PAGE O well-a-day, Mistress Ford, having an honest man to
your husband, to give him such cause of suspicion!

MISTRESS FORD What cause of suspicion?

MISTRESS PAGE What cause of suspicion? Out upon you! How am I
mistook in you!   80

MISTRESS FORD Why, alas, what's the matter?

MISTRESS PAGE Your husband's coming hither, woman, with all the
officers in Windsor, to search for a gentleman that he says is here
now in the house, by your consent, to take an ill advantage of his
absence. You are undone.   85

MISTRESS FORD 'Tis not so, I hope.

MISTRESS PAGE Pray heaven it be not so that you have such a man
here! But 'tis most certain your husband's coming, with half Windsor at his heels, to search for such a one. I come before to tell you.
If you know yourself clear, why, I am glad of it; but if you have a   90
friend here, convey, convey him out. Be not amazed, call all your
senses to you, defend your reputation, or bid farewell to your good
life forever.

MISTRESS FORD What shall I do? There is a gentleman, my dear
friend; and I fear not mine own shame so much as his peril. I had   95
rather than a thousand pound he were out of the house.

MISTRESS PAGE For shame, never stand 'you had rather' and 'you had
rather'! Your husband's here at hand! Bethink you of some conveyance. In the house you cannot hide him. – O, how have you deceived me! – Look, here is a basket. If he be of any reasonable   100
stature, he may creep in here, and throw foul linen upon him, as if
it were going to bucking; or – it is whiting-time – send him by your
two men to Datchet Mead.

MISTRESS FORD He's too big to go in there. What shall I do?

[FALSTAFF *rushes out of hiding*]

FALSTAFF Let me see't, let me see't! O, let me see't! I'll in, I'll in!   105
Follow your friend's counsel. I'll in!

79–80] *As prose, Rowe; as two lines of verse, divided after* upon you F **84** house ... to] *Pope;* house; by your consent to
F **104** SD] *Craik, as Capell; not in* F **105–6**] *As prose, Pope; as two lines of verse, divided between* see't *and* I'll F

90 **clear** innocent.
91 **friend** lover.
91 **amazed** bewildered.
92–3 **good life** life as a respectable woman.
97 **stand** waste time saying.

98 **Your ... hand** Of course, this is just a story
devised between Mistress Page and Mistress Ford;
but is overtaken by events when Ford does actually
appear, as it were on cue.
102 **whiting** bleaching.

MISTRESS PAGE What, Sir John Falstaff! [*Aside to him*] Are these your
    letters, knight?

FALSTAFF I love thee. Help me away. Let me creep in here. I'll never –
    [*Falstaff gets into the basket; they cover him with clothes*]

MISTRESS PAGE [*To Robin*] Help to cover your master, boy. – Call your   110
    men, Mistress Ford. – You dissembling knight!

                                         [*Exit Robin*]

MISTRESS FORD What, John! Robert! John!

             [*Enter* JOHN *and Robert*]

    Go, take up these clothes here quickly. Where's the cowl-staff?
    Look how you drumble! [*They fit the cowl-staff*] Carry them to the
    laundress in Datchet Mead. Quickly, come!   115

      [*Enter* FORD, PAGE, CAIUS, *and* EVANS]

FORD [*To his companions*] Pray you, come near. If I suspect without
    cause, why then make sport at me, then let me be your jest, I
    deserve it. – How now? Whither bear you this?

JOHN To the laundress, forsooth.

MISTRESS FORD Why, what have you to do whither they bear it? You   120
    were best meddle with buck-washing!

FORD Buck? I would I could wash myself of the buck! Buck, buck, buck!

---

107 SD] *Aside.* Q; *not in* F   **109** thee] F; thee, and none but thee Q   **109** SD] *Sir John goes into the basket, they put cloathes ouer him, the two men carries it away: Foord meetes it, and all the rest, Page, Doctor, Priest, Slender, Shallow.* Q; *not in* F   **110** SD] *Hibbard; not in* F   **111** SD] *As Capell; Oliver (after 124); not in* F   **112** SD] *As Capell; not in* F   **114** SD] *As NS; not in* F   **115** SD] *Rowe; not in* F   **116** SD] *Hibbard; not in* F   **116–18**] *As prose, Pope; as three lines of verse, divided after* cause *and* jest F   **119** SH JOHN] *Oliver; Ser.* F

---

108 letters Mistress Page reproaches Falstaff not for having written letters to herself and Mistress Ford, but for having written a love-letter to her when he is found courting Mistress Ford. 'The plural is intensive and expresses indignation' (Craik).

109 I love thee Q's reading here repeats the phrase Falstaff had used to Mistress Ford at 57. Q's double use of exactly the same phrase is neatly comic, and it may be, as Craik suggests, that the omission here in F is because of eye-skip; but it also seems perfectly possible on the stage that Falstaff in his panic has only time to get out a minimal and hopelessly ill-disguised response to Mistress Page's private reproach, and not the more elaborate and courtly phrase said aside to her that Craik supposes.

111 SD It is better, as Craik suggests, that Robin (who is not in Q's version of the scene) should exit here than with John and Robert carrying the basket at 124, so that he is not too closely associated with the basket and its burden.

113 cowl-staff pole on which a 'cowl' or basket is borne between two persons.

114 drumble move sluggishly, dawdle.

120 what . . . do what business is it of yours?

120–1 You . . . meddle O yes, for sure, it is for you to concern yourself with . . . !

122 Buck? Ford takes this not in the sense 'washing' but as referring to the stag in rutting season, whose horns symbolised the cuckold deceived by such sexual energy.

Ay, buck! I warrant you, buck – and of the season too, it shall
appear.
> [*Exeunt John and Robert with the basket*]

Gentlemen, I have dreamed tonight. I'll tell you my dream. Here,   125
here; here be my keys. Ascend my chambers. Search, seek, find out.
I'll warrant we'll unkennel the fox. Let me stop this way first.
> [*He locks the door*]

So; now escape.

PAGE Good Master Ford, be contented. You wrong yourself too much.

FORD True, Master Page. – Up, gentlemen, you shall see sport anon.   130
Follow me, gentlemen.   [*Exit*]

EVANS This is fery fantastical humours and jealousies.

CAIUS By gar, 'tis no the fashion of France. It is not jealous in France.

PAGE Nay, follow him, gentlemen. See the issue of his search.
> [*Exeunt Caius and Evans, followed by Page*]

MISTRESS PAGE Is there not a double excellency in this?   135

MISTRESS FORD I know not which pleases me better, that my husband
is deceived, or Sir John.

MISTRESS PAGE What a taking was he in when your husband asked
who was in the basket!

MISTRESS FORD I am half afraid he will have need of washing, so   140
throwing him into the water will do him a benefit.

122–4] *As prose, F3; as three lines of verse, divided after* the buck *and* you, buck F   124 SD] *As Rowe; not in* F   127 SD] *As Capell; not in* F   128 escape] *Daly;* vncape F; uncouple *Hanmer;* uncope *NS;* uncase *Sisson;* uncoop *Oxford*   129] *As prose, Pope; as two lines of verse, divided after* contented F   130–1] *As prose, F3; as three lines of verse, divided after* Up, gentlemen *and* anon F   131 SD] *Capell; not in* F   133] *As prose, F3; as two lines of verse, divided after* of France F   134 SD] *Craik; Exit omnes.* Q *(after 132, omitting F's 133–4); Exeunt* F2 *(after 133); Exeunt Page, Caius, and Evans / Capell; not in* F   136–7] *As prose, F3; as two lines of verse, divided after* better F   139 who] F; what *Harness*

125 **tonight** this past night.

126 **here be my keys** Ford flourishes his freedom to lock and unlock anything in his house in the search. In Q he gives his keys to one of his companions: 'Maister *Page* take my keyes: helpe to search'; but this is clearly not so in F, because shortly afterwards he locks a door and then himself leads the way upstairs.

127 **unkennel** unearth (*OED v* 1).

128 ***So; now escape*** There, that's done; now escape if you can (referring to Falstaff who has in fact just escaped). It is unclear what F's 'vncape' could mean, and the various emendations beginning 'un-' do not seem very satisfactory. Craik's suggestion that the compositor of F set 'vn' automatically because he had set the 'vn' of 'vnkennell' immediately above it at the beginning of the preceding line is very attractive, and allows us to keep the dominant second syllable of the word as it appears in F.

129 **be contented** calm yourself.

130 **True** Ford in his rage has only half heard the last words spoken by Page, about wronging too much, and takes them as applying to the wrong he fancies he suffers.

132–3 Evans and Caius have forgotten their own recent passions.

138–9 Neither in F nor Q does Ford actually ask *who* or *what* is in the basket (though in Q he does ask more vigorously about what is *happening* to it), in spite of the fact that Falstaff at 3.5.82–3, when boasting to Brook about his sufferings on his behalf, says Ford asked his servants *what* they had in it; neither was there any opportunity for Mistress Page to know (though she could certainly guess) the kind of state Falstaff was in.

138 **taking** state of fear.

140 **will . . . washing** Because fear will have made him piss or shit uncontrollably.

MISTRESS PAGE Hang him, dishonest rascal! I would all of the same strain were in the same distress.

MISTRESS FORD I think my husband hath some special suspicion of Falstaff's being here, for I never saw him so gross in his jealousy till   145
now.

MISTRESS PAGE I will lay a plot to try that, and we will yet have more tricks with Falstaff. His dissolute disease will scarce obey this medicine.

MISTRESS FORD Shall we send that foolish carrion, Mistress Quickly,   150
to him, and excuse his throwing into the water, and give him another hope, to betray him to another punishment?

MISTRESS PAGE We will do it. Let him be sent for tomorrow eight o'clock, to have amends.

[*Enter* FORD, PAGE, CAIUS, *and* EVANS]

FORD I cannot find him. Maybe the knave bragged of that he could not   155
compass.

MISTRESS PAGE [*Aside to Mistress Ford*] Heard you that?

MISTRESS FORD You use me well, Master Ford, do you?

FORD Ay, I do so.

MISTRESS FORD Heaven make you better than your thoughts!   160

FORD Amen!

MISTRESS PAGE You do yourself mighty wrong, Master Ford.

FORD Ay, ay, I must bear it.

EVANS If there be anypody in the house, and in the chambers, and in the coffers, and in the presses, heaven forgive my sins at the day of   165
judgement!

---

150 foolish] F2; foolishion F   154 SD] *Capell; Enter all.* Q; *not in* F   157 SD] *As Capell; not in* F   158] F; You serue me well, do you not? Q *(evidently equivalent to* F's *line but attached to its version of the end of Evans' speech at 166);* You use me well, Master Ford, do you not? *Craik*   159] F; Ay, ay: do, do *conj. Craik*   160 you] F; me *Oxford, conj. Capell*

143 **strain** disposition.
147 **try** test.
148 **obey** respond to.
150 ***foolish** F's 'foolishion' is easily explained as an eye-skip to the end of the following word.
150 **carrion** old bag, old witch. This is a general term of contempt, particularly used of a woman, but clearly here not violent invective.
154 **amends** amends made.
155 **that** that which.
156 **compass** accomplish.
158–9 I think sense can be made of this exchange as it stands in F. Mistress Ford is saying with vigorous indignation: 'It is the case that you are using me

well, is it?'; and Ford replies impeniently: 'Yes, it is' (in the sense that this is good and proper treatment of an unfaithful wife). As in Q, Ford begins this dialogue after the search impenitent and changes his attitude as a result of the onslaught upon him.
163 Ford's attitude is in process of change. He is half saying 'I must bear the wrong done to me' and half saying 'I must bear the wrong I have done'.
165 **presses** cupboards (compare the modern term 'linen press').
165 **heaven . . . sins** Evans has his usual fine disregard for precise logic; logic would demand he should say 'heaven retain my sins'.

CAIUS By gar, nor I too. There is nobodies.

PAGE Fie, fie, Master Ford, are you not ashamed? What spirit, what
 devil suggests this imagination? I would not ha' your distemper in
 this kind for the wealth of Windsor Castle.   170

FORD 'Tis my fault, Master Page. I suffer for it.

EVANS You suffer for a pad conscience. Your wife is as honest a 'omans
 as I will desires among five thousand, and five hundred too.

CAIUS By gar, I see 'tis an honest woman.

FORD Well, I promised you a dinner. Come, come, walk in the Park. I   175
 pray you pardon me. I will hereafter make known to you why I have
 done this. – Come, wife, come, Mistress Page, I pray you pardon
 me. Pray heartily pardon me.

PAGE [*To Caius and Evans*] Let's go in, gentlemen; but trust me, we'll
 mock him. [*To Ford, Caius, and Evans*] I do invite you tomorrow   180
 morning to my house to breakfast. After, we'll a-birding together. I
 have a fine hawk for the bush. Shall it be so?

FORD Anything.

EVANS If there is one, I shall make two in the company.

CAIUS If there be one or two, I shall make-a the turd.   185

FORD Pray you go, Master Page.

                    [*Exeunt all but Evans and Caius*]

EVANS I pray you now, remembrance tomorrow on the lousy knave
 mine host.

CAIUS Dat is good, by gar; with all my heart!

EVANS A lousy knave, to have his gibes and his mockeries!   190

                                    Exeunt

178 heartily] hartly F; heartly *Oliver*   179 SD] *Oxford; not in* F   179 go in] F; go *conj. Craik*   180 SD] *Oxford; not in* F   186
SD] *Hibbard; not in* F

167 nor I too 'Caius's confirmation . . . is
splendidly independent of syntactic coherence with
Evans's speech' (Craik).

169 imagination delusion.

173 desires desire to find.

179 Let's go in This seems a little odd after
Ford has just invited them to go out for a walk
before dinner. Oliver suggests that 'going in' means
simply leaving the stage, and this would be the
normal phrase; but it seems better, with the NS
editors, to assume Page is saying 'Let's accept the
invitation to go in to dinner after we have had our
walk.'

181 a-birding go killing small birds with the
aid of sparrow-hawks. Hart describes in some detail
how the sparrow-hawk was used to drive small birds
into the leafless bushes of late winter or early spring,
where they could be shot by the hunter. This is not
to be confused with the more noble art of falconry,
where the falcon itself killed for the amusement of
the onlookers.

184 make two 'Evans' attempt to pick up the
English idiom "make one" ' (Hart).

185 turd Caius describes himself accidentally
in a way he had not intended.

187–90 We are reminded of the similar ending
to 3.1.

3.4 [*Enter* FENTON *and* ANNE PAGE]

FENTON   I see I cannot get thy father's love;
        Therefore no more turn me to him, sweet Nan.
ANNE   Alas, how then?
FENTON   Why, thou must be thyself.
        He doth object I am too great of birth,
        And that, my state being galled with my expense,   5
        I seek to heal it only by his wealth.
        Besides these, other bars he lays before me –
        My riots past, my wild societies –
        And tells me 'tis a thing impossible
        I should love thee but as a property.   10
ANNE   Maybe he tells you true.
FENTON   No, heaven so speed me in my time to come!
        Albeit I will confess thy father's wealth
        Was the first motive that I wooed thee, Anne,
        Yet, wooing thee, I found thee of more value   15
        Than stamps in gold or sums in sealèd bags.
        And 'tis the very riches of thyself
        That now I aim at.
ANNE   Gentle Master Fenton,
        Yet seek my father's love, still seek it, sir,
        If opportunity and humblest suit   20
        Cannot attain it, why then – hark you hither! [*They talk aside*]

[*Enter* SHALLOW, SLENDER, *and* MISTRESS QUICKLY]

Act 3, Scene 4   3.4] *Scæna Quarta.* F   0 SD] *Rowe; Enter Fenton, Anne, Page, Shallow, Slender, Quickly, Page, Mist. Page.* F; *Enter* M. *Fenton, Page, and mistresse Quickly.* Q   7 Besides these,] F; Besides, these *Craik, conj. Walker*   12 SH FENTON] Q3; *not in* F   20 opportunity] F; importunity *Hanmer*   21 then – hark] *Theobald;* then harke F   21 SD.1 *They . . . aside*] *Rowe; not in* F   21 SD.2] *As Theobald; Enter* M. *Page his wife,* M. *Shallow, and Slender.* Q; *not in* F

10 **a property** (1) a mere means to an end (*OED sb* 4), (2) wealth owned.

16 **stamps in gold** stamped gold coins.

20 **opportunity . . . suit** 'the most humble suit, made at the most favourable opportunity' (Craik).

21 **hark . . . hither** Anne sees company coming and takes Fenton aside.

Act 3, Scene 4
3 **be thyself** act independently of your father.
5 **state** estate.
5 **galled** chafed into a sore, i.e. damaged.
7 **bars** impediments, obstacles.
8 **societies** companionships.

SHALLOW Break their talk, Mistress Quickly. My kinsman shall speak
for himself.

SLENDER I'll make a shaft or a bolt on't. 'Slid, 'tis but venturing.

SHALLOW Be not dismayed.   25

SLENDER No, she shall not dismay me. I care not for that, but that I am
afeard.

MISTRESS QUICKLY [*To Anne*] Hark ye, Master Slender would speak
a word with you.

ANNE I come to him. [*Aside to Fenton*] This is my father's choice.   30
O, what a world of vile ill-favoured faults
Looks handsome in three hundred pounds a year!

MISTRESS QUICKLY And how does good Master Fenton? Pray you, a
word with you.

                    [*She draws Fenton aside*]

SHALLOW She's coming. To her, coz! O boy, thou hadst a father!   35

SLENDER I had a father, Mistress Anne; my uncle can tell you good
jests of him. – Pray you, uncle, tell Mistress Anne the jest how my
father stole two geese out of a pen, good uncle.

SHALLOW Mistress Anne, my cousin loves you.

SLENDER Ay, that I do, as well as I love any woman in Gloucestershire.   40

SHALLOW He will maintain you like a gentlewoman.

SLENDER Ay, that I will, come cut and long-tail, under the degree of a
squire.

SHALLOW He will make you a hundred and fifty pounds jointure.

ANNE Good Master Shallow, let him woo for himself.   45

SHALLOW Marry, I thank you for it. I thank you for that good comfort.

22–3] *As prose, Pope; as two lines of verse, divided after* Quickly F   24] *As prose,* F4; *as a single line of verse, with the last four
letters of* venturing *turned down* F   26–7] *As prose, Pope; as two lines of verse, divided after* me F   28 SD] *Oliver; not in* F   30
SD] *Craik, as NS; not in* F   31 F; O God how many grosse faults are hid, Q   33–4] *As prose, Pope; as two lines of verse,
divided after* Fenton F   34 SD] *As Capell; not in* F   35] *As prose, Pope; as two lines of verse, divided after* coz F

22 Break Interrupt.

24 I'll . . . on't I'll manage it one way or another (proverbial, from the saying which contrasts
the longbow shaft with the crossbow bolt; Tilley
s264).

24 'Slid By God's (eye)lid.

24 'tis . . . venturing it's only a matter of making the attempt.

31 See Textual Analysis, p. 161.

35 thou . . . father Shallow is encouraging
Slender by bidding him remember his (valiant)
father; but Slender takes this as a hint to begin
talking about his father.

42–3 come . . . squire 'i.e. as well as anyone

else of a squire's rank can do, whoever he may be'
(Craik). The phrase 'come cut and long-tail' refers
proverbially to dogs with docked and undocked
tails, and means 'in all circumstances' (Tilley c938).

44 jointure the part of the husband's estate settled on the wife, to give her an income if widowed.
As Craik notes, a widow's usual entitlement was to
one-third of her husband's estate, i.e. an income of
£100 a year in this case (see 32), so £150 represents
a generous settlement here.

46 good comfort Shallow hopes he sees interest in Slender on Anne's part because she asks for
him to woo in his own person.

– She calls you, coz. I'll leave you. [*He stands aside*]

ANNE Now, Master Slender.

SLENDER Now, good Mistress Anne.

ANNE What is your will?   50

SLENDER My will? 'Od's heartlings, that's a pretty jest indeed! I ne'er
  made my will yet, I thank heaven. I am not such a sickly creature, I
  give heaven praise.

ANNE I mean, Master Slender, what would you with me?

SLENDER Truly, for mine own part, I would little or nothing with you.   55
  Your father and my uncle hath made motions. If it be my luck, so;
  if not, happy man be his dole! They can tell you how things go
  better than I can.

[*Enter* PAGE *and* MISTRESS PAGE]

You may ask your father; here he comes.

PAGE Now, Master Slender. – Love him, daughter Anne. –   60
  Why, how now? What does Master Fenton here?
  You wrong me, sir, thus still to haunt my house.
  I told you, sir, my daughter is disposed of.

FENTON Nay, Master Page, be not impatient.

MISTRESS PAGE Good Master Fenton, come not to my child.   65

PAGE She is no match for you.

FENTON Sir, will you hear me?

PAGE   No, good Master Fenton, –
  Come, Master Shallow, come, son Slender, in. –
  Knowing my mind, you wrong me, Master Fenton.
                    [*Exeunt Page, Shallow, and Slender*]

MISTRESS QUICKLY Speak to Mistress Page.   70

---

47 SD] *NS; not in* F   52, 53 heaven] F; God *Oxford*   58 SD] *Rowe (after 59); not in* F   61 Fenton] Q3; *Fenter* F   69 SD]
Rowe; not in F

47 She calls you We must suppose that Slender turned back to Shallow, moving away from
Anne, at 37, and that the following exchange takes
place with Slender and Shallow together a little way
apart from Anne.

50 will Anne's use of 'will' to mean 'wish' is
taken in an extravagantly silly way by Slender.
There lurks beneath this exchange of 'will' the sense
of the word as carnal desire (*OED sb*¹ 2), conceivably
a challenge from Anne met by an embarrassed
escape by Slender, who feels no desire (see also
1.1.165–206).

51 'Od's heartlings God's little heart (a mild
oath).

52, 53 heaven See Textual Analysis, p. 161.

56 motions proposals.

57 happy . . . dole may that man's destiny
(*OED* Dole *sb*¹ 4) be to be fortunate, i.e. good luck to
the winner.

60 Now . . . Slender It cannot be accident that
Page begins with the same words as Anne at 48.
Poor Slender is batted like a shuttlecock between
opposing wills.

FENTON Good Mistress Page, for that I love your daughter
            In such a righteous fashion as I do,
            Perforce against all checks, rebukes, and manners
            I must advance the colours of my love
            And not retire. Let me have your good will.   75
ANNE Good mother, do not marry me to yond fool.
MISTRESS PAGE I mean it not; I seek you a better husband.
MISTRESS QUICKLY That's my master, Master Doctor.
ANNE Alas, I had rather be set quick i'th'earth,
            And bowled to death with turnips.   80
MISTRESS PAGE Come, trouble not yourself. – Good Master Fenton,
            I will not be your friend nor enemy.
            My daughter will I question how she loves you,
            And as I find her, so am I affected.
            Till then, farewell, sir. She must needs go in;   85
            Her father will be angry.
                              [*Exeunt Mistress Page and Anne*]
FENTON Farewell, gentle mistress; farewell, Nan.
MISTRESS QUICKLY This is my doing now. 'Nay', said I, 'will you cast
        away your child on a fool and a physician? Look on Master Fenton.'
        This is my doing.   90

77] *As a single line of verse, Rowe; as prose,* F   81–2] *As two lines of verse divided thus / Rowe³; as two lines of verse, divided after* Master F   81 yourself. – Good] your self; good *Warburton;* your selfe good F   86 SD] *Rowe; not in* F   89 and] F; or *Hanmer, conj. Johnson*   89–90 Look . . . doing] *As prose, Pope; as a single line of verse,* F

73 **against** (1) resisting, (2) contrary to.
73 **checks** obstacles.
74 **colours** flag.
79 **set . . . earth** buried up to the neck alive in the earth.
81 *It seems better here to suppose, following Warburton's punctuation, that Mistress Page's first four words are addressed to Anne. There seems no compelling reason why the immediately preceding exchange between Anne and Mistress Quickly should be aside, as Craik has it, since Mistress Quickly's openness here could well be part of her strategy to help Anne and Fenton, as she describes it at 88–90. Anne's instant reaction to the prospect of Caius could then be what changes Mistress Page's mind temporarily (if it is indeed a temporary change of mind and not deliberate deceiving). At 4.4.80–1 she is strongly in favour of Caius, as before.
84 **affected** inclined.

86 SD The *Exeunt* is better here than after the following line, since otherwise it seems a little odd that Anne does not answer Fenton's farewell.
87 **gentle mistress** i.e. Mistress Page.
88 **This** i.e. Mistress Page's temporary (or pretended) change of mind. Mistress Quickly may be a silly woman, but she has the wisdom of a kind heart (even if we find it difficult to believe she said to Mistress Page the words she quotes here), and hardly merits the description of her by Mistress Ford at 3.3.150, whereas arguably Mistress Page is both foolish and malign in her later championing of Caius.
89 **a fool . . . physician** i.e. Caius. Johnson's conjectured 'or' makes Mistress Quickly refer to both Slender and Caius, but that would be pointless, since it is Page who favours Slender. So Mistress Quickly is adapting the usual proverb here: 'Every man is either a fool or a physician to himself' (Tilley M125).

FENTON   I thank thee, and I pray thee once tonight
Give my sweet Nan this ring. There's for thy pains.
[He gives her a ring and money]
MISTRESS QUICKLY   Now Heaven send thee good fortune!
[Exit Fenton]
A kind heart he hath. A woman would run through fire and water
for such a kind heart. But yet I would my master had Mistress   95
Anne; or I would Master Slender had her; or, in sooth, I would
Master Fenton had her. I will do what I can for them all three, for
so I have promised, and I'll be as good as my word – but speciously
for Master Fenton. Well, I must of another errand to Sir John
Falstaff from my two mistresses. What a beast am I to slack it!   100
[Exit]

3.5   *[Enter* FALSTAFF]

FALSTAFF   Bardolph, I say!

[Enter BARDOLPH]

BARDOLPH   Here, sir.
FALSTAFF   Go fetch me a quart of sack; put a toast in't.
[Exit Bardolph]
Have I lived to be carried in a basket like a barrow of butcher's offal,
and to be thrown in the Thames? Well, if I be served such another   5
trick, I'll have my brains ta'en out and buttered, and give them to a
dog for a new year's gift. The rogues slighted me into the river with
as little remorse as they would have drowned a blind bitch's pup-

---

92 SD] *Craik, as NS; not in* F   93 SD] F2 *(after 92); not in* F   100 SD] *Exeunt* F   **Act 3, Scene 5**   0] *Scena Quinta.* F   0
SD] *Enter Sir Iohn Falstaffe.* Q; *Enter Falstaffe, Bardolfe, Quickly, Ford.* F; *Enter Sir Iohn Falstaffe and Bardolfe.* Q2   1 SD]
As NS; not in F   3] *As prose,* F3; *as a single line of verse,* F   3 SD] *Theobald; not in* F   7 The rogues] F; Sblood, the rogues
Q   7 slighted] F; slided Q   8 blind bitch's] F, Q; bitch's blind *Theobald*

91 **once** some time.
92 **There's … pains** In Q, Fenton's gift of
money is specified as 'a brace of angels', a good sum.
98 **speciously** Quickly-speech for 'specially'
(as again at 4.5.87–8).
99 **of** on.
100 **slack** neglect.

Act 3, Scene 5
3 **toast** piece of hot toast.
4 **barrow** barrow-load.
7 **The rogues** See Textual Analysis, p. 161.

7 **slighted** slid me contemptuously. Q's 'slided'
makes better sense in an obvious way, but it is not
difficult perhaps to imagine Falstaff obliging the
verb 'slight' (= to treat disrespectfully) to do duty
also as 'slide'. It is better, I think, to treat this word
as, strictly speaking, an impossible formation than
to suppose with the *OED* (Slight *v* 3c) that we have
here a legitimate sense for the verb as meaning 'to
throw contemptuously'.
8 **blind bitch's** Theobald's emendation must
give the correct sense (the puppies would be blind
because so young), but both F and Q agree that

pies, fifteen i'th'litter! And you may know by my size that I have a
kind of alacrity in sinking. If the bottom were as deep as hell, I   10
should down. I had been drowned but that the shore was shelvy and
shallow – a death that I abhor, for the water swells a man, and what
a thing should I have been when I had been swelled! I should have
been a mountain of mummy.

       [*Enter* BARDOLPH *with two tankards of sack*]

BARDOLPH Here's Mistress Quickly, sir, to speak with you.   15
FALSTAFF Come, let me pour in some sack to the Thames water, for my
  belly's as cold as if I had swallowed snowballs for pills to cool the
  reins. Call her in.
BARDOLPH Come in, woman.

       [*Enter* MISTRESS QUICKLY]

MISTRESS QUICKLY By your leave; I cry you mercy. Give your wor-   20
  ship good morrow.
FALSTAFF [*To Bardolph*] Take away these chalices. Go, brew me a
  pottle of sack finely.
BARDOLPH With eggs, sir?
FALSTAFF Simple of itself. I'll no pullet-sperm in my brewage.   25

              [*Exit Bardolph with the tankards*]

  How now?
MISTRESS QUICKLY Marry, sir, I come to your worship from Mistress
  Ford.

13–14 I should . . . been] F; By the Lord Q   14 mummy] F; money Q   14 SD] *As NS; not in* F   19 SD] Q; *not in* F   20–1]
As prose, Pope; as two lines of verse, divided after mercy F   22 SD] *Craik; not in* F   22–3] *As prose, Pope; as two lines of verse,
divided after* chalices F   25 no pullet-sperm] no Pullet-Spersme F; none of these pullets sperme Q; no pullet-sperms
Oxford   25 SD] *As Capell; not in* F

Falstaff simply switches the words to give an easier
passage to the sound of what he says. Here, as with
'slighted', we have Falstaff in command of the language he uses, not only (as always with him) in
making it serve his imagination, but in making it
yield sense and shape out of his distortions of it. See
Introduction, p. 11.
  9 you Falstaff addresses the audience in this
soliloquy.
  11 shelvy gradually sloping.
  13–14 I should . . . been See Textual Analysis,
p. 162.
  14 mummy dead flesh. Egyptian mummies
were brought back to Europe at this time either

(rarely) intact or in fragments 'because of their supposed medicinal value, greatest, it was thought,
in virgin mummies' (E. S. Bates, *Touring in 1600*,
Century, repr. 1987, p. 222).
  14 SD *two tankards* Bardolph is commanded to
take away 'chalices' at 22, no doubt holding a pint
each, since Falstaff has called for a quart of sack at 3.
  17–18 cool the reins cool the kidneys (to prevent lust).
  23 pottle four pints (the first two not being
enough).
  23 finely i.e. probably heated with spices.
  25 Simple of itself Unmixed (i.e. with eggs).

FALSTAFF Mistress Ford? I have had ford enough. I was thrown into
   the ford. I have my belly full of ford.   30
MISTRESS QUICKLY Alas, the day, good heart, that was not her fault.
   She does so take on with her men; they mistook their erection.
FALSTAFF So did I mine, to build upon a foolish woman's promise.
MISTRESS QUICKLY Well, she laments, sir, for it, that it would yearn
   your heart to see it. Her husband goes this morning a-birding. She   35
   desires you once more to come to her, between eight and nine. I
   must carry her word quickly. She'll make you amends, I warrant
   you.
FALSTAFF Well, I will visit her. Tell her so. And bid her think what a
   man is. Let her consider his frailty, and then judge of my merit.   40
MISTRESS QUICKLY I will tell her.
FALSTAFF Do so. Between nine and ten, sayst thou?
MISTRESS QUICKLY Eight and nine, sir.
FALSTAFF Well, be gone. I will not miss her.
MISTRESS QUICKLY Peace be with you, sir.   [*Exit*]   45
FALSTAFF I marvel I hear not of Master Brook. He sent me word to stay
   within. I like his money well. – O, here he comes.

                 [*Enter* FORD *disguised as Brook*]

FORD God bless you, sir.
FALSTAFF Now, Master Brook, you come to know what hath passed
   between me and Ford's wife?   50
FORD That, indeed, Sir John, is my business.
FALSTAFF Master Brook, I will not lie to you. I was at her house the
   hour she appointed me.
FORD And how sped you, sir?

33] *As prose, Rowe; as a single line of verse, with the last word turned up,* F   **45** SD] Q; *not in* F   **47** O . . . comes] *As prose, Pope;*
as a single line of verse, F   **47** SD] *Enter Brooke.* Q; *not in* F   **48** God bless] God saue Q; Blesse F   **49–50**] *As prose,* F3; *as*
two lines of verse, divided after know F   **52–3**] *As prose, Pope; as two lines of verse, divided after* you F   **54** And . . . sped] Q;
And sped F

30 belly full (1) belly filled with, (2) fill of (i.e.
enough of). Falstaff plays with the name Ford here
as he did with Brook at 2.2.122, though the pleasant
rivulet of sack has become a dangerous and unpleas-
ant river in which a man could drown.
  31 good heart poor thing, poor woman.
  32 take on with berate.
  32 erection Mistress Quickly's mistake for
'direction' (i.e. instruction), which leads to a nice
double entendre at Falstaff's next words. Falstaff not
only mistook his direction in relying on Mistress
Ford, but also mistakenly trusted that his sexual

arousal (his erection builded up) would lead to its
gratification (*OED* Erection *sb* 4).
  34 yearn move to compassion (*OED v* 7).
  40 his frailty man's usual moral frailty (by
contrast with Falstaff's admirable resolution in
keeping his sinful promise to visit her, his 'merit').
  44 miss fail.
  48 *God See Textual Analysis, p. 161.
  54 *how sped you how well did you do?
Falstaff's reply at 55 is to this question in the form
of Q's reading and not to the question 'did you or
did you not' as envisaged by F.

FALSTAFF Very ill-favouredly, Master Brook.   55

FORD How so, sir? Did she change her determination?

FALSTAFF No, Master Brook, but the peaking cornuto her husband,
Master Brook, dwelling in a continual 'larum of jealousy, comes me
in the instant of our encounter, after we had embraced, kissed,
protested, and, as it were, spoke the prologue of our comedy; and at   60
his heels a rabble of his companions, thither provoked and insti-
gated by his distemper, and, forsooth, to search his house for his
wife's love.

FORD What, while you were there?

FALSTAFF While I was there.   65

FORD And did he search for you, and could not find you?

FALSTAFF You shall hear. As good luck would have it, comes in one
Mistress Page, gives intelligence of Ford's approach, and, in her
invention and Ford's wife's distraction, they conveyed me into a
buck-basket.   70

FORD A buck-basket?

FALSTAFF By the Lord, a buck-basket! Rammed me in with foul shirts
and smocks, socks, foul stockings, greasy napkins, that, Master
Brook, there was the rankest compound of villainous smell that ever
offended nostril.   75

FORD And how long lay you there?

FALSTAFF Nay, you shall hear, Master Brook, what I have suffered to
bring this woman to evil for your good. Being thus crammed in the
basket, a couple of Ford's knaves, his hinds, were called forth by

---

67 good luck] F; God Q   68 gives] F; Giues her Q   68 in] F; by Q   72 By the Lord] Q; Yes F   74 smell] F, Q; smells
Hanmer

---

55 **ill-favouredly** badly.

57 **peaking** skulking (*OED a* 1).

57 **cornuto** cuckold (lit. Italian = horned man).

58 **'larum** alarum, alarm.

58–9 **comes me in** comes in.

59 **the . . . encounter** at the very moment of
our meeting.

60 **protested** proclaimed (our love).

62 **distemper** deranged condition (i.e. rage of
jealousy).

67 **good luck** See Textual Analysis, p. 162.

68 **in** with.

71 **A buck-basket?** Many editors interpret F's
'?' as exclamatory here, but it seems better to print
this phrase as one of the long series of questions
which Ford asks as his part of this exchange with
Falstaff. His dawning realisation of the way Falstaff

escaped and his request for more information could
both be conveyed by a question.

72 ***By the Lord** See Textual Analysis, p. 160.

72 **Rammed** From the 'buck' of the previous
word to the 'ram' of this cannot be accidental: very
much rutting images to describe the failure of
Falstaff's attempt at love.

73 **that** so that.

74 **of villainous smell** This has no need to be
simply an adjectival phrase meaning 'stinking', as
Craik suggests; but 'smell' may instead be taken as a
strongly emphatic and idiosyncratic singular for the
plural 'smells'. Q has a slightly weakened version of
this phrase ('of the most / Villanous smel'), which
may more easily be taken as adjectival.

78 **to evil** to comply with your evil desires.

79 **hinds** servants (*OED sb*[2] 1). There is no ety-

their mistress to carry me in the name of foul clothes to Datchet   80
Lane. They took me on their shoulders, met the jealous knave their
master in the door, who asked them once or twice what they had in
their basket. I quaked for fear lest the lunatic knave would have
searched it; but fate, ordaining he should be a cuckold, held his
hand. Well, on went he for a search, and away went I for foul   85
clothes. But mark the sequel, Master Brook. I suffered the pangs of
three several deaths: first, an intolerable fright to be detected with a
jealous rotten bell-wether; next, to be compassed like a good bilbo
in the circumference of a peck, hilt to point, heel to head; and then,
to be stopped in like a strong distillation with stinking clothes that   90
fretted in their own grease. Think of that – a man of my kidney –
think of that – that am as subject to heat as butter, a man of
continual dissolution and thaw. It was a miracle to 'scape suffoca-
tion. And in the height of this bath, when I was more than half
stewed in grease like a Dutch dish, to be thrown into the Thames,   95
and cooled, glowing hot, in that surge, like a horseshoe. Think of
that – hissing hot – think of that, Master Brook!

FORD In good sadness, sir, I am sorry that for my sake you have suffered
all this. My suit, then, is desperate? You'll undertake her no more?

FALSTAFF Master Brook, I will be thrown into Etna, as I have been into   100
Thames, ere I will leave her thus. Her husband is this morning gone
a-birding. I have received from her another embassy of meeting.
'Twixt eight and nine is the hour, Master Brook.

FORD 'Tis past eight already, sir.

87 several] F; egregious Q   96 surge] serge F   98–9] F3; *as prose, but with the second sentence beginning on a new line* F

mological connection between this and the word for
the female of the deer, but we may nevertheless note
that at 88 Falstaff describes Ford as a 'bell-wether'
and that by the end of the play Falstaff is, as it were,
the failed stag and Ford the successful one.

80 **in the name of** as being apparently.

84 **fate . . . cuckold** 'Cuckolds come by destiny' (Tilley c889).

87 **with** by.

88 **rotten** rotting, diseased.

88 **bell-wether** ram with a bell round its neck
(sometimes castrated), selected to lead the flock of
sheep, who in this case are Ford's companions.

88 **compassed** curved (*OED v*[1] 14).

88 **good bilbo** A good sword could be well bent
without breaking. See 1.1.128 n.

89 **peck** a vessel to hold a 'peck', a quarter of a
bushel, of dry goods, the circumference about the
magnitude of a sword's length.

90 **strong distillation** strongly smelling dis-
tilled odour (which might be kept in a stoppered
bottle).

91 **fretted** seethed; the sense is of an internal
consuming away, a kind of fermentation (*OED v*[1] 7,
10).

91 **kidney** nature (*OED sb* 2).

93 **dissolution** dissolving.

95 **Dutch dish** The Dutch were proverbially
addicted to butter.

96 **surge** The waters of the Thames surging
round Falstaff as he disturbed their placid flow.

98 **good sadness** all seriousness.

100 **Etna** The Sicilian volcano. Oliver comments on Etna and Thames here, 'a brilliant adaptation of "go through fire and water"'.

102 **embassy** message.

FALSTAFF Is it? I will then address me to my appointment. Come to me   105
  at your convenient leisure, and you shall know how I speed; and the
  conclusion shall be crowned with your enjoying her. Adieu. You
  shall have her, Master Brook; Master Brook, you shall cuckold
  Ford.   [*Exit*]
FORD Hum! Ha! Is this a vision? Is this a dream? Do I sleep? Master   110
  Ford, awake! Awake, Master Ford! There's a hole made in your best
  coat, Master Ford. This 'tis to be married; this 'tis to have linen
  and buck-baskets! Well, I will proclaim myself what I am. I will
  now take the lecher. He is at my house. He cannot 'scape me. 'Tis
  impossible he should. He cannot creep into a halfpenny purse, nor   115
  into a pepperbox. But lest the devil that guides him should aid him,
  I will search impossible places. Though what I am I cannot avoid,
  yet to be what I would not shall not make me tame. If I have horns
  to make one mad, let the proverb go with me – I'll be horn-mad.
                                                              [*Exit*]

4.1 [*Enter* MISTRESS PAGE, MISTRESS QUICKLY, *and* WILLIAM]

MISTRESS PAGE Is he at Mistress Ford's already, think'st thou?
MISTRESS QUICKLY Sure he is by this, or will be presently. But truly
  he is very courageous mad about his throwing into the water. Mistress Ford desires you to come suddenly.
MISTRESS PAGE I'll be with her by and by. I'll but bring my young man   5
  here to school. Look where his master comes. 'Tis a playing day, I
  see.
                       [*Enter* EVANS]

109 SD] Q; *not in* F   119 one] F; me *Halliwell, conj. Dyce (Remarks)*   119 SD] *Exeunt.* F   Act 4, Scene 1   4.1] *Actus Quartus, Scœna Prima.* F   0 SD] *Rowe; Enter Mistris Page, Quickly, William, Euans.* F   1 Mistress] M. F   7 SD] *Rowe (after 8); not in* F

111–12 hole . . . coat 'To pick a hole in a man's coat' (Tilley H522) meant to spy out a fault in another, here adapted by Ford to his situation.
  115 halfpenny purse small purse for small coins.
  117 what I am i.e. being a cuckold.
  118 what . . . not i.e. a cuckold.
  118–9 horns . . . mad i.e. the horns that make one mad, the proverbial cuckold's horns. Craik accepts Dyce's emendation of 'one' to 'me' here, but the phrase 'to make one mad' could just be a kind of adjectival epithet.

Act 4, Scene 1
  1 Mistress Craik expands F's 'M.' convincingly

to 'Mistress' not 'Master', pointing out that F uses the same abbreviation for both titles. This is talk between women about what concerns them, Falstaff's visit to Mistress Ford. There is about this whole scene a certain gender distinction between male and female. The boy, William, is taught by his master, Evans, things that his father, Ford, thinks he should know. By contrast, Mistress Quickly misunderstands, and Mistress Page thinks little of the whole enterprise, which is presented as an absurd raggle-taggle of assorted bits of information.
  2 presently directly.
  3 courageous The word is used here in a loosely intensive sense: 'very mad indeed'.
  4 suddenly immediately.

How now, Sir Hugh, no school today?

EVANS No. Master Slender is let the boys leave to play.

MISTRESS QUICKLY Blessing of his heart!   10

MISTRESS PAGE Sir Hugh, my husband says my son profits nothing in the world at his book. I pray you, ask him some questions in his accidence.

EVANS Come hither, William. Hold up your head. Come.

MISTRESS PAGE Come on, sirrah. Hold up your head. Answer your   15
master, be not afraid.

EVANS William, how many numbers is in nouns?

WILLIAM Two.

MISTRESS QUICKLY Truly, I thought there had been one number more, because they say "'Od's nouns'.   20

EVANS Peace your tattlings! – What is 'fair', William?

WILLIAM *Pulcher.*

MISTRESS QUICKLY Polecats? There are fairer things than polecats, sure.

EVANS You are a very simplicity 'oman. I pray you peace. – What is   25
lapis, William?

WILLIAM A stone.

EVANS And what is 'a stone', William?

WILLIAM A pebble.

EVANS No, it is *lapis*. I pray you remember in your prain.   30

WILLIAM *Lapis.*

EVANS That is a good William. What is he, William, that does lend articles?

---

10 Blessing] 'Blessing F

---

9 is . . . play has given the boys a holiday. A distinguished visitor to a school, then as now, could clearly ask for a holiday for the children. Perhaps behind Evans' slightly odd formulation 'let . . . leave' we are to discern some such formulation from the visitor as 'let the boys play' or 'let the boys have leave to play'.

10 Blessing See Textual Analysis, p. 161.

13 accidence rudiments of Latin grammar (properly speaking, the introductory part of grammar which deals with inflections). The standard textbook in use would have been *A Short Introduction of Grammar* by William Lilly and John Colet, first published in 1549.

18 Two As the standard textbook said: 'In Nounes be two Numbers, the Singular and the Plural.'

20 'Od's nouns i.e. God's wounds. The diphthong in 'nouns' would have been pronounced as in 'wounds', and Mistress Quickly mistakes the lexical origin of this common oath.

21 tattlings prattling.

23 Polecats The word would have been pronounced to chime approximately with *pulcher*. Polecats were regarded as vermin, and Ford uses the word abusively at 4.2.151.

26 *lapis* Lapis, like *pulcher*, is an example drawn from Lilly, who also recommends that the pupil should be tested, as here, on translation both into and from Latin. At 29 William mistakes the procedure and fails to translate back into Latin.

WILLIAM Articles are borrowed of the pronoun, and be thus declined:
    Singulariter, nominativo, hic, haec, hoc.   35

EVANS *Nominativo, hig, hag, hog.* Pray you mark: *genitivo, huius.* Well,
    what is your accusative case?

WILLIAM *Accusativo, hinc.*

EVANS I pray you have your remembrance, child. *Accusativo, hung,*
    hang, hog.   40

MISTRESS QUICKLY 'Hang-hog' is Latin for bacon, I warrant you.

EVANS Leave your prabbles, 'oman. – What is the focative case,
    William?

WILLIAM O – *vocativo* – O.

EVANS Remember, William: focative is *caret.*   45

MISTRESS QUICKLY And that's a good root.

EVANS 'Oman, forbear.

MISTRESS PAGE Peace!

EVANS What is your genitive case plural, William?

WILLIAM Genitive case?   50

EVANS Ay.

WILLIAM *Genitivo, horum, harum, horum.*

MISTRESS QUICKLY Vengeance of Jenny's case! Fie on her! Never
    name her, child, if she be a whore.

EVANS For shame, 'oman!   55

MISTRESS QUICKLY You do ill to teach the child such words. He
    teaches him to hic and to hac, which they'll do fast enough of
    themselves, and to call 'horum'. Fie upon you!

---

39 *hung*] Pope; *hing* F   52 *Genitivo*] Singer; *Genitiue* F   53 Jenny's] Ginyes F

34–5 William has learnt this word for word from Lilly.

35 *Singulariter, nominativo* In the singular, in the nominative (Lilly regularly uses the ablative form of the case heading to denote the cases in his paradigms).

38 *hinc* William mistakenly says *hinc* for *hunc*, and is immediately interrupted and corrected by Evans. Pope's emendation at 39 is essential, to prevent Evans making the mistake he is correcting.

42 *prabbles* trivial chatter. The word has usually a more quarrelsome sense (see 1.1.43), but here seems to convey no more than that Mistress Quickly is irritating.

42 *focative case* Evans' pronunciation of 'vocative' introduces the notion 'fuck' and suggests the slang sense of 'case' as meaning 'vagina' (Mistress Quickly at 53 has taken 'genitive case' to mean 'Jenny's vagina'). The tissue of innuendo is extended by William's 'O' (another term for the

vagina) and Mistress Quickly's mishearing of *caret* at 45 as 'carrot' (also slang for penis).

44 William is trying to remember, but there is no vocative. This is a trick question. 'O' is the usual prefix for the vocative form (as in 'table, o table, of a table' etc.).

45 *caret* is lacking. There can be no doubt that Evans knows perfectly well that '*caret*' is a fully sufficient verbal form; it is just that he does not mind the redundancy of 'is is lacking'.

53 *Vengeance of* A plague on.

53 *Jenny* i.e. this woman Jenny.

54 *whore* Mistress Quickly has misinterpreted '*horum*' at 52.

57 *to hic . . . hac* Mistress Quickly takes the Latin pronouns to be a kind of compound English verb 'to hick and to hack', which no doubt has the sense for her of 'hack' (= go whoring, fuck). See 2.1.41 n.

58 '*horum*' See 54 n.

EVANS 'Oman, art thou lunatics? Hast thou no understandings for thy
     cases, and the numbers of the genders? Thou art as foolish Chris-   60
     tian creatures as I would desires.
MISTRESS PAGE [*To Mistress Quickly*] Prithee hold thy peace.
EVANS Show me now, William, some declensions of your pronouns.
WILLIAM Forsooth, I have forgot.
EVANS It is *qui, quae, quod*. If you forget your *quis*, your *quaes*, and your   65
     quods, you must be preeches. Go your ways and play, go.
MISTRESS PAGE He is a better scholar than I thought he was.
EVANS He is a good sprag memory. Farewell, Mistress Page.
MISTRESS PAGE Adieu, good Sir Hugh.

                                        [*Exit Evans*]
     Get you home, boy.   70

                                        [*Exit William*]
     Come, we stay too long.

                                        Exeunt

4.2 [*The buck-basket brought out*]
     [*Enter* FALSTAFF *and* MISTRESS FORD]

FALSTAFF Mistress Ford, your sorrow hath eaten up my sufferance. I
     see you are obsequious in your love, and I profess requital to a hair's
     breadth, not only, Mistress Ford, in the simple office of love, but in

---

59 lunatics] *Capell; Lunaties* F   62 SD] *Munro; not in* F   69–71] *As prose, Pope; as two lines of verse, divided after* Hugh
F   69 SD] *Steevens³; not in* F   70 SD] *Oxford; not in* F   **Act 4, Scene 2**   4.2] *Scena Secunda.* F   0 SD.1] *Craik; not in* F   0
SD.2] *Rowe;* Enter Falstaffe, Mist. Ford, Mist. Page, Seruants, Ford, Page, Caius, Euans, Shallow. F; Enter misteris Ford and
her two men. Q

---

59 lunatics Evans uses a similar formulation at
4.2.103.
66 preeches breeched (= whipped with
breeches down). See Nashe in *Summer's Last Will
and Testament* (1592): 'Nouns and pronouns, I pro-
nounce you as traitors to boys' buttocks.'
68 is i.e. has, or perhaps 'is a boy with'.
68 sprag alert, clever. *OED* suggests (Sprag *a*)
that this is a mispronunciation of 'sprack', and that
later instances of 'sprag' as an adjective derive from
this Shakespeare passage.

Act 4, Scene 2
0 SD.1 The buck-basket needs to be onstage at
the beginning of the scene, since it is clear that John
and Robert do not bring it with them at 88 SD. In Q
it seems clear that Mistress Ford's short exchange

with her servants before Falstaff enters is to give
them the opportunity to bring on the basket.
1 eaten . . . sufferance i.e. made my suffering
insignificant by comparison.
2 obsequious compliant to my wishes (*OED
adj* 1).
2–3 to . . . breadth fully the same (Tilley
H29).
3 simple . . . love unadorned act or function of
love. There is a distinction here between what be-
longs centrally to love (probably the simple act of
copulation) and the elaborate accompanying courte-
sies, the 'accoutrement, complement, and ceremony'. Since 'complement' occurs among the
accompaniments, we should take it as meaning
'ceremonious completeness' and not 'consumma-
tion' in any sexual sense.

all the accoutrement, complement, and ceremony of it. But are you
sure of your husband now?   5

MISTRESS FORD He's a-birding, sweet Sir John.

MISTRESS PAGE [*Within*] What ho, gossip Ford! What ho!

MISTRESS FORD Step into the chamber, Sir John.

                                                          [*Exit Falstaff*]

                        [*Enter* MISTRESS PAGE]

MISTRESS PAGE How now, sweetheart, who's at home besides
yourself?   10

MISTRESS FORD Why, none but mine own people.

MISTRESS PAGE Indeed?

MISTRESS FORD No, certainly. [*Aside to her*] Speak louder.

MISTRESS PAGE Truly, I am so glad you have nobody here.

MISTRESS FORD Why?   15

MISTRESS PAGE Why, woman, your husband is in his old lines again.
He so takes on yonder with my husband, so rails against all married
mankind, so curses all Eve's daughters of what complexion soever,
and so buffets himself on the forehead, crying 'Peer out, peer out!',
that any madness I ever yet beheld seemed but tameness, civility,   20
and patience to this his distemper he is in now. I am glad the fat
knight is not here.

MISTRESS FORD Why, does he talk of him?

MISTRESS PAGE Of none but him, and swears he was carried out, the
last time he searched for him, in a basket; protests to my husband he   25
is now here, and hath drawn him and the rest of their company from
their sport to make another experiment of his suspicion. But I am
glad the knight is not here. Now he shall see his own foolery.

MISTRESS FORD How near is he, Mistress Page?

---

7 SD] *Rowe; not in* F   8] F; *Step behind the arras good sir* *Iohn* Q   8 SD.1] *Rowe; He steps behind the arras.* Q; *not in* F   8
SD.2] *As* F2; *Enter mistresse Page. (after line corresponding to 6)* Q; *not in* F   13 SD] *As Theobald; not in* F   16 lines] F; *vaine*
Q; *lunes Theobald*

7 **gossip** friend (particularly a term of endearment between women; *OED sb* 2).

8 **chamber** Compare the use of the closet in
1.4. At this point in Q Falstaff hides again behind
the arras, as he had done at 3.3.71. As Craik notes,
Mistress Ford's aside at 13 is appropriate to
Falstaff's greater distance from the action here in F.

11 **people** servants.

12 **Indeed?** Are you sure? (expressing relief
that the coast is clear, for Falstaff's benefit).

16 **in . . . lines** up to his old tricks (*OED* Line
*sb*² 29 = caprices, fits of temper). Theobald's emendation to 'lunes' (=fits of madness), though adopted
by the NS editors and by Craik, seems unnecessary,
and the Q reading 'in his old vaine' (*OED* Vein *sb*
14b = humour, mood) seems to have lying behind it
the relatively colourless 'lines' rather than a more
specific reference to madness.

19 **Peer out** Show yourselves (Ford to his
cuckold's horns; *OED* v² 2 = peep out).

MISTRESS PAGE Hard by, at street end. He will be here anon.   30
MISTRESS FORD I am undone. The knight is here.
MISTRESS PAGE Why then you are utterly shamed, and he's but a dead
  man. What a woman are you! Away with him, away with him!
  Better shame than murder.
MISTRESS FORD Which way should he go? How should I bestow him?   35
  Shall I put him into the basket again?

[*Enter* FALSTAFF]

FALSTAFF No, I'll come no more i'th'basket. May I not go out ere he
  come?
MISTRESS PAGE Alas, three of Master Ford's brothers watch the door
  with pistols, that none shall issue out; otherwise you might slip   40
  away ere he came. But what make you here?
FALSTAFF What shall I do? I'll creep up into the chimney.
MISTRESS FORD There they always use to discharge their birding-
  pieces.
MISTRESS PAGE Creep into the kiln-hole.   45
FALSTAFF Where is it?
MISTRESS FORD He will seek there, on my word. Neither press, coffer,
  chest, trunk, well, vault, but he hath an abstract for the remembrance of such places, and goes to them by his note. There is no
  hiding you in the house.   50
FALSTAFF I'll go out, then.
MISTRESS PAGE If you go out in your own semblance, you die, Sir John
  – unless you go out disguised.

36 SD] *Rowe; not in* F   37–8] *As prose, Pope; as two lines of verse, divided after* basket F   43–5] *Dyce, conj. Malone; Mist.
Ford.* There they alwaies vse to discharge their Birding-peeces: creepe into the Kill-hole. F   45 kiln-hole] Kill-hole F   52
SH PAGE] *Malone; Ford* F

30 anon straightaway.

34 Better ... murder i.e. Shame (which you
cannot avoid) is at any rate better than murder
(which you may perhaps avoid).

41 But ... here? But what are you doing here?
In the analogous situation at 3.3.107–9, Mistress
Page clearly speaks aside to Falstaff, and Falstaff
struggles unsuccessfully to do so in return (see
3.3.109 n.); but here there seems less pretence of
privacy on Mistress Page's part, and no attempt on
Falstaff's to reply directly to her.

43–4 use ... birding-pieces 'Because it was a
safe way to discharge the fire-arms or to dislodge the
soot (or both)' (Oliver).

45 SH *MISTRESS PAGE This extra speech
heading seems to be required here. It is just possi-

ble, but seems unlikely, that Mistress Ford should
make the suggestion about the kiln-hole and then
immediately and emphatically deny that there could
be any hiding place for Falstaff in the house. The
insertion of this heading also maintains the regular
alternation in speech between Mistress Ford and
Mistress Page that persists unbroken, in spite of the
verbal presence of Falstaff, from the beginning of
the scene until the entrance of the servants at 88. On
the stage this emphatic and undisturbed alternation
can act as a sort of verbal upstaging of the fat knight.

45 kiln-hole oven entrance.

48 abstract list.

52 SH *PAGE F has two consecutive speech
headings for Mistress Ford, at 52 and 54. The
change here to Mistress Page preserves the speech

MISTRESS FORD How might we disguise him?

MISTRESS PAGE Alas the day, I know not. There is no woman's gown   55
big enough for him; otherwise he might put on a hat, a muffler, and
a kerchief, and so escape.

FALSTAFF Good hearts, devise something; any extremity rather than a
mischief.

MISTRESS FORD My maid's aunt, the fat woman of Brentford, has a   60
gown above.

MISTRESS PAGE On my word, it will serve him. She's as big as he is;
and there's her thrummed hat and her muffler too. – Run up, Sir
John.

MISTRESS FORD Go, go, sweet Sir John! Mistress Page and I will look   65
some linen for your head.

MISTRESS PAGE Quick, quick! We'll come dress you straight. Put on
the gown the while.

[Exit Falstaff]

MISTRESS FORD I would my husband would meet him in this shape.
He cannot abide the old woman of Brentford. He swears she's a   70
witch, forbade her my house, and hath threatened to beat her.

MISTRESS PAGE Heaven guide him to thy husband's cudgel, and the
devil guide his cudgel afterwards!

MISTRESS FORD But is my husband coming?

MISTRESS PAGE Ay, in good sadness is he, and talks of the basket too,   75
howsoever he hath had intelligence.

MISTRESS FORD We'll try that; for I'll appoint my men to carry the
basket again, to meet him at the door with it as they did last time.

MISTRESS PAGE Nay, but he'll be here presently. Let's go dress him
like the witch of Brentford.   80

MISTRESS FORD I'll first direct my men what they shall do with the
basket. Go up; I'll bring linen for him straight.   *[Exit]*

---

60 the fat woman] F; *Gillian* Q   60 Brentford] *Brainford* F (*and so thereafter*)   68 SD] *Exit* F2; *Exit Mis. Page, & Sir Iohn.*
Q; *not in* F   81 direct] Q3; *direct direct* F   82 SD] *Capell; not in* F

---

alternation in this part of the scene (see 45 SH n.),
and gives her plainly appropriate words about the
situation outside the house, which she can report on
(as she has done at 39–41). The equivalent speech in
Q is also Mistress Page's.

    57 kerchief linen for the head (as at 66), to go
under the hat.

    60 fat . . . Brentford Brentford is a town about
twelve miles east of Windsor. See Introduction,
p. 25.

63 thrummed fringed.

65 look look out (*OED v* 6d).

69 shape outward appearance.

75 good sadness 'all seriousness' (Hibbard).

77 try make experiment of.

82 SD Exit 'Mistress Ford goes out to fetch
Falstaff's head-linen and to summon John and
Robert' (Craik).

MISTRESS PAGE Hang him, dishonest varlet! We cannot misuse him
  enough.
                    We'll leave a proof, by that which we will do,   85
                    Wives may be merry and yet honest too.
                    We do not act that often jest and laugh;
                    'Tis old but true: 'Still swine eats all the draff.'   [*Exit*]

          [*Enter* MISTRESS FORD, JOHN, *and* ROBERT]

MISTRESS FORD Go, sirs, take the basket again on your shoulders.
  Your master is hard at door. If he bid you set it down, obey him.   90
  Quickly, dispatch!   [*Exit*]
JOHN Come, come, take it up.
ROBERT Pray heaven it be not full of knight again!
JOHN I hope not. I had as lief bear so much lead.
          [*John and Robert lift the basket*]

          [*Enter* FORD, PAGE, SHALLOW, *Caius, and* EVANS]

FORD Ay, but if it prove true, Master Page, have you any way then to   95
  unfool me again? – Set down the basket, villain!
          [*John and Robert set down the basket*]
  Somebody call my wife. Youth in a basket! O you panderly rascals!
  There's a knot, a ging, a pack, a conspiracy against me. Now shall

83–4] *As prose, Pope; as two lines of verse, divided after* varlet F   83 misuse him] F2; misuse F   88 SD.1 *Exit*] Capell; *not in* F   88 SD.2] *As Capell; Enter Ser.* F2 *(after 91); not in* F   91 SD] Capell; *not in* F   92 SH JOHN] Oliver; 1 Ser. F   93 SH ROBERT] Oliver; 2 Ser. F   94 SH JOHN] Oliver; 1 Ser. F   94 as lief] F2; liefe as F   94 SD.1] *As NS; not in* F   94 SD.2] Rowe; *Enter M. Ford, Page, Priest, Shallow, the two men carries the basket, and Ford meets it.* Q *(after 68); not in* F   96 villain] F; you ssaue Q; villains Collier²   96 SD] Oxford; *not in* F   98 ging] F2; gin F

83 *misuse him* The pronoun has plainly fallen out in F.
87 *act* i.e. act immorally.
88 *Still . . . draff* i.e. it is the pig who is making no noise or fuss who actually has his snout in the feed (proverbial; Tilley s681).
90 *hard at door* right at the doorstep.
94 SD.2 *Caius* Even though Caius does not speak in this scene, he is part of Page's birding party (3.3.185) and was present at Ford's previous attempt to expose Falstaff in 3.3. He also appears in F's 'massed entry' at the beginning of this scene.
95–6 *Ay . . . again?* We may suppose that Page has just said to Ford: 'If it prove false, then you will be shown to be a fool.' Ford thinks the risk of mistakenly supposing himself cuckolded less than the risk of being a cuckolded fool indeed.

96 *villain* It is tempting to emend to 'villains', but we may suppose that Ford here addresses the servant carrying the front end of the basket as he comes towards him.
97 *Somebody . . . wife* Nobody does this for him, so he must do it himself at 99.
97 *Youth . . . basket* 'Youth' has almost allegorical force here, in this proverbial evocation of the cunning young lover successfully escaping (Tilley Y51). What we have, of course, is a fat old lover unsuccessfully escaping.
98 *ging* gang (*OED* Ging sb 3). F's 'gin' is just possible, as meaning 'snare', but seems unlikely, since the whole run of Ford's nouns here refers to a group of conspirators.

the devil be shamed. – What, wife, I say! Come, come forth! Behold
what honest clothes you send forth to bleaching!   100
PAGE Why, this passes, Master Ford. You are not to go loose any
   longer, you must be pinioned.
EVANS Why, this is lunatics. This is mad as a mad dog.
SHALLOW Indeed, Master Ford, this is not well, indeed.
FORD So say I too, sir!   105

               [*Enter* MISTRESS FORD]

Come hither, Mistress Ford! Mistress Ford the honest woman, the
modest wife, the virtuous creature, that hath the jealous fool to her
husband! I suspect without cause, mistress, do I?
MISTRESS FORD Heaven be my witness you do, if you suspect me in
   any dishonesty.   110
FORD Well said, brazen-face, hold it out. – Come forth, sirrah!
          [*He opens the basket and begins pulling out clothes*]
PAGE This passes!
MISTRESS FORD Are you not ashamed? Let the clothes alone.
FORD I shall find you anon.
EVANS 'Tis unreasonable. Will you take up your wife's clothes? Come, 115
   away.
FORD [*To John and Robert*] Empty the basket, I say!
PAGE Why, man, why?
FORD Master Page, as I am a man, there was one conveyed out of my
   house yesterday in this basket. Why may not he be there again? In   120
   my house I am sure he is. My intelligence is true, my jealousy is
   reasonable. [*To John and Robert*] Pluck me out all the linen.
MISTRESS FORD If you find a man there, he shall die a flea's death.
          [*John and Robert empty the basket*]
PAGE Here's no man.
SHALLOW By my fidelity, this is not well, Master Ford. This wrongs   125
   you.

105 SD] *Hanmer; not in* F   111 SD] *As Rowe; not in* F   117 SD] *As NS; not in* F   118 SH PAGE] *Oxford, conj. Lambrechts; M.
Ford.* F   122 SD] *Oxford; not in* F   123 SD] *Craik; not in* F

99 **devil be shamed** i.e. by the truth coming to
light. The proverb is 'Speak the truth and shame
the devil' (Tilley T566).
101 **passes** is beyond what is acceptable.
107 **to** as.
111 **hold it out** keep up the pretence.
118 SH *PAGE The words of this speaker are in
Page's style and not Mistress Ford's. Again, Ford in
addressing Page at the beginning of the following

speech is plainly replying to the immediately preceding words, as we see from the echo of 'man',
which continues echoing in the next two speeches.
121 **intelligence** information.
123 **he . . . death** 'i.e. I'll undertake to kill him
by crushing him with my finger-nails (for he will be
small enough)' (Craik).
125 **fidelity** faith.

EVANS Master Ford, you must pray, and not follow the imaginations of
your own heart. This is jealousies.

FORD Well, he's not here I seek for.

PAGE No, nor nowhere else but in your brain.   130

FORD Help to search my house this one time. If I find not what I seek,
show no colour for my extremity. Let me for ever be your table-
sport. Let them say of me, 'As jealous as Ford, that searched a
hollow walnut for his wife's leman'. Satisfy me once more. Once
more search with me.   135

[John and Robert refill the basket and carry it out]

MISTRESS FORD What ho, Mistress Page! Come you and the old
woman down. My husband will come into the chamber.

FORD Old woman? What old woman's that?

MISTRESS FORD Why, it is my maid's aunt of Brentford.

FORD A witch, a quean, an old cozening quean! Have I not forbid her   140
my house? She comes of errands, does she? We are simple men; we
do not know what's brought to pass under the profession of fortune-
telling. She works by charms, by spells, by the figure, and such
daubery as this is, beyond our element; we know nothing. *[He takes
a cudgel]* Come down, you witch, you hag, you! Come down, I say!   145

MISTRESS FORD Nay, good sweet husband! – Good gentlemen, let him
not strike the old woman.

MISTRESS PAGE *[Within]* Come, mother Pratt; come, give me your
hand.

135 SD] *Craik; not in* F   139 my . . . of] F; my maidens Ant, *Gillian* of Q   144 daubery] dawbry F   144 is,] F; is
Wheatley   144–5 SD] *As* NS; *not in* F   146–7 him not] Q3; him F   148 SD] *Craik; not in* F   148 Pratt] *Prat* F

127 **pray** i.e. against possession by the devil.

127–8 **follow . . . heart** Evans derives his litur-
gical sounding formulation from the Anglican General Confession ('We have followed too much the
devices and desires of our own hearts') and the
Magnificat ('he hath scattered the proud in the imagination of their hearts'), with a touch of his own
style in the plural 'imaginations'.

132 **show . . . extremity** allege no reasonable
ground for my extreme behaviour (*OED* Colour *sb*
12b).

132–3 **table-sport** 'the subject of your dinner-
table jokes' (Oliver).

133 **Let . . . Ford** Compare *Tro.* 3.2.195–6: 'let
them say . . . "As false as Cressid." '

134 **leman** lover.

140 **quean** disreputable, impudent woman
(*OED sb* 1).

140 **cozening** cheating.

141 **of errands** i.e. on someone else's (dubious)
business.

141 **simple men** 'i.e. men, and therefore, in
the eyes of women, simple' (Craik). Ford appeals by
implication to his birding-party companions, as his
wife appeals to them on the other side at 146–7.

142 **under the profession** in the name.

143 **figure** horoscope (*OED sb* 14).

144 **daubery** coarse and specious outward
show (*OED* Daub *v* 7).

144 **our element** the range of our
understanding.

148 **Pratt** This is the usual spelling of the English surname. The name suits Ford's estimate of the
old woman, as probably derived from the noun
meaning 'a piece of trickery or fraud' (*OED sb*¹); but
I think Craik is right to suggest (with Hart) that
Ford's threat at 150 is not using a verbal sense
derived from the common noun (though there may
be some hint from *OED* Prat *sb*² = buttocks) but
rather converting the woman's surname into a
nonce-word used as a threat. Compare *1H4* 2.2.91–
2: 'You are grandjurors, are ye? We'll jure ye, faith',

FORD I'll pratt her.   150

[*Enter* MISTRESS PAGE *leading Falstaff disguised as an old woman*]

[*Ford beats Falstaff*]

Out of my door, you witch, you rag, you baggage, you polecat, you
runnion! Out, out! I'll conjure you, I'll fortune-tell you!

[*Exit Falstaff*]

MISTRESS PAGE Are you not ashamed? I think you have killed the poor
woman.

MISTRESS FORD Nay, he will do it. – 'Tis a goodly credit for you.   155

FORD Hang her, witch!

EVANS By yea and no, I think the 'oman is a witch indeed. I like not
when a 'oman has a great peard. I spy a great peard under her
muffler.

FORD Will you follow, gentlemen? I beseech you, follow. See but the   160
issue of my jealousy. If I cry out thus upon no trail, never trust me
when I open again.

PAGE Let's obey his humour a little further. Come gentlemen.

[*Exeunt Ford, Page, Shallow, Caius, and Evans*]

MISTRESS PAGE Trust me, he beat him most pitifully.

MISTRESS FORD Nay, by the mass, that he did not: he beat him most   165
unpitifully, methought.

MISTRESS PAGE I'll have the cudgel hallowed and hung o'er the altar.
It hath done meritorious service.

MISTRESS FORD What think you? May we, with the warrant of woman-
hood and the witness of a good conscience, pursue him with any   170
further revenge?

---

150 pratt] *Prat* F   150 SD.1, 150 SD.2; 152 SD] *Enter Falstaffe disguised like an old woman, and misteris Page with him, Ford
beates him, and hee runnes away.* Q; *not in* F   151 rag] *Ragge* F; *Hagge* Q3; *Rag* F2; *Hag* F3   153–4] *As prose, Pope; as two
lines of verse, divided after* ashamed F   158 spy] *spie* F; *espied* Q; *spied Craik*   158 her] Q; *his* F   163] *As prose, Pope; as two
lines of verse, divided after* further F   163 SD] *Exit omnes.* Q; *not in* F

and Ford's similar use of 'conjure' and 'fortune tell'
at 152.

151 **rag** A term of contempt deriving from the
sense of 'rag' as a worthless piece of material (*OED
sb*[1] 3b). There is a case for reading 'hag', however,
since Ford has already used the phrase 'you witch,
you hag' at 145.

152 **runnion** A term of abuse of obscure origin
applied to a woman (*OED*).

158 **spy** The past tense would certainly seem
more appropriate here since Falstaff has left the
stage, but perhaps the present tense is an example of
Evans' linguistic eccentricity.

158 ***her** On balance Q's reading seems prefer-

able here. It may be that it is Evans who allows a
suspicion that the old woman is a man to affect the
possessive (though it was thought common for a
witch to have a beard), but it is more likely that the
scribe or the compositor allowed his knowledge of
the situation to lead him to the error.

160 **follow** i.e. follow me.

161–2 **cry . . . again** Ford uses hunting terms:
'cry out' and 'open' = give tongue, and 'trail' =
scent.

163 **obey . . . humour** humour   his   strange
mood.

167 **cudgel . . . altar** Falstaff's threat at 2.2.219
has been reversed.

MISTRESS PAGE The spirit of wantonness is sure scared out of him. If the devil have him not in fee-simple, with fine and recovery, he will never, I think, in the way of waste attempt us again.

MISTRESS FORD Shall we tell our husbands how we have served him?   175

MISTRESS PAGE Yes, by all means, if it be but to scrape the figures out of your husband's brains. If they can find in their hearts the poor unvirtuous fat knight shall be any further afflicted, we two will still be the ministers.

MISTRESS FORD I'll warrant they'll have him publicly shamed, and   180 methinks there would be no period to the jest should he not be publicly shamed.

MISTRESS PAGE Come, to the forge with it, then shape it. I would not have things cool.

Exeunt

4.3 *Enter* HOST *and* BARDOLPH

BARDOLPH Sir, the German desires to have three of your horses. The Duke himself will be tomorrow at court, and they are going to meet him.

HOST What duke should that be comes so secretly? I hear not of him in the court. Let me speak with the gentlemen. They speak English?   5

BARDOLPH Ay, sir. I'll call him to you.

HOST They shall have my horses, but I'll make them pay; I'll sauce

184 SD] F; *Exit both.* Q   **Act 4, Scene 3 4.3**] *Scena Tertia.* F   1 German desires] F; Germans desire *Capell*   6 him] F; them Q

172 **spirit of wantonness** devil of lust.

173 **in . . . recovery** in absolute possession, beyond possibility of change (legal terminology).

174 **waste** act of damage by a tenant (*OED sb* 7), one who does not own the property (as Falstaff does not own the women). This is legal terminology again.

176 **scrape the figures** erase the imaginings.

179 **ministers** agents.

181 **period . . . jest** proper and just conclusion to the joke.

Act 4, Scene 3

1 **German desires** There are fairly plainly three Germans wanting horses in this scene, but Bardolph speaks, here and at 6, in the singular, as

though perhaps one of the Germans was the spokesman for the others. I feel that one should resist the easy course of emending away Bardolph's singular use (which does not appear in Q, which reads instead 'heere be three Gentlemen . . . would haue your horse', with an inversion of the grammatical number of subject and object in F), that 'where all is so cryptic, alteration is most unwise' (Oliver). See Introduction, p. 3.

4 **comes** that comes (Abbott 244).

7–8 **sauce them** charge them extortionate prices (*OED v* 4a). *OED* cites only the instance here of this jocular meaning, but the meaning is not in doubt, since at 7 and 9 the Host glosses his own phrase with 'I'll make them pay' and 'They must come off' (*OED* Come *v* 61k = pay).

them. They have had my house a week at command. I have turned
away my other guests. They must come off; I'll sauce them. Come.

Exeunt

4.4 *Enter* PAGE, FORD, MISTRESS PAGE, MISTRESS FORD, *and* EVANS

EVANS 'Tis one of the best discretions of a 'oman as ever I did look
upon.

PAGE And did he send you both these letters at an instant?

MISTRESS PAGE Within a quarter of an hour.

FORD Pardon me, wife. Henceforth do what thou wilt.   5
    I rather will suspect the sun with cold
    Than thee with wantonness. Now doth thy honour stand
    In him that was of late an heretic,
    As firm as faith.

PAGE   'Tis well, 'tis well. No more.
    Be not as extreme in submission as in offence.   10
    But let our plot go forward. Let our wives
    Yet once again, to make us public sport,
    Appoint a meeting with this old fat fellow,
    Where we may take him and disgrace him for it.

FORD There is no better way than that they spoke of.   15

PAGE How? To send him word they'll meet him in the Park at midnight? Fie, fie, he'll never come.

EVANS You say he has been thrown in the rivers, and has been grievously peaten as an old 'oman. Methinks there should be terrors in
him, that he should not come. Methinks his flesh is punished; he   20
shall have no desires.

PAGE So think I too.

---

8 house] Q; houses F   Act 4, Scene 4   4.4] *Scena Quarta.* F   6 cold] *Rowe;* gold F

---

8 ***house** F's reading 'houses' is plainly a mistake caused by the persistence in the scribe's or
compositor's mind of 'horses' from the beginning of
the speech.

8 **at command** at their disposal (*OED sb* 4b).
The situation with the other guests is not quite
clear, and at any rate we know that Falstaff is still
lodging at the Garter. Craik suggests that the Host
means 'that he has kept one or more rooms empty
and reserved for the coming Germans, and has
refused bookings from intending guests'.

Act 4, Scene 4

1 **discretions . . . 'oman** examples of wom-
anly good sense.

6 ***cold** The NS editors suggest that the evident mistake in F here is 'surely an error of dictation'; and this may well be so, provided that we
allow for the kind of aural error where the compositor 'dictates' to himself, the words from his text
echoing in his mind. We may suppose that (as with
a modern audience) the verb 'suspect' earlier in the

MISTRESS FORD Devise but how you'll use him when he comes,
    And let us two devise to bring him thither.
MISTRESS PAGE There is an old tale goes that Herne the Hunter,   25
    Sometime a keeper here in Windsor Forest,
    Doth all the winter-time, at still midnight,
    Walk round about an oak, with great ragg'd horns;
    And there he blasts the trees, and takes the cattle,
    And makes milch-kine yield blood, and shakes a chain   30
    In a most hideous and dreadful manner.
    You have heard of such a spirit, and well you know
    The superstitious idle-headed eld
    Received and did deliver to our age
    This tale of Herne the Hunter for a truth.   35
PAGE Why, yet there want not many that do fear
    In deep of night to walk by this Herne's oak.
    But what of this?
MISTRESS FORD   Marry, this is our device:
    That Falstaff at that oak shall meet with us,
    Disguised like Herne, with huge horns on his head.   40
PAGE Well, let it not be doubted but he'll come;
    And in this shape when you have brought him thither,
    What shall be done with him? What is your plot?
MISTRESS PAGE That likewise have we thought upon, and thus:
    Nan Page my daughter, and my little son,   45
    And three or four more of their growth we'll dress

25–6] *As two lines of verse divided thus, Pope; divided after* the F   **29** trees] *Hanmer;* tree F   **30** makes] F2*;* make F   **40**]
Disguised like *Horne*, with huge horns on his head, Q (Q *uses the spelling 'Horne' for* F*'s 'Herne' throughout); not in* F

line did not establish a firm enough meaning in context to prevent a usual kind of association between the sun and gold at the end of the line. Had the words read 'accuse the sun of cold' the error could hardly have occurred.

25 Herne the Hunter See Introduction, p. 22.

26 Sometime Once upon a time.

28 ragg'd ragged, wild and irregular in shape.

29 blasts blights.

29 *trees F's singular 'tree' would mean that Herne repeatedly blighted the single oak (though it is just possible that 'tree' could be taken as a kind of generic singular). It seems better to emend to suggest Herne's general habit with trees, and to suggest that the scribe or compositor was falsely led

to a singular tree here by the oak in the preceding line.

29 takes affects, attacks (*OED* Take *v* 7).

30 *makes F's 'make' is clearly a slip.

30 milch-kine dairy cows.

33 idle-headed eld foolish people of old (*OED* Eld *sb*² 5b).

36 want not are not lacking.

40 *Disguised . . . head Page's 'in this shape' at 42 makes it certain that something has dropped out of Mistress Ford's immediately preceding speech in F. The line inserted from Q's substantially differing version of the Herne the Hunter plan supplies what is essential.

46 growth size.

Like urchins, oafs, and fairies, green and white,
With rounds of waxen tapers on their heads,
And rattles in their hands. Upon a sudden,
As Falstaff, she, and I are newly met,   50
Let them from forth a sawpit rush at once
With some diffusèd song. Upon their sight,
We two in great amazedness will fly.
Then let them all encircle him about,
And fairy-like to pinch the unclean knight,   55
And ask him why, that hour of fairy revel,
In their so sacred paths he dares to tread
In shape profane.

MISTRESS FORD   And till he tell the truth,
Let the supposèd fairies pinch him sound
And burn him with their tapers.

MISTRESS PAGE   The truth being known,   60
We'll all present ourselves, dis-horn the spirit,
And mock him home to Windsor.

FORD   The children must
Be practised well to this, or they'll ne'er do't.

EVANS I will teach the children their behaviours, and I will be like a
jackanapes also, to burn the knight with my taber.   65

FORD That will be excellent. I'll go buy them vizards.

MISTRESS PAGE My Nan shall be the Queen of all the Fairies,
Finely attirèd in a robe of white.

PAGE That silk will I go buy. [*Aside*] And in that time
Shall Master Slender steal my Nan away   70

---

47 oafs] Ouphes F   55 to pinch] F; to-pinch *Steevens²*, conj. *Tyrwhitt*   58 SH MISTRESS FORD] *Rowe; Ford.* F   66] *As prose,*
Pope; as two lines of verse, divided after excellent F   67–8] *As verse, Rowe³; as prose,* F   69 SD] *Pope (after 71); not in* F

---

47 **urchins . . . fairies** These are in this context clearly roughly synonomous terms for elvish
beings (oaf = elvish child; urchin = elf (*OED sb*
1c)).

51 **sawpit** pit across which timber was laid to
be sawn.

52 **diffusèd** confused, disordered, wild.

55 **to pinch** The infinitive marker 'to' is gram-
matically redundant and only inserted for the metre. Tyrwhitt's conjecture that 'to' is an intensive
prefix (to-pinch = to pinch thoroughly) is decisively rejected by *OED* but is not intrinsically impossible. Fairies, too, were traditionally vicious and
not amateurish pinchers.

58 SH *MISTRESS FORD Rowe's emendation

is plainly correct. This speech is part of the plan
concerted by the two women.

61 **dis-horn** Horns on a cuckold's head sym-
bolise his overmastering by the virility of another;
on a stag's head they are symbols of sexual power. It
is appropriate, then, that Falstaff is only *dressed as* a
stag, and that he loses his horns. Compare also
5.2.11.

61 **spirit** wicked spirit.

64–5 **be . . . jackanapes** i.e. act mischievously
(not be costumed) like a monkey. It is plain from
5.5.74 that Evans is in fairy dress like the children.

66 **vizards** visors, masks. See 4.6.39.

70 **Master Slender** A discredited symbol of
sexual potency, like the dis-horned Falstaff or

And marry her at Eton. [*To Mistress Page and Mistress Ford*]
　　　　　　　Go, send to Falstaff straight
FORD Nay, I'll to him again in name of Brook;
　　He'll tell me all his purpose. Sure he'll come.
MISTRESS PAGE Fear not you that. [*To Page, Ford, and Evans*]
　　　　　　　Go get us properties
And tricking for our fairies.   75
EVANS Let us about it. It is admirable pleasures and fery honest
　　knaveries.   [*Exeunt Page, Ford, and Evans*]
MISTRESS PAGE Go, Mistress Ford,
　　Send quickly to Sir John, to know his mind.
　　　　　　　　　　　　　　　　　　[*Exit Mistress Ford*]
I'll to the Doctor. He hath my good will,   80
And none but he, to marry with Nan Page.
That Slender, though well landed, is an idiot;
And he my husband best of all affects.
The Doctor is well moneyed, and his friends
Potent at court. He, none but he, shall have her,   85
Though twenty thousand worthier come to crave her.
　　　　　　　　　　　　　　　　　　　　　　　　[*Exit*]

4.5 [*Enter* HOST *and* SIMPLE]

HOST What wouldst thou have, boor? What, thick-skin? Speak, breathe,
　　discuss; brief, short, quick, snap.
SIMPLE Marry, sir, I come to speak with Sir John Falstaff from Master
　　Slender.

71 SD] *Craik; not in* F   74 SD] *Craik; not in* F   76–7] *As prose, Pope; as two lines of verse, divided after* it F   77 SD] *Rowe;*
not in F   79 SD] *Rowe; not in* F   81 he, to] *Pope;* he to F   86 SD] F2; *not in* F   **Act 4, Scene 5**   4.5] *Scena Quinta.* F   0
SD] Q; *Enter Host, Simple, Falstaffe, Bardolfe, Euans, Caius, Quickly.* F

(at 85) the French doctor with potent friends at
court.
　71 **Eton** A village on the north side of the
Thames, immediately opposite Windsor.
　71 SD *To . . . Ford* It is clear, here and at 74,
that the plotters are divided into two distinct parties, men and women.
　72 **Nay** And in addition to that.
　74 **properties** props, i.e. the tapers and rattles.
　75 **tricking** finery, costume.
　83 **he** i.e. him (Abbott 207).
　86 **worthier** more deserving (i.e. for reasons
other than the wealth in land that attracts Page or
the wealth in money that attracts Mistress Page).

Act 4, Scene 5
　1 **thick-skin** blockhead.
　1 **breathe** use your breath to utter (synonymous with 'Speak' and 'discuss' in the Host's reduplicating style).
　2 **snap** Synonymous with the three preceding
words. As Craik notes, the reduplicating steadily
intensifies through these first words of the Host,
with two nouns (boor, thick-skin), three verbs, and
then four adverbs; and the Host's next speech begins with five nouns.

HOST There's his chamber, his house, his castle, his standing-bed and   5
truckle-bed. 'Tis painted about with the story of the Prodigal, fresh
and new. Go, knock and call. He'll speak like an Anthropophaginian
unto thee. Knock, I say.

SIMPLE There's an old woman, a fat woman, gone up into his chamber.
I'll be so bold as stay, sir, till she come down. I come to speak with   10
her, indeed.

HOST Ha? A fat woman? The knight may be robbed. I'll call. – Bully
knight! Bully Sir John! Speak from thy lungs military. Art thou
there? It is thine host, thine Ephesian, calls.

FALSTAFF [*Within*] How now, mine host?   15

HOST Here's a Bohemian Tartar tarries the coming down of thy fat
woman. Let her descend, bully, let her descend. My chambers are
honourable. Fie! Privacy? Fie!

[*Enter* FALSTAFF]

FALSTAFF There was, mine host, an old fat woman even now with me,
but she's gone.   20

SIMPLE Pray you, sir, was't not the wise woman of Brentford?

FALSTAFF Ay, marry, was it, mussel-shell. What would you with her?

SIMPLE My master, sir, my Master Slender, sent to her, seeing her go
through the streets, to know, sir, whether one Nim, sir, that beguiled him of a chain, had the chain or no.   25

---

15 SD] *Oxford; he speakes aboue* Q2   18 SD] *Enter Sir Iohn.* Q *(after 20); not in* F   23 my Master Slender] F; *my maister Slender* Q

6 **truckle-bed** small additional bed on truckles
or castors which could be stored under the main bed
(standing-bed).

6 **'Tis . . . Prodigal** The chamber walls are
painted with the parable of the Prodigal Son (Luke
15), appropriately for Falstaff.

7 **Anthropophaginian** Strictly speaking, can-
nibal; but here in reality just a good, strange,
mouth-filling word for the Host to use to the diminutive Slender.

13 **lungs military** The inversion of noun and
adjective gives a portentous air.

14 **Ephesian** In the Host's use this has as little
meaning and as much style as 'Anthropophaginian'.
That St Paul warned the Ephesians against drunkenness (Eph. 5.18) may explain Shakespeare's
choice of the epithet as appropriate.

16 **Bohemian Tartar** Nothing to do with
either Bohemia or the Tartars, save that these no-
tions in the Host's mind make a splendidly inappropriate title of barbaric splendour for Simple.

18 **Privacy** Concealment (i.e. of immoral
goings-on; *OED* 3).

21 **wise** skilled in magic arts.

22 **mussel-shell** Appropriate epithet for Slender: open, empty, worthless.

23 **my Master Slender** As Craik points out,
this is a strange use of the possessive pronoun, and
'Master' hovers between simple repetition of the
second word of the speech and being Slender's title.
There is no need to emend, however, because Simple's speech is full of trailing repetitions and of
linguistic shapes that half slip from his grasp.

24–5 **beguiled . . . chain** Although in   1.1
Slender is shown at the mercy of the trickery of
Falstaff and his companions, the incident Simple
mentions here makes no appearance. The chain
perhaps lingered in Shakespeare's mind from
4.4.30.

25 **no** There can be little doubt that 'no' here
chimes slackly in Simple's mind with 'know' at
24.

FALSTAFF I spake with the old woman about it.

SIMPLE And what says she, I pray, sir?

FALSTAFF Marry, she says that the very same man that beguiled Master
Slender of his chain cozened him of it.

SIMPLE I would I could have spoken with the woman herself. I had   30
other things to have spoken with her too, from him.

FALSTAFF What are they? Let us know.

HOST Ay, come. Quick!

SIMPLE I may not conceal them, sir.

HOST Conceal them, or thou diest.   35

SIMPLE Why, sir, they were nothing but about Mistress Anne Page, to
know if it were my master's fortune to have her or no.

FALSTAFF 'Tis; 'tis his fortune.

SIMPLE What, sir?

FALSTAFF To have her or no. Go, say the woman told me so.   40

SIMPLE May I be bold to say so, sir?

FALSTAFF Ay, sir; like who more bold.

SIMPLE I thank your worship. I shall make my master glad with these
tidings.   [*Exit*]

HOST Thou art clerkly, thou art clerkly, Sir John. Was there a wise   45
woman with thee?

FALSTAFF Ay, that there was, mine host, one that hath taught me more
wit than ever I learned before in my life. And I paid nothing for it
neither, but was paid for my learning.

[*Enter* BARDOLPH]

BARDOLPH Out, alas, sir, cozenage, mere cozenage!   50

HOST Where be my horses? Speak well of them, varletto.

---

34 SH SIMPLE] *Rowe; Fal.* F   42] F; *I tike, who more bolde* Q   44 SD] *Rowe; not in* F   45 Thou art] Q; Thou are F   49
SD] Q; *not in* F

---

28 beguiled cheated.

29 cozened cheated.

30–1 Simple's speech seems to peter out, characteristically, in a morass of loosely assembled
prepositions, because on the stage 'too' is easily
heard as 'to'.

34 SH *SIMPLE F's speech heading is simply a slip; and Simple's use of 'conceal' for
'reveal' in his reply to the Host here is fully characteristic.

38 'This speech is best delivered as a one-word
reply, followed by a three-word amplification as
Simple looks uncomprehendingly at Falstaff'
(Craik).

42 like . . . bold i.e. 'as bold as the boldest'
(Sisson).

45 *Thou art F's reading here is an easy slip.

45 clerkly learned (because of the way Falstaff
has twice, at 28–9 and 40, cheated Simple with an
answer that gives no answer, in the way that oracles
or wise women often did).

49 was . . . learning i.e. by being beaten. To
the Host though not to the audience Falstaff's
words have an oracular quality, darkly mysterious
and wise.

50 mere absolute.

51 varletto The Host's italianised form of
'varlet'.

BARDOLPH Run away with the cozeners. For so soon as I came beyond
　　Eton, they threw me off from behind one of them in a slough of
　　mire, and set spurs and away, like three German devils, three
　　Doctor Faustuses.   55
HOST They are gone but to meet the Duke, villain. Do not say they be
　　fled. Germans are honest men.

　　　　　　　　　　　[*Enter* EVANS]

EVANS Where is mine host?
HOST What is the matter, sir?
EVANS Have a care of your entertainments. There is a friend of mine   60
　　come to town tells me there is three cozen-Germans that has coz-
　　ened all the hosts of Readings, of Maidenhead, of Colnbrook, of
　　horses and money. I tell you for good will, look you. You are wise,
　　and full of gibes and vlouting-stocks, and 'tis not convenient you
　　should be cozened. Fare you well.   [*Exit*]   65

　　　　　　　　　　　[*Enter* CAIUS]

CAIUS Vere is mine host de Jarteer?
HOST Here, Master Doctor, in perplexity and doubtful dilemma.
CAIUS I cannot tell vat is dat; but it is tell-a me dat you make grand
　　preparation for a duke de Jamanie. By my trot, dere is no duke that
　　the court is know to come. I tell you for good will. Adieu.   [*Exit*] 70

---

57 SD] Q *(which transposes the order of entry of Evans here and Caius at 65); not in* F   61 three cozen-Germans] three Cozen-
Iermans F; three sorts of cosen garmombles Q   62 Readings] Readins F; Readings Q   65 SD.1] Q; *not in* F   65 SD.2] Q; *not
in* F   70 SD] Q; *not in* F

52 **Run away with** This is a humorously literal
way of describing the thieves running away with the
horses.
　53 **threw . . . them** Bardolph was evidently
riding pillion so as to be on hand to bring the horses
back after the Germans had finished with them.
　55 **Doctor Faustuses** i.e. Germans possessed
by the devil, as in Marlowe's play. See 1.1.105 n.
　60 **your entertainments** the hospitality you
extend to guests.
　61 **cozen-Germans** This nonce-word (=
cheating Germans) involves a quibble with 'cousin-
german' (= first cousin). Q's reading may be a play
on the name Mömpelgard (see Introduction,
p. 3).
　62 **Readings . . . Colnbrook** Readings (i.e.
Reading), Maidenhead, and Colnbrook were all
smaller places near the town of Windsor.
　63 **wise** The word is used in a very ironic and

undermined sense, as with the 'wise woman' of
Brentford.
　64 **vlouting-stocks** We are perhaps to remember the last time Evans used this word (see 3.1.93
and n.), as he and Caius resolved to revenge themselves upon the Host. They have clearly arranged
the whole incident of the horse-stealing 'Germans'.
The word in this context should mean 'floutings'
rather than 'objects of flouting', but Shakespeare
uses to his advantage Evans' characteristically loose
speech habits in making him repeat the term the
audience will remember.
　68 **grand** Although this could stand as an
English word, it is no doubt spoken with a French
accent by Caius, and so becomes the French word
meaning 'great', which is the adjective one would
more readily expect here.
　69 **Jamanie** Germany.
　70 **is know to** knows to have.

HOST [*To Bardolph*] Hue and cry, villain, go! – [*To Falstaff*] Assist me,
knight, I am undone! – [*To Bardolph*] Fly, run, hue and cry, villain!
I am undone!

[*Exeunt Host and Bardolph*]

FALSTAFF I would all the world might be cozened, for I have been
cozened and beaten too. If it should come to the ear of the court how   75
I have been transformed, and how my transformation hath been
washed and cudgelled, they would melt me out of my fat drop by
drop, and liquor fishermen's boots with me. I warrant they would
whip me with their fine wits till I were as crestfallen as a dried pear.
I never prospered since I forswore myself at primero. Well, if my   80
wind were but long enough, I would repent.

[*Enter* MISTRESS QUICKLY]

Now, whence come you?

MISTRESS QUICKLY From the two parties, forsooth.

FALSTAFF The devil take one party, and his dam the other, and so they
shall be both bestowed. I have suffered more for their sakes, more   85
than the villainous inconstancy of man's disposition is able to bear.

MISTRESS QUICKLY And have not they suffered? Yes, I warrant; speciously one of them. Mistress Ford, good heart, is beaten black and
blue, that you cannot see a white spot about her.

FALSTAFF What tell'st thou me of black and blue? I was beaten myself   90
into all the colours of the rainbow; and I was like to be apprehended
for the witch of Brentford. But that my admirable dexterity of wit,
my counterfeiting the action of an old woman, delivered me, the

---

71–2 SD *To Bardolph / To Falstaff / To Bardolph*] Oxford; *not in* F   71 Hue] *Rowe;* Huy F   72 hue] *Rowe;* huy F   73 SD]
Capell; Exit. Q; *not in* F   81 long enough] F; long inough to say my prayers Q   81 SD] Q *(after 82); not in* F   92 Brentford.
But] *As Theobald;* Braineford, but F

---

71 **Hue and cry** Clamorous pursuit of an offender (i.e. Raise the alarm!)

71 **villain** There is no hostile intent about the
Host's form of address to Bardolph, either here or at
56.

76 **my transformation** Falstaff's metamorphosis first into dirty washing and then an old
woman.

78 **liquor** grease (to waterproof).

79 **crestfallen . . . pear** Falstaff pictures himself fallen from triumph and shrivelled to a nothing-
ness in a mixed image that has lost no energy in
defeat.

80 **forswore . . . primero** cheated at the popular card game of primero and then swore I had not.

81 **long enough** Q's expanded version is what
an actor might well say onstage to make sure the
audience understood. See Textual Analysis, p. 155.

84 **devil . . . dam** See 1.1.118 n.

85 **bestowed** lodged, catered for.

86 **inconstancy** fickleness (i.e. the disposition
to change one's mind as a consequence of the pres-
sure of events).

87–8 **speciously** for 'specially'.

93 **counterfeiting . . . woman** Falstaff's account is that, after being publicly hounded out of
Ford's house as a witch, he escaped, and made his
way back to his lodgings doing an admirable impression of an innocent old woman.

knave constable had set me i'th'stocks, i'th'common stocks, for a
witch.   95
MISTRESS QUICKLY Sir, let me speak with you in your chamber. You
shall hear how things go, and, I warrant, to your content. Here is a
letter will say somewhat. Good hearts, what ado here is to bring you
together! Sure, one of you does not serve heaven well, that you are
so crossed.   100
FALSTAFF Come up into my chamber.

Exeunt

4.6 *Enter* FENTON *and* HOST

HOST Master Fenton, talk not to me. My mind is heavy. I will give over
    all.
FENTON Yet hear me speak. Assist me in my purpose,
        And, as I am a gentleman, I'll give thee
        A hundred pound in gold more than your loss.   5
HOST I will hear you, Master Fenton; and I will, at the least, keep your
    counsel.
FENTON From time to time I have acquainted you
        With the dear love I bear to fair Anne Page,
        Who mutually hath answered my affection,   10
        So far forth as herself might be her chooser,
        Even to my wish. I have a letter from her,
        Of such contents as you will wonder at,
        The mirth whereof so larded with my matter
        That neither singly can be manifested   15
        Without the show of both. – Fat Falstaff
        Hath a great scene. The image of the jest

Act 4, Scene 6   4.6] *Scena Sexta.* F

98 Good hearts Poor things.
98 here is This slightly unidiomatic formulation is just Mistress Quickly getting stuck in the
form of words with which she began the previous
sentence.
100 crossed thwarted (*OED* Cross *v* 14).

Act 4, Scene 6
1–2 give ... all give up all effort (and in this
particular case, on Fenton's behalf). The Host was
in favour of Fenton's suit at 3.2.51–4.

14 The mirth whereof i.e. the account of the
plan against Falstaff.
14 larded ... matter so bound up with my
own concern (the plan to steal away with Anne)
(*OED* Lard *v* 4 = intersperse, garnish; the connection of 'lard' in its primary sense with 'fat' at 16 is a
happy one).
16 show revealing.
17 great scene prominent part to play.

I'll show you here at large. Hark, good mine host:
Tonight at Herne's Oak, just 'twixt twelve and one,
Must my sweet Nan present the Fairy Queen –   20
The purpose why is here – in which disguise,
While other jests are something rank on foot,
Her father hath commanded her to slip
Away with Slender, and with him at Eton
Immediately to marry. She hath consented. Now, sir,   25
Her mother, ever strong against that match
And firm for Doctor Caius, hath appointed
That he shall likewise shuffle her away,
While other sports are tasking of their minds,
And at the dean'ry, where a priest attends,   30
Straight marry her. To this her mother's plot
She, seemingly obedient, likewise hath
Made promise to the Doctor. Now thus it rests:
Her father means she shall be all in white,
And in that habit, when Slender sees his time   35
To take her by the hand and bid her go,
She shall go with him. Her mother hath intended,
The better to denote her to the Doctor –
For they must all be masked and vizarded –
That quaint in green she shall be loose enrobed,   40
With ribbons pendent flaring 'bout her head;

---

26 ever strong against] *Pope;* euen strong against F; still against Q   27–8 hath . . . away] F; in a robe of red / By her deuice, the Doctor must steale her thence Q   38 denote] *Capell, conj. Steevens;* deuote F

18 **here at large** i.e. in this letter in more detail.

20 **present** play the part of.

21 **here** i.e. in the letter. The audience already knows the essentials of the plan against Falstaff, and will see onstage the detail of it, so Fenton's letter from Anne is only for the Host's eye.

22 **something . . . foot** 'somewhat abundantly in progress' (Craik).

26 ***ever** F's 'euen' makes weak sense, and 'ever' (supported by Q's 'still') would need only to be slightly misread to produce the error.

28 **shuffle her away** hurry her secretly away (*OED* Shuffle *v* 5b).

29 **tasking of** taxing, occupying.

30 **dean'ry** dean's house. Hart's suggestion that this is the deanery attached to St George's Chapel in the grounds of Windsor Castle can be accepted. Shakespeare never uses the word in the general sense of a parsonage, but only with apparent specific reference here and at 5.3.2 and 5.5.178.

33 **thus it rests** the situation, then, is this.

38 ***denote** F's 'deuote' makes little sense, and 'u' for 'n' is a particularly easy compositorial mistake.

40 **quaint** handsomely, prettily.

40 **in green** At 4.4.67–8, for the benefit of her husband, Mistress Page had decided that her daughter should be in white as the Queen of Fairies. Her private plan here is that someone else (a 'postmaster's boy' as it turns out; see 5.5.165–6) will play that part in white, while Anne Page becomes a green fairy. See 5.5.177.

41 **pendent flaring** hanging loosely down and blowing in the wind.

And when the Doctor spies his vantage ripe,
To pinch her by the hand, and, on that token,
The maid hath given consent to go with him.

HOST Which means she to deceive, father or mother? 45

FENTON Both, my good host, to go along with me.
And here it rests, that you'll procure the vicar
To stay for me at church 'twixt twelve and one,
And, in the lawful name of marrying,
To give our hearts united ceremony. 50

HOST Well, husband your device. I'll to the vicar.
Bring you the maid, you shall not lack a priest.

FENTON So shall I evermore be bound to thee;
Besides, I'll make a present recompense.

Exeunt

5.1 [*Enter* FALSTAFF *and* MISTRESS QUICKLY]

FALSTAFF Prithee, no more prattling; go. I'll hold. This is the third
time; I hope good luck lies in odd numbers. Away, go! They say
there is divinity in odd numbers, either in nativity, chance, or
death. Away!

MISTRESS QUICKLY I'll provide you a chain, and I'll do what I can to 5
get you a pair of horns.

FALSTAFF Away, I say; time wears. Hold up your head, and mince.

[*Exit Mistress Quickly*]

45] *As verse, Rowe; as prose,* F   Act 5, Scene 1   5.1] *Actus Quintus. Scæna Prima.* F   0 SD] *Rowe; Enter Falstaffe, Quickly, and Ford.* F   7 SD.1] *Rowe (after 6); not in* F

43 To He is to.

45 As Craik notes, the Host here and in his next speech uncharacteristically uses verse, 'being subdued to the style of the scene'.

47 here it rests i.e. here is the help I need from you.

50 give . . . ceremony ceremoniously unite our hearts.

51 husband . . . device take care of (your part of) your plan, with a glance at the husband Fenton is to become.

52 Bring you This embraces both the conditional ('If you bring') and the imperative.

54 make . . . recompense give you an immediate reward. See 5.

Act 5, Scene 1

1 hold keep the appointment.

1–2 third time As we say, 'third time lucky':

the proverbs cluster round Falstaff's revived hope ('All things thrive at thrice' Tilley T175; 'There is luck in odd numbers' Tilley L582; 'The third time pays for all' Tilley T319).

3 divinity divine power (*OED* 3).

3–4 either . . . death i.e. it is lucky to be born or to die on an odd-numbered day, and other lucky things also happen on odd-numbered days.

5 chain See 4.4.30. 'No dramatic use is made of this chain, nor is it referred to in 5.5' (Craik).

7 Craik notes that this line is actually a hexameter, but it is perhaps best thought of as 'accidentally' metrical, to be distinguished, for instance, from the more deliberate random metrics of Pistol's habitual speech.

7 wears wastes, runs on, runs out (*OED v*[1] 19).

7 Hold . . . mince i.e. we're back in business, let that put pride into your carriage as you mince off (the tone is affectionately disparaging).

[*Enter* FORD *disguised as Brook*]

How now, Master Brook! Master Brook, the matter will be known
tonight or never. Be you in the Park about midnight, at Herne's
Oak, and you shall see wonders.   10

FORD Went you not to her yesterday, sir, as you told me you had
appointed?

FALSTAFF I went to her, Master Brook, as you see, like a poor old man,
but I came from her, Master Brook, like a poor old woman. That
same knave Ford, her husband, hath the finest mad devil of jealousy   15
in him, Master Brook, that ever governed frenzy. I will tell you he
beat me grievously, in the shape of a woman; for in the shape of
man, Master Brook, I fear not Goliath with a weaver's beam, because I know also life is a shuttle. I am in haste. Go along with me.
I'll tell you all, Master Brook. Since I plucked geese, played truant,   20
and whipped top, I knew not what 'twas to be beaten till lately.
Follow me. I'll tell you strange things of this knave Ford, on whom
tonight I will be revenged, and I will deliver his wife into your hand.
Follow. Strange things in hand, Master Brook! Follow.

Exeunt

5.2 *Enter* PAGE, SHALLOW, [*and*] SLENDER

PAGE Come, come, we'll couch i'th'Castle ditch till we see the light of
our fairies. Remember, son Slender, my –

SLENDER Ay, forsooth, I have spoke with her, and we have a nay-word

---

7 SD.2] *As Rowe; not in* F   18 Goliath] Goliah F   **Act 5, Scene 2**   5.2] *Scena Secunda.* F   2 my –] my. F; my daughter.
F2; my daughter – *Craik*

18 **Goliath . . . beam** 'And the shaft of his
spear was like a weaver's beam' (1 Sam. 17.7).

19 **life . . . shuttle** 'My days are swifter than a
weaver's shittle' (Job 7.6). The weaving image has
clearly led Falstaff from the Goliath quotation to
the other.

20 **plucked geese** Hart cites evidence suggesting that it was a boy's game (and it would have been
quite a daring one) to pluck feathers from a live
goose.

21 **whipped top** To keep a top spinning with a
whip was a common children's game.

24 **Strange . . . hand** Strange happenings
afoot. Falstaff draws his phrase from 'strange

things' at 22 and 'into your hand' at 23, but instead
of a feeble Shallow-like repetition, produces a resonant variation.

Act 5, Scene 2
1 **couch** lie hidden.
2 **my** – F's lack of punctuation suggests that
Slender interrupts Page as he is about to remind
him of the plan (i.e. 'my daughter will be in white').
There seems no reason why Slender (even Slender)
should need reminding that Page has a daughter, as
suggested by the reading of F2, often followed by
editors. See Textual Analysis, p. 151.

how to know one another. I come to her in white and cry 'mum'; she
cries 'budget'; and by that we know one another.   5

SHALLOW That's good too. But what needs either your 'mum' or her
'budget'? The white will decipher her well enough. – It hath struck
ten o'clock.

PAGE The night is dark. Light and spirits will become it well. Heaven
prosper our sport! No man means evil but the devil, and we shall   10
know him by his horns. Let's away. Follow me.

Exeunt

5.3 *Enter* MISTRESS PAGE, MISTRESS FORD, [*and*] CAIUS

MISTRESS PAGE Master Doctor, my daughter is in green. When you
see your time, take her by the hand, away with her to the deanery,
and dispatch it quickly. Go before into the Park. We two must go
together.

CAIUS I know vat I have to do. Adieu.   5

MISTRESS PAGE Fare you well, sir.

[*Exit Caius*]

My husband will not rejoice so much at the abuse of Falstaff as he
will chafe at the Doctor's marrying my daughter. But 'tis no matter.
Better a little chiding than a great deal of heartbreak.

MISTRESS FORD Where is Nan now, and her troop of fairies, and the   10
Welsh devil Hugh?

MISTRESS PAGE They are all couched in a pit hard by Herne's Oak,
with obscured lights, which, at the very instant of Falstaff's and our
meeting, they will at once display to the night.

MISTRESS FORD That cannot choose but amaze him.   15

MISTRESS PAGE If he be not amazed, he will be mocked. If he be
amazed, he will every way be mocked.

Act 5, Scene 3   5.3] *Scena Tertia.* F   6 SD] F2 *(after 5); not in* F   11 Welsh devil Hugh] *Capell;* Welch-deuill Herne F

4 her in white the girl in white.

4–5 'mum' . . . 'budget' *OED* conjectures that
'mumbudget' was 'the name of some children's
game in which silence was required'.

9 become it grace it.

11 know . . . horns As in the proverb 'The
devil is known by his horns' (Tilley D252).

Act 5, Scene 3

7 abuse ill-treatment.

11 *Welsh devil Hugh F's reading 'Herne' is
perhaps an error deriving from the immediately

preceding reference to the devil (5.2.10), which
linked him with Herne/Falstaff. The word 'devil'
must here be used in a weakened sense as meaning a
mischievous spirit (*OED sb* 4b). Compare *Mac.*
2.3.17: 'I'll devil-porter it no further.'

15 cannot . . . amaze cannot fail to terrify.

16–17 If he be not . . . way be mocked 'Even
if he is not terrified, he will be mocked (for his
misbehaviour); and if he is terrified he will be
mocked for his credulity as well as for his misbehaviour' (Craik).

MISTRESS FORD We'll betray him finely.
MISTRESS PAGE Against such lewdsters and their lechery,
        Those that betray them do no treachery.   20
MISTRESS FORD The hour draws on. To the Oak, to the Oak!

Exeunt

5.4 *Enter* EVANS [*like a satyr,*] *and* [*boys dressed like*] *fairies*

EVANS Trib, trib, fairies! Come, and remember your parts. Be pold, I
    pray you. Follow me into the pit, and when I give the watch-'ords,
    do as I pid you. Come, come; trib, trib!

Exeunt

5.5 [*Enter* FALSTAFF *disguised as Herne with a buck's head upon him*]

FALSTAFF The Windsor bell hath struck twelve; the minute draws on.
    Now, the hot-blooded gods assist me! Remember, Jove, thou wast a

---

Act 5, Scene 4   5.4] *Scena Quarta.* F   0 SD] Q *(part of a longer stage direction, at a point in* Q*'s different management of the plot at the end of the play, corresponding to 5.5.29* SD*); Enter Evans disguised, and William Page and other children disguised as fairies, with rattles in their hands / Craik; Enter Euans and Fairies.* F   Act 5, Scene 5   5.5] *Scena Quinta.* F   0 SD] *Enter sir Iohn with a Bucks head vpon him.* Q; *Enter Falstaffe, Mistris Page, Mistris Ford, Euans, Anne Page, Fairies, Page, Ford, Quickly, Slender, Fenton, Caius, Pistoll.* F; *Enter Falstaff disguised as Herne, with a buck's horns upon his head, and with a chain in his hand / Craik*   2 hot-blooded gods] hot-bloodied-Gods F

19 lewdsters lewd persons.

Act 5, Scene 4
0 SD Although Q's account of the stage business in this plot at the end of the play is garbled (in particular in the matter of the various colours Anne Page is supposed to be wearing), it seems important to distinguish carefully between what could be easily muddled in a memorial reconstruction and what would be easily remembered. That Evans was dressed 'like a Satyre' would be just such a detail; and all the more interesting to preserve it because neither the spoken text of F nor Q mentions it. The word 'satyr' in Elizabethan literature usually meant a kind of woodland god (in Roman art a figure with 'the ears, tail, and legs of a goat, and budding horns', *OED sb* 1), and this would seem an appropriate role for the adult among his boy fairies. Editors often identify one of the boys here as William Page (see 4.4.45), but this is arguably unnecessary since no part of the boy's character as William is of dramatic consequence (as is not the case, for instance, with Evans in his disguise). On the rattles, see 5.5.23 SD n. See Textual Analysis, p. 156.
1 Trib Trip.
2 into the pit i.e. the sawpit (see 4.4.51). There

is a lightly meant underlying joke here, because 'pit' was also used to mean hell (*OED sb*¹ 4), and we remember that at 5.3.11 Parson Evans is the 'Welsh devil'.
2 watch-'ords watchword.

Act 5, Scene 5
0 SD As with the stage direction at the beginning of 5.4, it seems best to follow Q. Whether the 'Bucks head' of Q means just the horns (as is possible: *OED* Head *sb* 6 = the antlers of a deer) or a horned mask, in the form of a deer's head to cover the face as well, is not clear. The chain mentioned as part of Herne's usual attire at 4.4.30 and promised to Falstaff by Mistress Quickly at 5.1.5, as part of the disguise she will procure for him, nowhere appears in Q and has no stage function in F. It seems better to let it disappear after the last mention of it at 5.1.5, rather than to have to disentangle oneself from it later. See Textual Analysis, p. 156.
1 minute appointed moment (*OED sb*¹ 1c).
2 hot-blooded gods i.e. the lustful gods of pagan antiquity.
2–3 Jove . . . Europa Jove (or Jupiter) carried off Europa, daughter of Agenor, king of Phoenicia, by tempting her to sit upon his back while he was in

bull for thy Europa. Love set on thy horns. O powerful love, that in
some respects makes a beast a man, in some other a man a beast!
You were also, Jupiter, a swan for the love of Leda. O omnipotent   5
love, how near the god drew to the complexion of a goose! A fault
done first in the form of a beast: O Jove, a beastly fault! And then
another fault in the semblance of a fowl: think on't, Jove, a foul
fault! When gods have hot backs, what shall poor men do? For me,
I am here a Windsor stag, and the fattest, I think, i'th'forest. Send   10
me a cool rut-time, Jove, or who can blame me to piss my tallow?
Who comes here? My doe?

[*Enter* MISTRESS FORD *and* MISTRESS PAGE]

MISTRESS FORD Sir John! Art thou there, my deer, my male deer?
FALSTAFF My doe with the black scut! Let the sky rain potatoes, let
it thunder to the tune of 'Greensleeves', hail kissing-comfits,   15
and snow eryngoes; let there come a tempest of provocation, I will
shelter me here.

[*He embraces her*]

MISTRESS FORD Mistress Page is come with me, sweetheart.
FALSTAFF Divide me like a bribed buck, each a haunch. I will keep my

---

12 SD] *Enter mistris* Page, *and mistris* Ford. Q; *not in* F   13] *As prose*, Pope; *as two lines of verse, divided after* my deer F   17
SD] *As Capell; not in* F   18 sweetheart] sweet hart F

---

the shape of a bull, and then swimming across the
sea to Crete with her. See Textual Analysis, p. 160.
   3 set on caused you to assume.
   4 makes . . . beast At a surface level Falstaff is
saying that love may take a beast-like man and make
him more fully human, or may contrariwise reduce
a man to a morally bestial state; but the resonant
metamorphosis of Jove into a bull gives these words
more than a conventionally moralising tone, so that
they convey rather the wondrous power of love to
transform, as it has here transformed Falstaff himself.
   5 swan . . . Leda Jupiter disguised himself as a
swan to seduce Leda, wife of King Tyndarus of
Sparta.
   6 complexion . . . goose i.e. Jupiter in becom-
ing a swan for love came very near to assuming the
appearance (complexion) of a goose (a proverbially
stupid creature).
   7 beastly foul, filthy.
   9 hot backs lustful loins.
   11 rut-time mating time.
   11 piss my tallow The heat of the season and
the heat generated by the lust of the rutting stag was
said to make it piss frequently, and the stag at the

end of the rut, lean now because of the intent ex-
penditure of energy in mating, was said to have
pissed away its fat (tallow).
   13 deer There is a quibble on 'dear'.
   14 scut short tail (and with a clear sexual reference to Mistress Ford, by way of one of the meanings of 'tail' = cunt *OED sb*¹ 5c). As Craik notes,
here is the only reference in the play to the fact that
Mistress Ford is dark-haired.
   14–17 Let . . . here Falstaff wishes that the sky
should rain down potatoes (the sweet potato was
thought to be an aphrodisiac), thunder out a love
song ('Greensleeves'), hail down perfumed sweet-
meats for sweetening a lover's breath (kissing-
comfits), and snow down another kind of
aphrodisiac sweetmeat (eryngoes), so that in the
midst of this tempest of sexual provocation he could
take shelter in Mistress Ford's body.
   18 The night is dark (5.2.9) and Falstaff has not
seen Mistress Page.
   18 sweetheart The F spelling makes the heart/
hart quibble clear.
   19 Divide . . . buck The reference is to cutting
up a stolen deer quickly to hide the theft, perpe-
trated here in Falstaff's imagining with the conniv-

sides to myself, my shoulders for the fellow of this walk, and my   20
horns I bequeath your husbands. Am I a woodman, ha? Speak I like
Herne the Hunter? Why, now is Cupid a child of conscience: he
makes restitution. As I am a true spirit, welcome!

　　　　　　　　　　　　　　　　[A noise of horns within]

MISTRESS PAGE Alas, what noise?
MISTRESS FORD Heaven forgive our sins!   25
FALSTAFF What should this be?
MISTRESS FORD *and* MISTRESS PAGE Away, away!

　　　　　　　　　　　　　　　　　　　　　　　[They run off]

FALSTAFF I think the devil will not have me damned, lest the oil that's
in me should set hell on fire. He would never else cross me thus.

　　Enter [EVANS *like a satyr with a lighted taper in his hand, and
boys dressed like*] *fairies* [*with lighted tapers on their heads*; *the boy
who played the part of Mistress Quickly disguised as the* QUEEN OF
FAIRIES, *the actor who played the part of Pistol disguised as*
HOBGOBLIN, *and* ANNE PAGE *disguised as a fairy*]

23 SD] *This edn; There is a noise of hornes, the two women run away.* Q; *A noise of rattles within / Craik; not in* F   25] F; *Mis. Pa. God forgiue me, what noise is this?* Q   27 SD] *As* Q *(see 23 SD); not in* F   28–9] *As prose, Pope; as three lines of verse, divided after* damned *and* fire F   29 SD] *This edn; Enter sir Hugh like a Satyre, and boyes drest like Fayries, mistresse Quickly, like the Queene of* Fayries: *they sing a song about him, and afterward speake.* Q; *Enter Fairies.* F; *Enter Evans, William Page, and children, disguised as before, with lighted tapers; 'Mistress Quickly' disguised as the Queen of Fairies, 'Pistol' disguised as Hobgoblin, and Anne Page disguised as a fairy / Craik*

ance of the keeper (*OED* Bribe *v* 1 = steal). See 1.1.87; the play begins and ends with a stolen deer.

19 each a haunch The two women get a buttock each, as is appropriate because the buttocks thrust in the act of copulation.

19–20 my sides to myself Perhaps denoting 'I will keep on my own side', i.e. defend myself.

20 my shoulders . . . walk The shoulders go to 'the keeper responsible for this particular "walk" or part of Windsor Forest' (Oliver), who has presumably connived at the theft and who would ordinarily have the shoulders of a deer legitimately killed.

21 horns Falstaff wears the horns of a rutting stag, which become, when bestowed on the deceived husbands, symbols of their cuckolded inadequacy; but the tables are turned on him by the noise of horns of a different kind as his speech ends.

21 woodman (1) hunter (*OED* 1), (2) hunter of women (*OED* 1b).

22 of conscience who follows his conscience.

22–3 he . . . restitution i.e. he restores what has been wrongfully withheld, Falstaff's victory in love.

23 *SD As with the chain (5.5.0 SD n.), the rattles

mentioned at 4.4.49 nowhere appear in Q and have no explicitly indicated stage function in F. As the chain does, they have an editorial presence in Craik's stage directions at 5.4.0 SD and here, but it seems better to let them disappear from the text itself after 4.4.49. Falstaff's mention of horns at 5.5.21 gives colour to Q's account of an actual stage performance at this point. One may perhaps suppose that Q's stage direction here about horns simply omitted to mention that the fairies sounded their rattles as well, and there is no reason why they should not have rattles with them whenever they appear, simply as part of their costume; but unlike the tapers on their heads (4.4.48) and in Evans' hand (4.4.65), they are not essential to the action that follows. See 35 n.

25 See Textual Analysis, p. 162.

29 cross me i.e. prevent me from sinning.

29 *SD Evans and the fairies as before, but it seems worth mentioning the tapers since they are now, presumably for the first time, lit. I accept Craik's view that 'mistresse Quickly' here in Q and 'Quickly' and 'Pistoll' in F's massed entry at the beginning of the scene, as well as Quickly and Pistol speech headings in F from this point on, indicate not

QUEEN OF FAIRIES Fairies black, grey, green, and white,   30
You moonshine revellers, and shades of night,
You orphan heirs of fixèd destiny,
Attend your office and your quality.
Crier Hobgoblin, make the fairy oyes.
HOBGOBLIN Elves, list your names; silence, you airy toys.   35
Cricket, to Windsor chimneys shalt thou leap.
Where fires thou find'st unraked and hearths unswept,
There pinch the maids as blue as bilberry:
Our radiant Queen hates sluts and sluttery.
FALSTAFF [*Aside*] They are fairies; he that speaks to them shall die.   40
I'll wink and couch; no man their works must eye.
[*He lies down and hides his face*]
EVANS Where's Bead? Go you, and where you find a maid
That ere she sleep has thrice her prayers said,
Raise up the organs of her fantasy;

30 SH QUEEN OF FAIRIES] *This edn; Qui.* F *(thereafter Qui. or Qu.); Quic:* Q *(thereafter Quic.);* 'MISTRESS QUICKLY' *as Queen of Fairies / Craik; Quick. / Oliver* 35 SH HOBGOBLIN] *This edn; Pist.* F *(and so thereafter);* 'PISTOL' *as Hobgoblin / Craik; Pist. / Oliver* 36 leap] F; lep *Craik* 40 SD] *Oxford; not in* F 41 SD] *Oxford; Lies down upon his face. / Rowe; not in* F 42 Bead] *Bede* F; *Pead* Q 44 fantasy;] *Theobald;* fantasie, F

those characters but the actors who had been playing them. There is no dramatic function in what
follows for the Quickly or Pistol elements in the
Queen of Fairies or Hobgoblin, as there emphatically is for the Evans element in the satyr; and at 95
SD the Queen of Fairies, mistakenly carried off by
Slender who assumes she is Anne, must turn out to
be not Mistress Quickly but a 'postmaster's boy'
(165–6). See 95 SD n. and Textual Analysis, p. 158.
  31 shades spirits.
  32 orphan without parents; though fairies are
parentless by definition and not by accident.
  32 heirs . . . destiny inheritors of fixed functions; fairies being specialised in their various different activities, rather like bees.
  33 Attend Attend to.
  33 office function.
  33 quality particular employment.
  34 Hobgoblin (otherwise called Puck or Robin
Goodfellow) was the fairies' 'town crier', and
so uses the crier's call of 'oyes' (*oyez* is Old French
for 'hear ye'; in this line plainly pronounced as a
monosyllable).
  35 list listen for.
  35 silence . . . toys The 'airy toys' (i.e. insubstantial nothings) had clearly been making a noise
since they came onstage, perhaps with their voices
(4.4.52) and rattles, the rattles perhaps succeeding
the sound of horns that announced their coming.
  36 Cricket An appropriate name for a fairy

who, like a house-cricket, occupies himself with
fireplaces.
  36 leap The variant pronunciation 'lep' (which
Craik admits into his text) is required for the near-
rhyme with 'unswept'.
  37 unraked not banked up to keep them alight
until morning (*OED* Rake v^1 5).
  38 bilberry a plant with deep blue berries.
  39 Queen The Queen of Fairies, but with a
glance possibly at the Queen in Windsor Castle.
  41 wink and couch close my eyes and lie
hidden.
  42 Bead The two fairies Evans addresses in Q
are 'Peane' and 'Pead', and F's 'Bede' here is clearly
the second of these names, appropriate in its small-
ness for a fairy, and perhaps with associations with
a rosary bead and thus prayer. It is fitting that the
parson, albeit disguised as a satyr, should be concerned about religious observance in this speech;
and it is plain from Falstaff's reference to 'that
Welsh fairy' at 74 that Evans speaks with his distinctive accent when playing his fairy part, even
though F, unlike Q, makes no attempt to represent it
phonetically in the fairy verse parts of the text. It is
worth noting that even Falstaff is momentarily en-
tranced into unaccustomed verse at 40–1. He is, of
course, as much and as little in disguise as Evans.
  44 'Stimulate her imagination (so that she has
pleasant dreams)' (Hibbard).
  44 *fantasy; Theobald's punctuation allows us

Sleep she as sound as careless infancy.   45
But those as sleep and think not on their sins,
Pinch them, arms, legs, backs, shoulders, sides, and shins.
QUEEN OF FAIRIES About, about!
Search Windsor Castle, elves, within and out.
Strew good luck, oafs, on every sacred room,   50
That it may stand till the perpetual doom
In state as wholesome as in state 'tis fit,
Worthy the owner and the owner it.
The several chairs of order look you scour
With juice of balm and every precious flower.   55
Each fair instalment, coat, and several crest,
With loyal blazon, evermore be blest!
And nightly meadow-fairies, look you sing,
Like to the Garter's compass, in a ring.
Th'expressure that it bears, green let it be,   60
More fertile-fresh than all the field to see;
And *Honi soit qui mal y pense* write
In em'rald tufts, flowers purple, blue, and white,

---

50 oafs] Ouphes F   58 nightly meadow-fairies] Nightly-meadow-Fairies F; nightly, meadow-fairies *Capell*   63 em'rald tufts] Emrold-tuffes F

to read the beginning of the following line as 'May she sleep' rather than 'Even though she sleep'. The sleep of careless (i.e. carefree) infancy is to be accompanied, not interrupted, by sweet dreams.

46 those as those who (Abbott 112).

48 About, about! Bestir yourselves!

51 perpetual doom day of judgement.

52 'i.e. as "healthy" in state (condition) as it is fitting in state (dignity)' (Oliver).

53 The dignity of the castle is 'worthy of the owner (Queen Elizabeth), and the owner is worthy of it' (Craik).

54 chairs of order stalls assigned to each of the Knights of the Garter in the choir of St George's Chapel in Windsor Castle.

54 scour cleanse.

55 balm aromatic herb.

56 instalment stall (each one equipped with the particular knight's insignia).

56 coat coat of arms. Each knight's arms were displayed on the stall plate nailed at the back of his stall. It is interesting that the play begins with a discussion about Shallow's coat of arms, which has as little intrinsically to do with the main plot of the play as this passage about the Knights of the Garter. See Introduction, p. 1.

56 crest the device borne on top of the helmet. His helmet and crest were set above each knight's stall.

57 With Together with.

57 blazon banner bearing the coat of arms. Each knight's banner projected on a staff above his helmet and crest.

58 nightly meadow-fairies meadow fairies of the night. Ralph Crane, the inveterate hyphenator, has linked these three words together in his scribal text for F, which suggests that he took 'nightly' in this adjectival sense (*OED adj* 2), rather than in the adverbial sense of 'by night' or 'every night' (*OED adv* 2, 1).

59 compass circle.

60 expressure . . . bears picture it presents (*OED* Expressure c). The fairy ring, as it were the coat of arms of the fairy world, is greener and fresher than the grass about it.

62 Honi . . . pense Shamed be he who thinks evil of this matter: the French motto of the Order of the Garter, normally in gold lettering on the blue ground of the Garter ribbon. The traditional story is that Edward III, who founded the order, picked up the Countess of Salisbury's accidentally dropped garter and, noticing the knowing looks of the spectators, openly tied it round his own knee, saying as he did so the words preserved in the motto.

Like sapphire, pearl, and rich embroidery,
Buckled below fair knighthood's bending knee.   65
Fairies use flowers for their charactery.
Away, disperse! – But till 'tis one o'clock,
Our dance of custom round about the oak
Of Herne the Hunter let us not forget.
EVANS Pray you, lock hand in hand; yourselves in order set;   70
And twenty glow-worms shall our lanterns be,
To guide our measure round about the tree. –
But stay! I smell a man of middle earth!
FALSTAFF [*Aside*] Heavens defend me from that Welsh fairy, lest he
transform me to a piece of cheese!   75
HOBGOBLIN [*To Falstaff*]
Vile worm, thou wast o'erlooked even in thy birth.
QUEEN OF FAIRIES [*To Evans*] With trial-fire touch me his finger-end.
If he be chaste, the flame will back descend
And turn him to no pain; but if he start,
It is the flesh of a corrupted heart.   80
HOBGOBLIN A trial, come!
EVANS   Come, will this wood take fire?
[*Evans puts the taper to Falstaff's finger, and he starts*]
FALSTAFF O, O, O!
QUEEN OF FAIRIES Corrupt, corrupt, and tainted in desire!

74–5] *As prose, Pope; as two lines of verse, divided after* fairy F   74 SD] *Oxford; not in* F   74 Heavens . . . from] F; God blesse
me from Q   76 SD] *Oxford; not in* F   76] *As verse, Rowe*³; *as prose,* F   77 SD] *Craik; not in* F   81 SD] *They put the Tapers to
his fingers, and he starts.* Q; *Evans burns Falstaff's finger with his taper / Craik; not in* F

66 **charactery** writing (i.e. flowers not ink).
68 **of custom** customary.
73 **man . . . earth** mortal man (i.e. not a fairy),
belonging to the earth which hung midway between
heaven and hell.
74 **Heavens . . . fairy** Falstaff has as yet no
idea that the 'Welsh fairy' is Evans; it is only later he
begins to realise he has been fooled, at 112. See
Textual Analysis, p. 162.
75 **cheese** See 1.2.10 n.
76 **o'erlooked** looked upon with the 'evil eye',
bewitched (*OED* Overlook *v* 7).
77 This line must be addressed to Evans alone,
who has a taper in his hand, and not to the fairies
collectively, because the burning is here a delicate
and preliminary trial ('*touch* me his finger-*end*'), and

not part of Falstaff's punishment, as it is at 94 when
the boys dance round him pinching him and burning him with the tapers on their heads.
77 **trial-fire** 'testing fire (as in the trial by or-
deal)' (Hibbard).
78 **descend** return ('descend' is used in this
loose sense for the sake of the rhyme).
79 **turn him to** put him to (*OED v* 43b).
79 **start** flinch suddenly.
81 **this wood** Falstaff's finger is treated as a
piece of kindling wood.
81 *SD As in F, the text of Q at this point makes
it clear that Evans alone 'tries' Falstaff ('Giue me
the Tapers, I will try / And if that he loue venery'),
although Q's stage direction is loosely plural.

About him, fairies, sing a scornful rhyme,

And, as you trip, still pinch him to your time.   85

[*Fairies dance around Falstaff, pinching and burning him*]

FAIRIES [*Sing*] Fie on sinful fantasy!

Fie on lust and luxury!

Lust is but a bloody fire,

Kindled with unchaste desire

Fed in heart, whose flames aspire,   90

As thoughts do blow them, higher and higher.

Pinch him, fairies, mutually;

Pinch him for his villainy.

Pinch him, and burn him, and turn him about,

Till candles and starlight and moonshine be out.   95

[*During the song, enter* CAIUS *at one door and steals away a Fairy in green; enter* SLENDER *at another door and steals away the Queen of Fairies in white; enter* FENTON *and steals away Anne Page. After the song a noise of hunting horns within. The Fairies run away from Falstaff but do not exit. Falstaff pulls off his buck's head, and rises.*]

[*Enter* PAGE *and* MISTRESS PAGE, *and* FORD *and* MISTRESS FORD]

85 SD] *This edn; Fairies dance around Falstaff, pinching him / Craik; not in* F   86 SH FAIRIES SD *Sing*] *Craik; The Song.* F   86–9] *As four lines of verse, Pope; as two lines of verse, divided after* luxury F   92–3] *As two lines of verse, Pope; as a single line of verse,* F   95 SD] *This edn; Here they pinch him, and sing about him, & the Doctor comes one way & steales away a boy in red. And Slender another way he takes a boy in greene: And Fenton steales misteris Anne, being in white. And a noyse of hunting is made within: and all the Fairies runne away. Falstaffe pulles of his bucks head, and rises vp. And enters M. Page, M. Ford, and their wiues, M. Shallow, Sir Hugh.* Q; *While the Fairies sing, enter Caius at one door and exit stealing away a Fairy in green; enter Slender at another door and exit stealing away a Fairy in white; enter Fenton and exit stealing away Anne Page. After the song a noise of hunting horns within. The Fairies hastily retire. Falstaff rises and begins to run away. Enter Page and Mistress Page, and Ford and Mistress Ford. / Craik (the last sentence as Capell); not in* F

84 **About him** Circle round about him.

86 **fantasy** liking, desire (*OED sb* 7).

87 **luxury** lechery, lasciviousness (*OED* 1).

88 **bloody fire** fire in the blood.

90 **aspire** rise up like smoke or fire (*OED v* 5).

91 **blow** i.e. as a fire is made to blaze with bellows.

92 **mutually** all together (*OED adv* 2).

95 SD Q is muddled about the colours, but the spoken text of F is clear that Caius has the boy in green, it being Mistress Page's plan that Anne should be in green for Caius (4.6.40); and that Slender has the Queen of Fairies in white, that being Page's understanding of the disguise Anne will be wearing as his plan for Slender comes into operation (4.4.67–8; 4.6.34). Q has previously suggested (see Collation and Commentary at 29 SD) that 'mistresse Quickly' is playing the Queen of Fairies, and so cannot have Slender here stealing her and substitutes for her an ordinary fairy, since Slender

later (in Q as in F) is annoyed to have discovered his 'Anne' is a boy (not that she is Mistress Quickly). It seems possible that there is a later error in Q: the stage direction at 29 is a 'theatrical note' that the boy who plays Quickly is to play the Queen of Fairies; but a later hand has misunderstood this as a note of part of the plot of the play and so modified the stage direction here at 95 to prevent Slender from stealing Quickly (See Textual Analysis, p. 158). The remaining fairies in this stage direction do not leave the stage completely, as Craik rightly notes, because they are indicated as onstage at 112 (and see 112 n.). At the end of the stage direction, if the couples enter as couples, 'this . . . emphasises the final harmony that is approaching' (Craik); in F Evans is already onstage, and there is no dramatic function for Shallow (who does not appear in the 'massed entry' at the beginning of the scene), so that these two final characters in Q's direction can be omitted.

PAGE Nay, do not fly; I think we have watched you now.
Will none but Herne the Hunter serve your turn?

MISTRESS PAGE I pray you, come, hold up the jest no higher. –
Now, good Sir John, how like you Windsor wives?
[*Pointing to the horns*]
See you these, husband? Do not these fair yokes   100
Become the forest better than the town?

FORD Now, sir, who's a cuckold now? Master Brook, Falstaff's a knave,
a cuckoldy knave. Here are his horns, Master Brook. And, Master
Brook, he hath enjoyed nothing of Ford's but his buck-basket, his
cudgel, and twenty pounds of money, which must be paid to Master   105
Brook. His horses are arrested for it, Master Brook.

MISTRESS FORD Sir John, we have had ill luck; we could never meet. I
will never take you for my love again, but I will always count you my
deer.

FALSTAFF I do begin to perceive that I am made an ass.   110

FORD Ay, and an ox too. Both the proofs are extant.

FALSTAFF And these are not fairies. I was three or four times in the
thought they were not fairies; and yet the guiltiness of my mind, the

---

96–7] *As verse, Rowe; as prose,* F   100 SD] *Hanmer; not in* F   102–3 Now . . . Brook] *As prose, Pope; as three lines of verse,
divided after* now *and* cuckoldy knave F   112 And . . . fairies] *As prose, Pope; as a single verse line,* F   112 And . . . fairies.]
And these are not Fairies: F; Why then these were not F*airies?* Q   112 I was] F; By the Lord I was Q

---

96 watched spied upon (*OED* Watch *v* 11a).

98 hold . . . higher continue the joke no further.

100 these fair yokes i.e. the antlers which Falstaff is now holding in his hand. They are called 'yokes' because of their crescent shape, like a plough (*OED* Yoke *sb* 4).

101 i.e. are they not better as the emblem of a stag rather than of a cuckolded husband? As Craik notes, there is tact in giving this reference to cuckoldry to the wife who did not have the jealous husband, since all is now forgiven and forgotten between Ford and his wife.

102 Master Brook The frequent repetition of the name parodies Falstaff's pressing use of 'Master Brook' in 2.2, 3.5, and 5.1.

103 cuckoldy knave See 2.2.211.

106 arrested seized by legal warrant (*OED* Arrest *v* 11). This arrest of Falstaff's horses until the debt is paid to Ford (in Q he is released from the debt, but not in F) may owe something to Mistress Page's idea of running Falstaff into debt with the Host so that he has to pawn his horses to him (at 2.1.77–8), and is loosely connected thematically, though not in plot terms, with the episode of the

Host and the 'German' horse thieves in 4.3 and at 4.5.50–73.

107 meet physically come together (*OED* v 11e). In the more everyday sense of the word, of course, they have met three times.

109 deer Mistress Ford here precisely does not intend the quibble with 'dear' that she apparently allows at 13, and the firmly animal 'deer' leads on to the 'ass' and 'ox' of the next lines, the ass for stupidity and the ox for cuckoldry yielding up their animal status in a damaging image for Falstaff.

111 Both . . . extant i.e. The proofs of both ass-like stupidity and ox-like cuckoldry are to hand ('extant') in the horns (which are also double).

112–17 See Textual Analysis, p 162.

112 And . . . fairies The present tense in F makes it clear that the fairy boys are still onstage. Falstaff is quite clear he has been gulled, and it is not appropriate that these words should be a question. In Q the fairies have run off the stage (at the equivalent of 95 SD), and so a question here about the absent 'fairies' who are not now evidently boys to the eyes of all is appropriate. In Q Mistress Page answers the question: 'No sir *Iohn* but boyes'. See Textual Analysis, p. 162.

sudden surprise of my powers, drove the grossness of the foppery
into a received belief, in despite of the teeth of all rhyme and reason,   115
that they were fairies. See now how wit may be made a Jack-a-Lent
when 'tis upon ill employment!

EVANS [*Discarding his disguise*] Sir John Falstaff, serve Got, and leave
your desires, and fairies will not pinse you.

FORD Well said, fairy Hugh.   120

EVANS And leave you your jealousies too, I pray you.

FORD I will never mistrust my wife again till thou art able to woo her in
good English.

FALSTAFF Have I laid my brain in the sun and dried it, that it wants
matter to prevent so gross o'erreaching as this? Am I ridden with a   125
Welsh goat too? Shall I have a coxcomb of frieze? 'Tis time I were
choked with a piece of toasted cheese.

EVANS Seese is not good to give putter. Your belly is all putter.

FALSTAFF 'Seese' and 'putter'? Have I lived to stand at the taunt of one
that makes fritters of English? This is enough to be the decay of lust   130
and late-walking through the realm.

MISTRESS PAGE Why, Sir John, do you think, though we would have
thrust virtue out of our hearts by the head and shoulders, and have
given ourselves without scruple to hell, that ever the devil could
have made you our delight?   135

---

118 SD] *This edn; returns, without his satyr-mask* / NS

---

114 powers understanding, wits.

114 grossness . . . foppery crudeness of the hoax (*OED* Foppery 'cf. Ger. *fopperei*, Du. *fopperij*, hoaxing').

115 into . . . belief to a point where I believed absolutely (*OED* Received *ppl adj* = 'Generally . . . accepted . . . as true').

115 in . . . reason in spite of all that common sense might have told me ('in spite of one's teeth' and 'neither rhyme nor reason' are proverbial phrases; Tilley S764, R98).

116 wit intelligence.

116 Jack-a-Lent 'Butt for every one to throw at' (Onions). See 3.3.20 n.

118 SD Discarding . . . disguise This seems the most likely point for Evans to cease being a satyr, revealing himself as he addresses Falstaff. It is perhaps evident from 'fairy Hugh' at 120 that he has been standing with the boys, whose general behaviour, in spite of their disguises, will have made it clear they are not fairies.

122–3 able . . . English Falstaff is not wholly

isolated in his discomfiture. First he is admonished by Evans, then Ford is admonished not to be jealous, and then Evans here twitted for the absurdity of his English.

124–5 wants matter lacks capacity.

125 o'erreaching delusion.

125 ridden i.e. ridden like a horse, as witches and devils were said to ride on the backs of those they oppressed (*OED* Ride *v* 17a).

126 Welsh goat Evans perhaps in his costume looked like a devil or witch figure in a traditionally goat-like appearance (Wales was also noted for its abundance of goats). See 5.4.0 SD n.

126 coxcomb of frieze fool's cap made of frieze (coarse woollen cloth of a kind to be much found in poor regions like Wales).

127 toasted cheese See 1.2.10 and 5.5.75.

128 give add to.

130 fritters chopped up fragments fried in batter.

131 late-walking walking the night for lecherous purposes.

FORD What, a hodge-pudding? A bag of flax?

MISTRESS PAGE A puffed man?

PAGE Old, cold, withered, and of intolerable entrails?

FORD And one that is as slanderous as Satan?

PAGE And as poor as Job?   140

FORD And as wicked as his wife?

EVANS And given to fornications, and to taverns, and sack, and wine,
and metheglins, and to drinkings, and swearings and starings,
pribbles and prabbles?

FALSTAFF Well, I am your theme. You have the start of me. I am   145
dejected. I am not able to answer the Welsh flannel. Ignorance itself
is a plummet o'er me. Use me as you will.

FORD Marry, sir, we'll bring you to Windsor, to one Master Brook, that
you have cozened of money, to whom you should have been a
pander. Over and above that you have suffered, I think to repay that   150
money will be a biting affliction.

PAGE Yet be cheerful, knight. Thou shalt eat a posset tonight at my
house, where I will desire thee to laugh at my wife that now laughs
at thee. Tell her Master Slender hath married her daughter.

MISTRESS PAGE [*Aside*] Doctors doubt that. If Anne Page be my   155
daughter, she is, by this, Doctor Caius' wife.

[*Enter* SLENDER]

155 SD] *Theobald; not in* F   155 Doctors . . . that] *As prose, Pope; as a single line of verse,* F   156 SD] Q *(which transposes the order of entry of Slender here and Caius at 178); not in* F

136 **hodge-pudding** 'pudding made of a medley of ingredients' (*OED*).

137 **puffed** inflated.

138 **intolerable** insufferably great.

139 **slanderous** Used in a rather loose sense, relevant to both Falstaff and Satan, of 'spreading falsehood'.

140–1 In the first two chapters of Job, Satan persuades God to afflict Job with great poverty, and Job's wife counsels him that he should as a consequence curse God and die.

143 **metheglins** 'Spiced or medicated variety of mead, originally peculiar to Wales' (*OED*) (here with Evans' characteristic plural).

143 **swearings and starings** arrogant swearing behaviour (an established phrase, with Evans' plural; *OED* Stare *v* 3a = to glare with anger).

144 **pribbles and prabbles** This phrase of Evans' previously occurs at the beginning of the play, when the quarrel between Shallow and Falstaff is in question. See 1.1.43 and n.

145 **theme** subject-matter.

145 **start of** advantage over (a common phrase, derived from having an advantage in a race; Tilley s828).

146 **dejected** cast down.

146 **Welsh flannel** coarse Welsh cloth, used here to refer ludicrously to Evans himself (*OED* Flannel *sb* 1d). See 126 n.

146–7 **Ignorance . . . me** Ignorance itself stands over me, sounding the very depths with its lead weight (i.e. I am searched out to my depths by Ignorance in the figure of this Welshman).

149 **should** were to.

152 **eat a posset** Page's invitation to this spiced drink neatly recalls his similar invitation at 1.1.156–7.

153 **laugh . . . wife** Again, as at 122–3, Falstaff is not left alone in his discomfiture.

155 **Doctors . . . that** Doubt is proverbially associated with doctors, i.e. learned men of any sort ('That is but one doctor's opinion' Tilley D426 and

SLENDER Whoa, ho, ho, father Page!

PAGE Son, how now! How now, son! Have you dispatched?

SLENDER Dispatched? I'll make the best in Gloucestershire know on't.
Would I were hanged, la, else!   160

PAGE Of what, son?

SLENDER I came yonder at Eton to marry Mistress Anne Page, and
she's a great lubberly boy. If it had not been i'th'church, I would
have swinged him, or he should have swinged me. If I did not think
it had been Anne Page, would I might never stir! And 'tis a post-   165
master's boy!

PAGE Upon my life, then, you took the wrong.

SLENDER What need you tell me that? I think so, when I took a boy for
a girl. If I had been married to him, for all he was in woman's
apparel, I would not have had him.   170

PAGE Why, this is your own folly. Did not I tell you how you should
know my daughter by her garments?

SLENDER I went to her in white, and cried 'mum', and she cried
'budget', as Anne and I had appointed. And yet it was not Anne, but
a postmaster's boy.   [*Exit*]   175

158] *As prose, Pope; as two lines of verse, divided after* son F   171–2] *As prose, Pope; as three lines of verse, divided after* folly
and daughter F   173 white] *Rowe³; greene F; red Q*   175 SD] *Craik; not in* F

'You need not doubt, you are no doctor' Tilley
D425). There is here also a glance at Caius' own title
and particular medical profession.

157 father Page The plaintive Slender me-
chanically uses the son-in-law's form of address to
Page, even though he has not succeeded in marrying
Anne. See 3.2.46.

158 Son . . . son Not questions but triumphant
exclamations. Page is confident.

158 dispatched settled the matter (*OED* Dispatch *v* 10).

161 Of what i.e. know of what? (picking up
'know on't' at 159).

163 great lubberly big loutish. This cannot be
a reference to the boy's actual appearance, since the
boy fairies were to be of rather the same size as Anne
(see 4.4.45–7) and Slender has mistaken this boy for
Anne. It is rather an expression of Slender's embar-
rassment. The no doubt diminutive Slender is angry enough in his next words to have thrashed
('swinged') the boy, but not so decisively bigger
than the girl-like boy for the fight necessarily to
have gone his way ('or he should have swinged me').

165 would . . . stir! A conventional exclamation ('I would I might never stir else' Tilley S861).

165–6 postmaster's boy i.e. stable-boy working for the man in charge of post-horses.

167 you . . . wrong i.e. you failed to follow the
instructions (but Slender, who did follow the instructions precisely, takes Page to mean 'something
went wrong' in his reply).

170 I . . . him i.e. I would not have accepted
him as a wife, would not have copulated with him.
Behind the indignation of Slender and Caius at having been offered boys, there is a general excitement
at the prospect as both characters emphasise repeatedly that they were offered boys. The audience and
players could not have failed also to have in mind at
190–200 that the girl Fenton has accepted as his
wife was in reality a boy, since a boy was playing the
part. See 179n., Introduction, p. 20 and Textual
Analysis, p. 156.

173 *her in white Here and at 177 and 182 F
mistakenly transposes the colours, and Q as usual is
not helpful with them, introducing here, as in 4.6
(see Collation, 4.6.27–8), a confused memory that
red was one of the colours used in the plot against
Slender and Caius. See Textual Analysis, p. 158.

175 SD *Exit* I accept Craik's argument that
Slender's exit here is needed to balance Caius' exit

MISTRESS PAGE Good George, be not angry. I knew of your purpose,
    turned my daughter into green, and indeed she is now with the
    Doctor at the deanery, and there married.

[*Enter* CAIUS]

CAIUS Vere is Mistress Page? By gar, I am cozened. I ha' married *un*
    garçon, a boy; *un paysan*, by gar, a boy. It is not Anne Page. By gar,   180
    I am cozened.
MISTRESS PAGE Why? Did you take her in green?
CAIUS Ay, by gar, and 'tis a boy. By gar, I'll raise all Windsor.   [*Exit*]
FORD This is strange. Who hath got the right Anne?

[*Enter* FENTON *and* ANNE PAGE]

PAGE My heart misgives me. Here comes Master Fenton.   185
    How now, Master Fenton!
ANNE Pardon, good father. Good my mother, pardon.
PAGE Now, mistress, how chance you went not with Master Slender?
MISTRESS PAGE Why went you not with Master Doctor, maid?
FENTON You do amaze her. Hear the truth of it.   190
    You would have married her most shamefully
    Where there was no proportion held in love.
    The truth is, she and I, long since contracted,
    Are now so sure that nothing can dissolve us.
    Th'offence is holy that she hath committed,   195
    And this deceit loses the name of craft,

---

177 green] *Rowe³;* white F   178 SD] Q; *not in* F   179–80 *un garçon*] *Capell;* oon Garsoon F   180 *un paysan*] *Capell;*
oon pesant F   182 green] *Pope;* white F   183 SD] *Capell; not in* F   188] *As prose, Pope; as two lines of verse, divided after*
mistress F

at 183, so that neither unwanted suitor is onstage to
disturb the union of Anne and Fenton. Slender does
not speak words appropriate to an exit, as Caius
plainly does at 183; but it is rather suited to the
general lack of impression he makes on things in
this play that he should be left to edge awkwardly
off as Mistress Page diverts her husband's attention
away from him.
    179 married Caius got further with his boy
than Slender with his. In Q it is Slender who gets to
the point of marriage and not Caius. He says so
twice, and is then exclaimed against by Evans, who
is amazed that Slender could not perceive that he
had been offered just a boy playing the part of a girl:
'Ieshu M. S*lender*, cannot you see but marrie

boyes?' See Introduction, p. 20 and Textual Analysis, p. 156.
    180 *un paysan* (French) a peasant (and so prob-
ably a farmer's boy).
    188 This is not a verse line. Perhaps Page is too
angry in his question to keep within the constraint
of metre.
    190 amaze 'bewilder' (here by asking two
questions simultaneously' (Oliver).
    192 proportion . . . love 'proper loving rela-
tionship between the parties' (Craik).
    193 contracted betrothed (i.e. privately).
    194 sure firmly united together (i.e. in
marriage).

Of disobedience, or unduteous title,
Since therein she doth evitate and shun
A thousand irreligious cursèd hours
Which forcèd marriage would have brought upon her.   200
FORD   [*To Page and Mistress Page*]
Stand not amazed. Here is no remedy.
In love the heavens themselves do guide the state.
Money buys lands, and wives are sold by fate.
FALSTAFF   [*To Page and Mistress Page*] I am glad, though you have
ta'en a special stand to strike at me, that your arrow hath   205
glanced.
PAGE   Well, what remedy? Fenton, heaven give thee joy!
What cannot be eschewed must be embraced.
FALSTAFF   When night-dogs run, all sorts of deer are chased.
MISTRESS PAGE   Well, I will muse no further. – Master Fenton,   210
Heaven give you many, many merry days! –
Good husband, let us every one go home,
And laugh this sport o'er by a country fire,
Sir John and all.
FORD   Let it be so, Sir John.
To Master Brook you yet shall hold your word,   215
For he tonight shall lie with Mistress Ford.

Exeunt

---

201 SD] *Oxford; not in* F   **204** SD] *Craik; not in* F   **207–8**] *As verse, Rowe³; as prose,* F

197 unduteous title the name of undutiful-
ness.
 198 evitate avoid.
 201 Here In these circumstances.
 202 guide the state rule.
 203 i.e. money will only buy lands not wives;
wives are offered on different terms, offered by fate
('Marriage and hanging go by destiny' Tilley M682).
 205 stand Huntsman's place of vantage from
which to shoot.

206 glanced struck obliquely (without injury).
Falstaff is not mortally injured because the hunters
themselves have suffered.
 208 What cannot be avoided must be accepted
(compare 'What cannot be cured must be endured'
Tilley C922).
 209 'When dogs run loose at night, out of control, the hunting will not be according to the rules'
(Oliver).
 210 muse grumble, complain (*OED v* 6).

TEXTUAL ANALYSIS

The only two texts of any authority of *The Merry Wives of Windsor* are the first quarto (Q) of 1602, printed for Arthur Johnson by T[homas] C[reede], and the First Folio (F) of 1623, where the play appears third in the group of four comedies with which the volume opens, set by Compositors B and C, with some contribution from D,[1] from fair copy evidently provided, as for the whole of this group, by Ralph Crane.[2] The Q text of the play was reprinted in 1619 (Q2); and the F text in 1630 as a separate quarto (Q3), and again in the reprints of the complete First Folio in 1632 (F2), 1663 (F3), and 1685 (F4), each one of which is a direct reprint of the preceding text. These later, non-authoritative, seventeenth-century printings show, as one would expect, minor variation from the Q and F texts from which they derive, and can occasionally be cited in a Commentary note where they provide an evident printing-house correction of a typographical slip in F or Q (for example, at 1.3.63 and 2.2.27, but see Commentary at 2.1.19, 2.1.20, and 5.2.2), but they are of no interest beyond this.

The relationship of F and Q

The relationship between the F and Q texts of *The Merry Wives of Windsor* has been the subject of prolonged controversy.[3] We may approach the problem by describing in turn the characteristics of the two texts and trying to account for them.

Q (1602)

Q presents a version of *The Merry Wives of Windsor* of about 1600 lines, by contrast with the F text of about 2700 lines. The textual agreement between F and Q where there are lines in common varies from close to fairly remote, but about 500 lines of Q have no counterpart at all in F. However we hypothesise (and such hypotheses can only hope roughly to represent the actual complication of human events) about the process which produced Q, we must say that this version of the play undoubtedly bears the marks of considerable non-authorial intervention about it. Let us consider these non-authorial elements, in order to build up a picture of the kind of distance there is between Q and Shakespeare's own hand in the matter (this made up of his missing 'foul papers', i.e. his supposed completed authorial draft of the play, and also of any revisions he may have made to his work later).

There is clear evidence in Q that this text is a damaged version of some earlier state

---

[1] See Charles Hinman, *The Printing and Proof-Reading of the First Folio of Shakespeare*, 1963, and T. H. Howard-Hill, 'The compositors of Shakespeare's Folio comedies', *SB* 26 (1973), 61–106.
[2] See T. H. Howard-Hill, *Ralph Crane and Some Shakespearean First Folio Comedies*, 1972.
[3] See Jeanne A. Roberts, '*The Merry Wives* Q and F: the vagaries of progress', *S. St.* 8 (1975), 143–75.

of the text rather than simply an early draft of the play, Shakespeare's first thoughts, as was usually suggested before the present century. This is not to rule out the possibility that Shakespeare himself revised *The Merry Wives of Windsor*, nor is it to deny that in Q we have evidence of a hand, probably not Shakespeare's, deliberately revising. Evidence of damage, probably due to memorial report (and most likely, as Greg suggested,[1] with the actor who played the Host being the culprit, since his part is best remembered), is easy to instance. At 1.4.62–6 in F, Mistress Quickly explains to Caius that Simple has come with a message from Evans, and Simple adds that this is about Slender's proposal of marriage to Anne; whereupon Caius issues a challenge to Evans. In the Q version, Evans has dropped out altogether and the message comes direct from Slender; but still Caius writes out a challenge to Evans. The challenge to Evans now makes no sense. Again, much of Q is printed as verse, though it is evidently prose; and though it is conceivable that this is due to compositorial error, it seems more likely to be because an actor remembered this largely prose play in a rough form of verse (it may be that this was habitually the way in which actors learnt, or even delivered, prose parts, prose being so much more difficult to memorise than verse). On occasion, where verse does appear in F, the Q text's attempt at it is very instructive: Fenton's wooing of Anne at 3.4.13–18, for instance, appears in Q's text as:

> Thy father thinks I loue thee for his wealth,
> Tho I must needs confesse at first that drew me,
> But since thy vertues wiped that trash away,
> *I* loue thee *Nan*, and so deare is it set,
> That whilst I liue, I nere shall thee forget.

Q's version cannot be Shakespeare's first thoughts; rather it is an actor's last thoughts of something like the F text. And if we look at the rest of Q's version of the wooing scene at 3.4.1–21, immediately preceding the lines just quoted, we can see how likely it is that an actor's imperfect recall was pieced out with reference to Slender and Caius, and how Q fails to convey the doubtless original delicacy of the scene where it is Anne who suggests that Fenton first wooed her for her wealth:

> *Fen:* Tell me sweet *Nan*, how doest thou yet resolue,
> Shall foolish *Slender* haue thee to his wife?
> Or one as wise as he, the learned Doctor?
> Shall such as they enjoy thy maiden hart?
> Thou knowst that *I* haue alwaies loued thee deare,
> And thou hast oft times swore the like to me.
>   *An:* Good M. *Fenton*, you may assure your selfe
> My hart is setled vpon none but you,
> 'Tis as my father and mother please:
> Get their consent, you quickly shall haue mine.

---

[1] W. W. Greg, *Shakespeare's Merry Wives of Windsor 1602*, 1910, p. xli, and Oliver, p. xxvi.

The actor here could not remember enough of the original text, as is also evident, for instance, at Q's version of 2.2.32–63. In F, Falstaff has ample grounds for urging Mistress Quickly to be brief, but in Q where the same urging occurs, there are not really grounds for it because Mistress Quickly's long rambling approach to her news does not appear:

> Sir I would speake with you in priuate.
>> *Fal.* Say on I prethy, heeres none but my owne houshold.
>> *Quic.* Are they so? Now God blesse them, and make them his seruants.
> Syr I come from Mistresse *Foord.*
>> *Fal.* So from Mistresse *Foord.* Goe on.
>> *Quic.* I sir, she hath sent me to you to let you
> Vnderstand she hath receiued your Letter,
> And let me tell you, she is one stands vpon her credit.
>> *Fal.* Well, come Misteris F*ord*, Misteris F*ord*.
>> *Quic.* I sir, and as they say, she is not the first
> Hath bene led in a fooles paradice.
>> F*al* Nay prethy be briefe my good she *Mercury*.

And what of the Host's 'bullies taile' in Q, in place of F's 'bully stale' at 2.3.23? F's reading must be the original (see Commentary), but either the Host in learning his part aurally eased that easily mistaken expression into something a little different, or the scribe taking dictation from the Host for the compositor of Q did so.

If there is good evidence, then, that Q is the product of a corrupt memorial report of *The Merry Wives of Windsor* for a printer to produce a pirated or 'bad' quarto of the play for illicit profit, we must still ask whether the play the actor (or perhaps actors, for Falstaff's part is also remembered well) was trying to piece together was the version represented later by F, or some other. There is evidence that it was some other.

The evidence falls into two parts. Firstly, there are differences between the Q and F texts involving such considerable omission or reordering of material as to suggest that the text behind Q was already deliberately adapted. Secondly, there is frequently evidence at a local level in Q of a process of 'theatricalisation' that must often begin to occur as soon as a written text becomes an acted one (especially where, as is not now the case with Shakespeare's plays, there was no presence of a prestigious printed text in the actors' minds to inhibit a creative way with the words they spoke). There seems at first nothing against the supposition that the process of adaptation occurred *after* the 'memorial' stage, or as Jowett puts it, that the 'nature of the text indeed suggests that steps have been taken to turn a grossly inadequate report into a roughly intelligible and coherent text',[1] and indeed some work may have been necessary at this stage. But both the highly topical and localised nature of the supposed first performance of the play on the one hand,[2] which would encourage early (though perhaps not immediate)[3] revi-

---

[1] Jowett, p. 341.
[2] See Introduction, p. 1.
[3] See p. 160.

sion, either by Shakespeare or by another hand, of those parts of it which would not make sense on the public stage in London; and also on the other hand the evidence of that instantly beginning process of accommodation of a written text to the conditions of performance (at a less formal, more detailed and intimate level than that represented by the prompt-book's tidying up of original foul papers for production) which I call 'theatricalisation', suggest that the version the actor responsible for Q was trying to remember already differed from the version of the play behind F.

Signs of adaptation in the Q text when it is compared with an F text localised to quite specific conditions of early private performance at court are easy to adduce. It seems that some of the adaptation behind Q was intended to make the play more convenient for the company to perform (for instance, by reducing the number of speaking boy actors needed by omitting Robin's speeches), but the most striking adaptations are the omission of the heraldic joking in the first scene of the play, the omission of all reference to Windsor and the Order of the Garter in the last scene, and the dropping of William Page's Latin lesson at the beginning of Act 4 (thus also saving another speaking part for a boy). This is all educated and upper-class matter that would appeal to the supposed first audience. It is conceivable, of course, that changes of this kind were the result of memorial error in the reporting of the play for the pirated quarto; but the neatness and completeness of the excision of upper-class matter (none of which actually advances the plot) and the sense that, especially, reference to Windsor Castle and the Order of the Garter at 5.5.49–65 would have no attraction on the public stage, suggest revision, either by Shakespeare or another hand, and not lapses of memory.

Adaptation, even when non-authorial, is easy to understand as distinct from memorial garbling, but 'theatricalisation' needs to be more delicately distinguished and illustrated. We may say that adaptation is change made deliberately to the written version of the play with some overall considerations in mind, so that a new written version is produced by someone with ready access to the previous written version. Both memorial garbling and theatricalisation involve a similar departure from the written original, but in the first case this departure is accidental and in the second is deliberate but not intended to produce an adapted written version. A player faced with a certain set of circumstances in the theatre will, on occasion, move or speak in a way irresistibly dictated by his own sense of the situation on the stage, and not at the authoritative instance of the lines in his written part. It is in this way that a play grows into a stage presence (at a greater or lesser distance from its written original) and comes to accumulate round itself an acting tradition. Some of the detailed and localised change produced by this experience of *The Merry Wives of Windsor* on stage may have found its way into the prompt-book at an earlier or later moment, but some certainly would not have done. I suggest that we see in Q evidence of intimate and detailed response to theatrical circumstance, some of which may have been written down deliberately but some of which has involuntarily arrived at a written form because part of the reporting actor's memory of what *The Merry Wives of Windsor* was like in creative performance. A few instances must suffice here, but more are noted in the Commentary.

At the very beginning of the play in Q, Shallow strides out on to the stage and directly addresses the audience (see note at 1.1.1). F's first words suggest an exchange with Evans before the play began which reaches out to the first appearance of the actors on the stage, with Shallow addressing Evans by name as the two come on (a useful piece of exposition, one might think in the study, giving the audience Evans' name, which is immediately followed by information about Shallow and Slender). This carefully thought out exposition gives way in Q to a much bolder bid for solo status by Shallow, his first words being a refusal of dialogue ('NEre talke to me'), the actor having taken the hint in what was presumably his written text (F's 'persuade me not') and made it much more energetic and dramatic, so that in Q Page (brought in now at line 1) has to try to calm Shallow's extreme anger, while Evans attempts to reason with an equally upset Slender. It is, I suggest, easy to imagine a theatrical process which gradually allowed the energy implicit in F to expand into noise and activity on the stage, noise enough to quiet an audience into attention:

> *Shal.* NEre talke to me, Ile make a star-chamber matter of it.
>   The Councell shall know it.
> *Pag.* Nay good maister *Shallow* be perswaded by mee.
> *Slen.* Nay surely my vncle shall not put it vp so.
> *Sir Hu.* Wil you not heare reasons M. *Slenders?*
>   You should heare reasons.
> *Shal.* Tho he be a knight, he shall not thinke to carrie it so away.
>   M. *Page* I will not be wronged.

It is certainly true that these first lines of Q have also been adapted to excise the heraldic matter,[1] and one may see that in Q Shallow jumps from F's 1.1.3 to F's 1.1.27 in his first two lines; but I think the adaptation is not the only influence upon these first lines and that Shallow's first four words in Q are an actor's response to the conditions of the stage (probably the conditions of a public stage rather than the politer atmosphere of an earlier private performance), which can be distinguished from the adapter's hand.

Again at 1.1.96–7 (see Commentary) a joke has evidently gone missing, rather than being neatly excised by an adapter. This is surely an actor making the best of his text in circumstances where the audience (and perhaps he also) could not quite make out the sense. At 1.1.123, Q makes the reference to the Edward shovel-boards clearer with a chiming phrase that was surely in common use, 'shouell boord shillings'. At 1.2.1 the first reference to Caius is made more explicit as he is called 'the French Doctor', no doubt to allow the audience to practise their antagonism before he even appears. At 1.3.15 (see Commentary) the magnificently meaningless 'gongarian' looks like an actor's inspired rendering of a word that originally did mean something, and the mock-heroic joke about the spigot is underlined so the audience will get it. Another piece of underlining occurs at 4.5.81 (see Commentary). The Host's characteristic speech must have gone down very well onstage, because we find Q extending the joke

---

[1] See p. 154.

with a pun on a French word (see 1.4.75 n.); and the joke about marrying boys at the end of the play must have roused response, because Q makes more of it (see 5.5.170 n. and 179 n.).

Changes of the kind I have just described seem the type to have arisen spontaneously as the play went on being performed. We may contrast with these the kind of change that looks like the tidying-up of foul papers by the compiler of the prompt-book, concerned before the play began about certain practical stage matters. With variants of this last kind between Q and F we reach back in Q's line of descent to the point where it first became a fully practical theatrical text. Evidence of the prompt-book compiler's hand is to be found, for instance, among the stage directions. At 2.2.124 SD, Q's stage direction specifies disguise for Ford as Brook, although the text has only ever mentioned a false name (and we know from 2.2.211 that Falstaff and Ford have never actually met before, so that disguise is not strictly required). It seems very likely that the disguise is introduced here by the prompt-book compiler, who considered it theatrically appropriate and an effective communication with the audience to have Ford as Brook costumed differently. Again, it would have to be decided before the play was put on exactly how Evans was to be disguised in the fairy scene at the end. At 5.4.0 SD (see Commentary), Q's specifying of a satyr costume reflects a decision made in addition to what the text offers, a production decision. Q's description, too, of Caius' 'closet' (as it is described in F) as a 'counting house' (see 1.4.32 n.) looks like a textual change introduced in the prompt-book to make it quite clear to the audience what was being represented by the inner stage at this point in the actual production in hand (i.e. a room not a cupboard).

A final example of variance between F and Q that is to be referred to the prompt-book stage in Q's descent is of even more interest because here it is a question not of

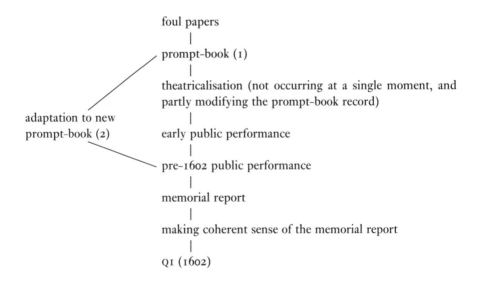

foul papers

|

prompt-book (1)

|

theatricalisation (not occurring at a single moment, and partly modifying the prompt-book record)

adaptation to new
prompt-book (2)

|

early public performance

|

pre-1602 public performance

|

memorial report

|

making coherent sense of the memorial report

|

Q1 (1602)

addition to or further specifying of what was already in the foul papers, but of correction of what seems fairly evidently a mistake in Shakespeare's own completed version of the play (see 1.3.73 n.). Such a tidying-up of an easily made (though not so easily fully corrected) error seems a very typical prompt-book feature.

The line of descent argued for Q here can be represented schematically. No doubt this stemma gives a simplified picture of what actually happened, but I would want to suggest that essentially the process represented in the diagram on the previous page produced Q, a much-distorted text, but a text close to the public theatrical experience of *The Merry Wives of Windsor* at every point.

F (1623)

By contrast, the F text of *The Merry Wives of Windsor* seems a product of the study rather than of the theatre. The logic, indeed, of noting that Q varies from F in ways that can be attributed to the prompt-book stage of Q's descent is to suggest that there is no prompt-book in F's line of descent, unless we are to suppose that at some stage prompt-book features were erased or reversed, which can hardly have been the case, for instance, with the error noted at the end of my discussion of Q, which it is inconceivable would have remained uncorrected even in some postulated early prompt-book stage.

Even if not in the sense of Q a theatrical text, F gives us a largely excellent account of the words we may suppose Shakespeare wrote down to be spoken. Some changes have, it seems, been made to Shakespeare's text, but the process of adaptation and in particular the memorial garbling, which make Q so unsatisfactory finally as an account of what Shakespeare wrote, are wholly absent in F. The unsatisfactory features of F, which any line of descent for the text has to account for, are chiefly the curious state of its stage directions, the confusion about costumes for the elopement in the last scene, the wholesale substitution of Broom for Brook as Ford's assumed name, and the fairly thorough expurgation of profanity.

There is good evidence that the F text of *The Merry Wives of Windsor*, in common with that of the other three comedies with which the First Folio begins, was set from a transcript provided by the professional scribe Ralph Crane,[1] whose scribal mannerisms in the use of parentheses and hyphens are clearly evident here. It is, however, too much to suppose that, if he was working from Shakespeare's own foul papers, he introduced all the unsatisfactory features which need to be explained, so that we need to speculate a little more about the copy for Crane's transcript.

It is often said that the 'massed entry' stage directions which are a feature of the F text, as well as of other (but not all) of the plays set from Crane's transcripts, can simply be referred to Crane's own idiosyncratic desire to present a classically formalised text, divided into acts and scenes and not cluttered by stage directions in the body of the text. Hence, in *The Merry Wives of Windsor*, with the single exception of '*Enter Fairies*' at 5.5.29 SD, stage directions simply consist of the names of all the characters

---

[1] See p. 151, n. 2.

who appear in a scene grouped together at the beginning of it, and an exit at the end. I think we may accept that Crane is responsible for the tidy scheme of acts and scenes, and for the stage directions as they finally appear in F, but I think it unlikely that he would have radically cast into this form a sequence of stage directions which, in the text he was copying, were already elaborately distributed through the text. In other words, the unsatisfactorily explicit stage directions of F are probably to be explained by the lack of a prompt-book stage between a Shakespearean manuscript that lacked them, at least in any elaborate form (possibly because completed in haste for a first private performance at court) and Crane's stylised and untheatrical presentation of entrances and exits.

The confusion about costumes in the last scene (see 5.5.173 n.) is also difficult to explain as an error arising somewhere in the process of transmission of F. It would indeed be an error typical of memorial garbling (as is undoubtedly Q's hopeless confusion about costumes for the disguising in the last act, although Q also preserves a possible memory of actual stage performance where the colour red was used in addition to the colours in use in F); but it is clear that F went through no memorial stage. By contrast, this is not an error likely to have remained uncorrected in any prompt-book version of the text (additional evidence that there was no such stage in F's descent). We are reduced to the possibility that this is a scribal or compositorial error, which seems unlikely, since the two words, white and green, are not easily confused by a scribe or compositor copying or following a text in front of him; or else to the possibility that this is Shakespeare's own mistake, an error easier to envisage on the part of a writer not following copy before him but writing hurriedly (to meet a deadline for a court performance, perhaps) in terms of a plot shape in his head.

The change from Brook to Broom and the fairly thorough expurgation of profanity are the remaining textual events in F's history which have to be fitted into the line of descent. The expurgation (which entails considerable editorial difficulty and which is considered in detail below) can be dated with reasonable certainty to about 1606 (i.e. later than Q, and conceivably because the foul papers were intended at that stage to serve as printer's copy for a 'good quarto'). The substitution of Broom for Shakespeare's clearly intended name of Brook (see 2.1.173 n. and Introduction, pp. 3–4) was probably an early and very temporary measure, recorded informally, as Craik suggests,[1] in Shakespeare's manuscript, which may have served as the theatrical text for a hastily produced first private performance of the play, but thereafter reversed. As a consequence Crane would, of course, have found the substitution there in Shakespeare's manuscript as he made his transcript. It is interesting to speculate that the 'theatrical note' that the actors playing Quickly and Pistol appear in other roles in the final scene (see notes at 5.5.29 SD and 95 SD) was, too, a hurried piece of doubling noted in the foul papers for the purposes of this first performance.

The following stemma represents the descent argued for F, together with that argued for Q:

---

[1] Craik, p. 57.

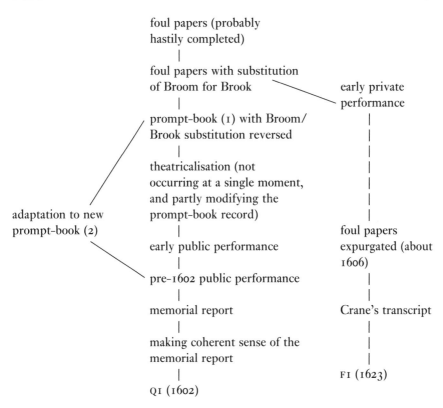

foul papers (probably
hastily completed)

|

foul papers with substitution
of Broom for Brook   early private
                                              performance
| |

prompt-book (1) with Broom/ |
Brook substitution reversed |
                                              |
| |

theatricalisation (not |
occurring at a single moment, |
and partly modifying the |
adaptation to new   prompt-book record) |
prompt-book (2) | |
                           early public performance   foul papers
                           | expurgated (about
                           pre-1602 public performance   1606)
                           | |
                           memorial report |
                           | Crane's transcript
                           making coherent sense of the |
                           memorial report |
                           | FI (1623)
                           Q1 (1602)

Editorial problems and solutions

The account so far given of the F and Q texts of *The Merry Wives of Windsor* plainly
presents editorial difficulties, and there are other editorial matters, too, which need
discussion and decision. The first decision to be made concerns the status of Shakespeare's own manuscript. Plainly, if we suppose that our sole duty is to present this, as
nearly as possible, then the argument of the preceding pages would lead us to print F,
with reversal of the Broom/Brook substitution and attempted reversal of the expurgation (turning to Q for help where it seems appropriate). But if we suppose that
Shakespeare envisaged, as part of what he was doing, the conversion of his manuscript
into a prompt-book easily usable onstage, then we must draw on Q more heavily
(notably for its stage directions, even though at times their garbled form and the
distortion of the text they appear in makes this difficult). If we suppose further that
Shakespeare envisaged his play acclimatised to the stage, then we must at least make
evident to the reader, even though not formally admitting into the text, aspects of the
theatrical experience of the play preserved for us in Q (more interestingly what the
actors did with it than the formal adaptation to the conditions of London public
performance). And this is what I have done. The text here presented is what I

conjecture Shakespeare would have found acceptable as the prompt-book (1) version of his play (the supposition being that the adaptation to prompt-book (2) only occurred after some attempt had been made onstage with the prompt-book most nearly representing Shakespeare's original intentions); but I suppose that neither he nor the reader would be uninterested in what happened to it less formally as it was played onstage in its adapted version, in the energy it provoked by the energy it offered, so that the notes often draw on Q's disreputable account of that energy.

This fundamental decision once made, it is easy to reverse the Broom/Brook substitution, and by contrast necessary to consider individually in context each of the alterations and additions made to stage directions in F. Beyond saying that stage directions printed here are such as the text seems to call for, and are heavily influenced by Q, nothing general can be said. With expurgation the case seems different, however, and a set of guiding principles leading to a variety of precise decisions can be elaborated.

EXPURGATION

There is no doubt that the Folio text of *The Merry Wives of Windsor* has been expurgated, probably as a result of the 1606 Act to Restrain Abuses of Players, which although it focused specifically upon performance and made it a punishable offence to use 'the holy Name of God or of Christ Jesus, or of the Holy Ghoste or of the Trinitie' on the stage, naturally had a consequent effect on play texts themselves. It is perhaps the case that the expurgating of the Folio *Merry Wives of Windsor* was done minimally and reluctantly, because on two occasions, it may be by careless oversight, the name of God is allowed to stand (1.1.147; 1.4.4), and it is used freely in the text where it appears in a technically different spelling, as Evans' 'Got' or Caius' 'gar' in particular, as well, of course, as where the word refers to a classical god (5.5.2–9). However, there are a number of places where it is very obvious that censoring has been done, to judge from the feeble or awkward or apologetic state of the text, and this plain evidence leads an editor to have suspicions also about other places, especially where the reading of Q, a text generous with its oaths, would undoubtedly have offended the censor. Examples of plain damage to the Folio text are:

2.2.18 This is one of a number of instances where F reads 'heaven' for 'God' with more or less awkward results. The phrase behind Falstaff's words here is undoubtedly 'the fear of God'.

2.3.14–17 See Commentary. The compositor's apostrophes here (as elsewhere in F) apologise for obvious absences, and even spill over to one instance where there probably was nothing omitted.

3.5.72 Falstaff's reply to Ford's incredulous question 'A buck-basket?' in F is the feeble 'Yes, a buck-basket!' Something more energetic than 'yes' is surely required.

The situation with *The Merry Wives of Windsor*, then, is that we have one otherwise generally reliable text which is clearly expurgated and one otherwise generally unreliable text which is unexpurgated. What is an editor to do? One easy course would be always to prefer the readings of F where they make sense. But expurgated texts usually do make sense, if sometimes at a little cost, because care has been taken to patch over their injuries, and it seems pusillanimous to accept a patch where the skin could be restored. On the other hand the Q text cannot be uncritically resorted to: sometimes there is not close enough (or indeed any) correspondence between the two texts to allow influence from Q to F, and there are other times when Q seems more generous with its oaths than the context calls for, at 2.2.139 and 3.4.31, for instance (as Oliver remarks, 'reporters improvise asseverations more readily than most other phrasing').[1]

My practice in this edition has been to emend F only where it seems unsatisfactory in one of the ways I have described above and where there is a reading of Q correspond-ing closely enough to suggest what has been deleted from F. This editorial decision accounts for Q readings at: 2.2.18; 2.2.42; 2.2.125; 2.2.241; 2.3.14; 2.3.15; 3.1.33; 3.1.34; 3.5.48; 3.5.72.

A further group of readings constitute what seem to me good cases for emendation to judge from the state of F, but in these cases I have not emended solely on the grounds that no Q reading corresponds or corresponds closely enough to them: 3.1.8; 3.1.11; 3.1.17; 3.1.25; 3.4.52; 3.4.53; 4.1.10.

This leaves a small group of cases where there seem no grounds for emendation, because F is satisfactory, but where nevertheless Q suggests interesting unexpurgated possibilities. I have not admitted any of these Q readings into the edited text, but they are worth looking at briefly here.

2.2.89 Q's oath sounds good and fits Mistress Quickly's character, although the vivid parallelism between the first and third sentences of the speech in F seems to have energy enough. Craik also interestingly suggests that Q here owes something to a line from Jonson's *Every Man in his Humour* and asks us to bear in mind that 'compilers of reported texts often introduce expressions from other plays'.[2]

3.1.71 Q's oath trips easily off the tongue, and would mark the transition from speech aside to Caius to public speech very well.

3.1.90 At first sight Q's 'Afore God' seems convincing; but this may well be a case where an oath came too easily to the mind of the reconstructor of the text, because Shallow's 'Trust me' in F seems tellingly to establish for him a different tone from the Host's madcap speech, and so gives him here an edge of independent authority. He is not simply an unthinking follower of the Host.

3.3.47 Falstaff perhaps does need a little more energy in his setting aside of Mistress Ford's good sense than F allows him. In Q the phrase 'By the Lord' is characteristic of Falstaff's speech, here and at 3.5.13–14, 3.5.72, and 5.5.112.

3.5.7 Q's oath seems appropriate to the situation, and is certainly an expression found in Falstaff's speech in *1H4*. As Jowett notes, 'Q's oath is one of the most objectionable in the period, and . . . was singled out for particular expurgation in the Folio.'[3]

[1] Oliver, p. xxxv.
[2] Craik, p. 61.
[3] Jowett, p. 346.

3.5.13–14 The repetitious words 'I should have been' in F are possibly weak rather than strong, and Q's direct attack by way of oath upon 'a mountain of mummy' better (Q's rendering of 'mummy' as 'money' is undoubtedly either a compositor's or dictation-taker's error, since it makes no sense).

3.5.67 F's 'good luck' is more convincing; Falstaff does not need to reach so high as God in thanks for his narrow escape, the moment is not so solemn as that.

5.5.25 Q has 'God' for F's 'Heaven', as in a number of previous cases where I have preferred Q's reading. I hesitate here. There seems a case for emending; there seems a case for not emending, but solely on the grounds that Q is not close enough; and there seems a case for suggesting that Mistress Ford's exclamation is a more satisfactory rhythmic unit than 'God forgive our sins', a little more ample and balanced in sound even if less emphatic in meaning.

5.5.74 Falstaff's 'Heavens' in F seems appropriately less urgent than Q's 'God'. Both the plural and the piece of cheese in the following line may persuade us that Falstaff, though the context suggests he is seriously frightened, is either pretending less fright to himself than he feels or that his words are the vehicle for a piece of lighter humour directed at Evans which the context strictly does not allow.

5.5.112 Falstaff's characteristic 'By the Lord' in Q seems heartier, but the rest of Falstaff's speech, in F though not in Q, is curiously unhearty, a momentarily genuinely repentant Falstaff. I think this brief change of tone would have been uninviting and difficult to do on the stage, and I can understand why there is wit and not repentance in Falstaff's discomfiture in Q:

> By the Lord I was twice or thrice in the mind
> They were not, and yet the grosnesse
> Of the fopperie perswaded me they were.
> Well, and the fine wits of the Court heare this,
> Thayle so whip me with their keene Iests,
> That thayle melt me out like tallow,
> Drop by drop out of my grease. Boyes!

CAIUS' FRENCH

Special problems are presented by the French doctor's French. The editorial aim has been to modernise into present-day French what has first been ascertained as correct sixteenth-century French (since Caius is a sixteenth-century native speaker). However, once scribal and compositorial error has been cleared aside and the plainly phonetic intention of some of F's readings has been accepted, there remains an unremovable obstacle in the way of total realisation of the editorial aim, and that is the fact that Shakespeare's own grasp of French was not that of a contemporary native speaker (and the assumption I have made is that Shakespeare's French was a good deal worse than, for instance, Craik supposes). Unavoidably then, Caius sometimes speaks as though he is an English speaker's notion of a native French speaker. One should not perhaps be too upset about this, because the stage aim of this play for an English audience is entirely satisfactorily accomplished by this linguistically imperfect means.

READING LIST

The selection of items in this list will give a sense of the diversity and range of approach to *The Merry Wives of Windsor* and will complement, I hope, the tenacity with which in this edition I have held to my own view of the kind of play it is.

Brown, John Russell. *Shakespeare and his Comedies*, 1957

Cotton, Nancy. 'Castrating (w)itches: impotence and magic in *The Merry Wives of Windsor*', *SQ* 38 (1987), 320–6

Craik, T. W. (ed.). *The Merry Wives of Windsor*, 1990 (Oxford Shakespeare)

Evans, Bertrand. *Shakespeare's Comedies*, 1960

Evans, Peter. '"To the oak, to the oak!" The finale of *The Merry Wives of Windsor*', *Theatre Notebook*, 40 (1986), 106–14

Freedman, Barbara. 'Falstaff's punishment: buffoonery as defensive posture in *The Merry Wives of Windsor*', *S.St.* 14 (1981), 163–74

Frye, Northrop. *Anatomy of Criticism*, 1957

Green, William. *Shakespeare's 'Merry Wives of Windsor'*, 1962

Gurr, Andrew. 'Intertextuality at Windsor', *SQ* 38 (1987), 190–200

Hinely, Jan Lawson. 'Comic scapegoats and the Falstaff of *The Merry Wives of Windsor*', *S.St.* 15 (1982), 37–54

Hotson, Leslie. *Shakespeare versus Shallow*, 1931

Leggatt, Alexander. *Citizen Comedy in the Age of Shakespeare*, 1973

Mace, Nancy A. 'Falstaff, Quin and the popularity of *The Merry Wives of Windsor* in the eighteenth century', *Theatre Survey* 31 (1990), 55–66

Melchiori, Giorgio. *Shakespeare's Garter Plays: Edward III to 'Merry Wives of Windsor'*, 1994

Oliver, H. J. (ed.). *The Merry Wives of Windsor*, 1971 (Arden Shakespeare)

Roberts, Jeanne Addison. *Shakespeare's English Comedy: 'The Merry Wives of Windsor' in Context*, 1979

Salingar, Leo. *Shakespeare and the Traditions of Comedy*, 1974

Scoufos, Alice-Lyle. *Shakespeare's Typological Satire*, 1979

Steadman, John M. 'Falstaff as Actaeon: a dramatic emblem', *SQ* 14 (1963), 230–44

Vickers, Brian. *The Artistry of Shakespeare's Prose*, 1968

White, R. S. 'Criticism of the comedies up to *The Merchant of Venice*, 1953–82', *S.Sur.* 37 (1984), 1–11